The Church of England in the First Decade of the 21st Century

Andrew Village

The Church of England in the First Decade of the 21st Century

Findings from the *Church Times* Surveys

Andrew Village
York St John University
York, UK

ISBN 978-3-030-04527-2   ISBN 978-3-030-04528-9 (eBook)
https://doi.org/10.1007/978-3-030-04528-9

Library of Congress Control Number: 2018962027

Cover credit: Rob Melnychuk/Getty Images

This Palgrave Macmillan imprint is published by the registered company Springer Nature Switzerland AG
The registered company address is: Gewerbestrasse 11, 6330 Cham, Switzerland

To Leslie J. Francis, Mentor, Colleague, and Friend

PREFACE

The start of the twenty-first century was an interesting time for the Church of England. Historians looking back at this period may draw attention to the major controversies that raged over issues such as how to move on from ordaining women as priests to also ordaining them as bishops, or what to do about the rapidly changing attitudes in Britain to same-sex relationships. They may note other important initiatives that the Church was trying to progress that tended not to make the headlines of the national press, such as Fresh Expressions of Church or the expansion of church secondary schools. If they are typical historians, they will glean their data from official documents, minutes of meetings, media reports and the like. While this may give a good idea of what the people who were in charge were thinking, it might miss out on understanding what the people who comprised the bulk of the Church of England made of all this. They might also miss out on what such people believed about more mundane matters that were not hitting the headlines at the time.

This book is about two surveys that were intended to try and understand the beliefs, attitudes and opinions of the grass roots of the Church of England. Both surveys sampled readers of the *Church Times* newspaper, which ran detailed questionnaires assessing a range of opinions, beliefs and attitudes in 2001 and 2013. The total returns of over 9000 in 2001 and just less than 5000 in 2013 represented about 27 and 21% of the readership of the newspaper at the time. While this sort of 'convenience' sample has its limitations, it is (as discussed in Chapter 2)

one of the best measures we currently have of what the rank and file of
the Church of England believe about their faith and their Church. The
first survey was organized by Leslie Francis, Mandy Robbins and Jeff
Astley; the results were reported in the *Church Times* in 2002 and subsequently in their book *Fragmented faith*. The data set also proved to
be a valuable resource for academic articles examining a range of more
specific questions about beliefs and attitudes in this part of the Anglican
Church. I began working on the 2001 data set in 2007 and appreciated
the way that Leslie and his co-workers made the data freely available.
We always felt that running a repeat survey would be invaluable, and the
opportunity came to do so at rather short notice in early summer 2013.
Leslie Francis and I organized this second survey, and I was responsible for collating and managing the data set. We had learnt from working
with the first survey which questions were the most useful, and although
there were some new things were wanted to do, we also recognized the
value of repeating some of the same items in the same form so that we
could see how opinions changed between the two surveys. That is what
this book is about. We decided that for this aspect of the data, I was
best placed to analyze and report the results, so while Leslie has offered
advice and help throughout, I am solely responsible for any errors or fail-
ings in this book.

This book is intended to report the second survey, but in a way that
asks two particular questions. The first is whether the differences in opinions between various groups in the Church that were noted in 2001
remain when the new data are added and subject to slightly more sophisticated statistical analysis. *Fragmented faith* took sections of the Church
at a time (e.g., lay people or clergy) and examined differences between
particular groups (e.g., young and old, Anglo-catholics and Evangelicals).
The presentation here treats the whole data set together and uses multiple regression analysis to test for differences after controlling for other
factors. This means overall differences between the surveys can be tested
after allowing for the different profiles of the two samples.

The second question looks in more detail at the changes between the
surveys. The Church of England certainly changed its practice in respect
of matters such as the remarriage of divorcees in church and was busy
debating the possibility of ordaining women as bishops or whether to
allow practicing homosexuals to be ordained. This sort of activity must
be accompanied by changes in beliefs, which might happen because
everyone shifts their opinion at the same time or because new ideas,

often held by younger people, gradually take over as one generation gives way to the next. As well as looking at the overall change in opinion between surveys, the data also allow us to see whether opinions shifted in particular birth cohorts, indicating that there has been a change of mind rather than just a change of the guard. This analysis is done separately among people from the three main traditions of the Church, namely Anglo-catholic, Broad church and Evangelical. This further allows us to see if opinions moved in the same way in these three traditions, or whether there were pockets of innovation or resistance.

The two surveys covered a lot of ground, asking questions on a wide range of matters that included personal details, worship patterns, theological beliefs and moral attitudes. Not all the items were repeated in the second survey, but a number were, and this book uses 28 such items. Chapters 3–10 report on different topics, and each gives the results of two or more items related to that topic. The introduction to the chapters sets the scene of what was happening in in the Church of England or more widely in England in the period before and after the turn of the century. The data are then reported using graphs rather than tables, and each chapter concludes by reflecting on what the results have shown. The final chapter slices the cake differently by first looking at the independent variables (sex, age, education, etc.) one at a time and asking how they generally related to opinions, and then by summarizing the changes in opinions between the two surveys.

This is a book of data, and there is lots of it. The aim has been to try and present it in a way that allows readers to grasp the key findings easily, without wading through detailed tables of numbers. Instead, I have used graphical presentation in a format that is repeated for each item being analyzed. I have in the past apologized for my use of statistics and graphs, especially when giving talks to church people, but have been chastised for perpetuating a fear of all things mathematical. Most people should be able to grasp the key features of the data from the two main types of graph used throughout the book once they understand what they each display. The analyses used to produce the figures are described in Chapter 2, and it is also worth looking at Appendix 2.1, which explains how to interpret the graphs. This is especially important for the cohort analysis because the presentation is not typical of most cohort graphs, which are based on much longer runs of surveys.

For those who prefer results in words rather than figures, I have tried to summarize the key points in the text of the 'Exploring the data' section in each chapter. This means the text can be read with little attention to the graphs and should still make some sense. Those who like to get a quick impression of what is going on will probably just use the graphs instead of reading the results sections in detail.

I was not involved in the first *Church Times* survey, and I thank Leslie Francis and his colleagues for giving me free access to all the data. Leslie in particular has been generous in encouraging me to use the data sets to produce articles and this book. I would also like to thank and congratulate those who edited the *Church Times* for supporting the survey and allowing the data to be used as it has been. Finally, it is most important to thank all those *Church Times* readers who took the time to complete and return the survey. It can be stimulating to complete questionnaires, as many have told me over the years. It can also be tedious and frustrating, as many have also told me over the years. We have been gifted a valuable historical and practical resource because those who participated generously shared their beliefs and opinions.

York, UK   Andrew Village

CONTENTS

List of Figures

LIST OF TABLES

CHAPTER 1

Introduction

This book is about two surveys of churchgoers in the Church of England. Both surveys sampled readers of the *Church Times* newspaper, which ran detailed questionnaires assessing a range of opinions, beliefs, and attitudes in 2001 and 2013. The results of the first survey have already been published in some detail (Francis, Robbins, & Astley, 2005). The aim here is twofold: first, to test differences in opinions between various groups in the Church[1] and, second, to explore in more detail changes between the two surveys. *Fragmented Faith*, the report on the first survey, showed clearly how opinions differed, sometimes markedly, across the Church in 2001, hence the title of the book. The treatment was admirably straightforward, looking at the percentages of people in various groups who agreed, disagreed or who were uncertain about different items in the survey. The results pointed to the way in which certain topics divided opinion between clergy and laity, men and women, young and old, Catholics and Evangelicals, or charismatics and non-charismatics. Part of what I do in this book is to ask those questions again but answer them in a slightly different way by including the results of the second survey. The statistical treatment tests if those differences are robust and remain when data from the two surveys are combined.

---

[1] In this book, I use 'Church' (with a capital letter) as shorthand for the Church of England.

© The Author(s) 2018
A. Village, *The Church of England
in the First Decade of the 21st Century*,
https://doi.org/10.1007/978-3-030-04528-9_1

The second feature of the analysis is an attempt to determine how changes in opinion were distributed across different birth cohorts. This is relevant because some of the changes that we see in the Church, and indeed in society generally, relate to matters such as attitudes towards gender roles, morals or sexual orientation. These have been changing rapidly over the last few decades, and sociologists have been interested in whether this is because everyone changes their mind simultaneously or because successive generations are different from their parents. With matters such as attitudes towards homosexuality, for example, some studies suggest that each generation tends to keep the same attitudes through life but more recent generations are more liberal, so that society is becoming more liberal as one generation replaces another (Crockett & Voas, 2003). In other cases, there is evidence that generations may shift opinion over their lifetime (Park & Rhead, 2013). The ideal data for this sort of analysis is taken from successive snapshots of opinion over many years, so that each birth cohort can be followed through its lifetime. This is not yet possible with *Church Times* survey data, but it is possible to compare different people from the same birth cohorts in 2001 and 2013. To make the analysis more useful, I have corrected for age-related patterns of change (opinions sometime change as people get older) and examined the pattern of change separately in different traditions within the Church. Although this is not ideal data for examining change within birth cohorts, it can nonetheless reveal something about what might be going on. Were people in the Church of England in the first century of the new millennium changing their beliefs and attitudes? If so, was this on all matters or just some, and were these changes uniformly spread across the Church?

Setting the Scene: The Context of Change

It is easy to imagine that things are changing more rapidly now than they ever have in the past: people have a tendency to imagine the past as being more stable than it probably was. Things certainly changed in the Church of England between 2001 and 2013 but only history will be able to tell if this was a time of 'unparalleled' or 'extraordinary' change or just part of a steady process of adaptation. The reality is that the years from 2001 to 2013 were set in a wider context of on-going change in society at large; that sort of change is sometimes rapid and associated with particular events, and sometimes incremental and not easily traceable to particular moments in time. Before looking at what was happening in the Church of England between the surveys, it is worth noting briefly some of the things that happened in Britain and the rest of the world that might have shaped the zeitgeist. Although most of the issues examined in Chapters 3–10 are not directly related to politics or events in society at large, these things do form the backdrop against which the opinions of churchgoers were being shaped.

The third millennium had been ushered in at the start of 2000 with a certain amount of 'millennium fever', suitably contextualized for the emerging digital age. Fears of the chaos and destruction that would be caused by computers crashing because their date systems could not cope with the change of year proved to be embarrassingly unfounded. Instead, the century started with celebrations and lots of fireworks. The Millennium Dome project, an attempt say something about British culture in the spirit of the London exhibitions of 1851 and 1951, courted more criticism over its expense than enthusiasm for the content (Bayley, 2007). Britain was not yet ready, it seemed, to rejoice in its identity in the same way that it would during the opening ceremony of the 2012 London Olympics. Elsewhere, the millennium was ushered in with huge celebrations in Bethlehem for Christmas 1999, but the 2000 Christmas celebrations were cancelled due to the breakdown of the Israeli–Palestinian peace talks and an upsurge of violence. At the time of the first *Church Times* survey in 2001, this ongoing conflict in the Middle-East dominated world news and would continue to do so for various reasons over the coming decade.

Several major events filled the news headlines in Britain in 2001. The foot and mouth outbreak started in March when the *Church Times* survey was published: it swept other issues aside for much of the summer and even caused the postponement of the general election. The virtual shutting down of swathes of countryside accompanied by gruesome pictures in the media of the mass funeral pyres of livestock lent a dystopic view to the season. The Church of England, with its presence across all parts of the countryside, had a key role in supporting farmers and others whose livelihoods could be shattered overnight, so the event featured prominently in many editions of the *Church Times*. In urban areas that summer, it was a different sort of bad news that captured the headlines. Violent disturbances in northern towns such as Bradford, Burnley and Oldham were attributed to racial tensions and disaffection among young Muslims (Cantle, 2001), something that was going to be a continuing theme in the years ahead.

If single events can be said to shape whole generations, then the simultaneous attacks on the World Trade Towers in New York and the Pentagon in Washington on 11 September (forever after referred to as '9/11') must surely be one such incident. America's shock and outrage at these terrorist attacks was nothing new for the general public in Britain, which had long endured equivalent horrors from the troubles in Northern Ireland. Nonetheless, the novelty of having the attacks unfold in real time on television screens around the world was a startling foretaste of how terrorism would interact with the burgeoning world of instant news and social media in the coming decade. The iPhone, Facebook and so much of the digital infrastructure that we now take for granted had not yet arrived, though they were just around the corner. The immediate consequence of 9/11 was the 'War on Terror' and everything that it implied for the changing relationships between Islam and the West. The US-led invasion of Afghanistan came a few weeks later, followed by the Iraq War in March 2003. In Britain, the long prelude to this latter invasion was marked by turmoil over the evidence for weapons of mass destruction and huge demonstrations against the war. The failure to find those weapons and the years of chaos and violence that subsequently plagued Iraq forever marred the image of Tony Blair and made Britain much more reluctant to intervene in subsequent overseas conflicts.

Britain's equivalent of the 9/11 attacks came in July 2005, the so-called 7/7 bombings in London. The realization that those involved were not foreign terrorists, but were instead Muslims who were born and raised in England, further reinforced the message of the 2001 race riots. The multiculturalism that had been a feature of the Labour government was called into question by some who wondered if there was a danger of fostering in sections of society values and beliefs that were fundamentally at odds with those of the majority. As we shall see in Chapter 10, this was the context that framed the intense debate about the role of faith schools in England.

Global terrorism seemed to form the backdrop for much of what happened in Britain in the first decade of this century. Nonetheless, it may not have been as important to most people as other political and social change. The financial crash of 2008, which came roughly halfway between the two *Church Times* surveys, may have had more far-reaching effects on the daily lives of most citizens. The loss of consumer confidence, reversal of economic growth, rise in unemployment and fall in living standards left many people struggling to make ends meet in the years leading up to the second survey. The effects on Church finances were evident from 2009 to 2012, during which time parish-level giving failed to keep up with expenditure (Research and Statistics, 2016). Food banks became commonplace across the country and many churches were involved in organizing the distribution of supplies to those who seem to have been failed by the welfare system. This was the time of David Cameron's rather short-lived notion of 'Big Society', a vision whereby the government would work hand in hand with the voluntary sector to encourage less dependence on the state and more self-support from the grass roots of communities (Cameron, 2010).

When Tony Blair's New Labour government came to power in 1997, the party moved quickly to fulfil its manifesto pledge to incorporate the European Convention of Human Rights into British law. This happened through the Human Rights Act 1998, which came into force in October 2000. This determined effort to remove discrimination in British society led to a wide-ranging reform of laws related to ethnicity, gender, and sexuality over the ensuing decade. The Equality Act 2010 was landmark legislation passed just before the demise of the Labour government led by Gordon Brown. It brought under one Act employment law related to race, gender, disability, age, and sexual orientation. The changes in law were ultimately driven by changes in public opinion: traditional beliefs and behaviours, which had long been enshrined in law or habit, were giving way to freedom of choice and equality of opportunity for all sections of society. As we shall see in Chapters 4–6, it was these changes in society that probably had the most profound effects on the Church of England in the period between the two surveys. This was a decade when the national church had to wrestle with the problems of serving a society whose beliefs and values no longer seemed to chime with some supposedly core pillars of Christian faith.

Evidence of the change was not necessarily obvious in 2001. In that year, the National Census included for the first time a question of religious affiliation, 'What is your religion?', followed by a list headed by 'Christian' and which included 'No religion'. The question was not compulsory, but completed on over 90% of returns, with 'Christian' being by far the largest response (72% in England and Wales). There was some surprise, and even shock, that this figure was so high, sparking considerable efforts by humanists and secularists to show that the question was biased or the affiliation meaningless. Nonetheless, it pointed to the reality that, despite the weight of political and media attention given to minority religions (especially Islam), most of the population, if asked, identified with their Christian heritage. By the 2011, census the proportion affiliating as Christian had fallen to 59%, and there was a corresponding rise in the 'No religion' category, which many saw as confirming a rapid move away from widespread identity with the Christian faith (Dawkins, 2012). The issue of how far Britain should be considered a 'Christian country' has long been debated in sociological and theological circles (Brown & Woodhead, 2016; Bruce, 2002; Davie, 1994, 2015; Gill, 2002) but it surfaces only occasionally in political debate. In his Christmas message in 2015, Prime Minister David Cameron spoke of Britain as a 'Christian country', provoking the inevitable backlash from secularists and those who wished to foster a more multicultural identity for the nation (Barnett, 2015).

If it was becoming more possible and acceptable to be non-religious as the decade progressed, there were also signs that being Christian could be difficult if privately held beliefs clashed with public expectations. In 2006 Nadia Eweida, an employee of British Airways, was told she could not wear a cross at work because this was not in line with the company's corporate image. Although the company changed the rule the following year, she took her case to the European Court of Human Rights, using the legislation designed to remove discrimination on the grounds of religion. In January 2013, the court ruled in her favour, but not in favour of three similar cases heard at the same time, including that of a Christian marriage counsellor sacked for refusing to give sex therapy advice to gay couples, and a Christian registrar who was disciplined for refusing to conduct same-sex civil partnership ceremonies. Robert Pigott, the BBC religious affairs correspondent, wrote at the time, 'Today's judgement sets the legal seal on years in which traditionalist Christians have tried, and failed, to defend their values against secular ones in British courts' (Pigott, 2013). The dispensation for religious groups in the legal framework allowed the Church of England to continue to discriminate against the employment of women as bishops or practicing homosexuals as clergy, but the legitimacy of this stance was increasingly being questioned both within and beyond the institution.

By 2013, the world was both changed from what it had been in 2001 and depressingly familiar. The Iraq War and western occupation had formally ended but tensions were still evident and suicide bombings were a constant reality. The renewal of war with the advent of the self-proclaimed Islamic State was an unseen peril that would not emerge until the following summer. The main focus in the Middle East was still the ongoing failure of Palestinians and Israelis to make lasting peace and also the failure of the Arab Spring, which had promised so much in 2011 but which by 2013 had led to civil war in Syria and a military coup that replaced Mohamed Morsi's democratically elected regime in Egypt. The British Parliament voted against David Cameron's motion calling for military action in Syria, despite allegations that the government there had used chemical weapons on civilians. The economic recession had abated in terms of its immediate threat to financial institutions, but the Conservative Liberal-Democrat Coalition government was three years into an austerity program aimed at reducing public spending and the national debt. This led to a rapid growth in 'food insecurity' and dependence on food banks among families in the worst-hit areas, something that would continue for years to come (Loopstra et al., 2015). In terms of social discrimination, the Equality Act 2010 and the Civil Partnership Act 2004 had begun to change the landscape. In July 2013, when the second *Church Times* survey was underway, legislation was passed in Parliament that would allow same-sex marriages in England and Wales. The social landscape of Britain in 2013 had certainly changed since the turn of the century, with shifts in public opinion and legal frameworks towards greater acceptance of diversity and minority rights.

THE CHURCH OF ENGLAND AT THE TURN OF THE CENTURY

Establishment and Governance

The Church of England is an established national church, which means its central rules and regulations are ultimately governed by Parliament and the 'Supreme Governor' is the monarch. If the Church of England underwent many changes in first decade or so of the twenty-first century, one symbol on continuity lay at the very top of the hierarchy. In 2012, Queen Elizabeth celebrated the diamond jubilee of her accession to the throne, and the following year she experienced as monarch another change in the Archbishop of Canterbury (her sixth) and another change of pope (also her sixth) when Benedict XVI abdicated and was succeeded by Francis.

The General Synod[2] is the main body that makes the regulations ('measures') that are then passed to Parliament for approval and Royal

[2] Also referred to here as 'Synod' with a capital letter to distinguish it from diocesan or deanery synods.

Assent. Synod was created in 1970 and by the turn of the century, it was well established, meeting usually twice a year, in London and in York. Of the three houses (bishops, clergy and laity), the House of Bishops often takes a key role in drafting measures, offering guidelines and commissioning reports. The Archbishops of the two English providences (Canterbury and York) provide oversight, and in 1998 the Archbishops' Council was formed to give a more directive and executive function than Synod could offer. The Council was barely established in 2000, but in the ensuing decade, it became a key body shaping the direction of change in the Church.

The role of Archbishop of Canterbury is crucial to both the Church of England and the Anglican Communion around the world. The period between the *Church Times* surveys roughly coincided with the time that Rowan Williams held this office. His predecessor, George Carey, was an Evangelical who was enthroned in 1991 and who announced his resignation in 2002. During his time in office, he had seen through the changes that allowed women to be ordained priests, the revision of liturgy that resulted in Common Worship in 2000, and drafts of a covenant of unity with the Methodist Church (which was passed by Synod in 2003). He also had to deal with a fractious Lambeth Conference in 1998 where the issue of homosexuality was debated and given much attention in the media (Bates, 2004).

Rowan Williams had not served as a bishop in England and was Bishop of Monmouth and Archbishop of Wales when elected. He was a very different sort of Archbishop to George Carey, being academic by nature and coming from a more Anglo-catholic background (Goddard, 2013). In choosing Williams, the Church had opted for a man who was an erudite, measured theologian whose writings could perplex even those trained in the same profession (Higton, 2004). He was perceived by some as a dangerous liberal, but his focus was less on trying to change tradition as on trying to faithfully interpret it in today's culture (Goddard, 2013). At his first press conference, he laid out (in typical erudite fashion) some of the things that would typify his tenure in office:

> My first task is that of any ordained teacher – to point to the source without which none of our activity would make sense, the gift of God as it is set before us in the Bible and Christian belief; and within the boundaries set by that, to try and help members of the Anglican family make sense to each other and work together for the honest and faithful sharing of our belief...

...And if there is one thing I long for above all else, it's that the years to come may see Christianity in this country able again to capture the imagination of our culture, to draw the strongest energies of our thinking and feeling into the exploration of what our creeds put before us. (Williams, 2002)

There are hints here of the difficulties he would face in the years ahead in trying to balance the desires of conservatives and liberals. He was sometimes defeated and sometimes his willingness to explore radical ideas, and express them in the carefully measured words of a trained academic, led him into trouble. A notorious incident was his speech at the Royal Courts of Justice in 2008, where his mention of the possibility of allowing some aspects of Sharia law to hold sway in Britain was greeted with howls of protest in the popular press (Goddard, 2013; Harden, 2008). Williams' tenure was marked by some fierce debates over homosexuality within the Church of England and the wider Anglican Communion, and it would take a great deal of diplomacy and careful footwork to prevent a complete schism. Although there were instances of breakaway bishops and churches across the Communion, the Church of England remained largely intact, despite some clergy and lay people leaving to join the Roman Catholic Church. In terms of change, much of the groundwork for the ordination of women bishops was laid before he retired, and his support for the Fresh Expressions movement enabled it to be properly funded and to flourish.

Rowan Williams resigned in March 2012 and was replaced by Justin Welby who took office a year later, just before the second *Church Times* survey was released. Welby was from an Evangelical background and was relatively unknown, having had only recently been elevated to the See of Durham (Atherstone, 2014). His tenure would see more change, with the advent of women bishops and adjustment to the growing acceptance of same-sex marriage within and beyond the Church.

Tradition

The Church of England has been evolving for the best part of 500 years and in that time it has produce a number of distinctive traditions. Two key traditions are the Anglo-catholic and the Evangelical, both of which have their roots in the eighteenth and nineteenth centuries (Hylson-Smith, 1989, 1993; Nockles, 1994; Scotland, 2004). Anglo-catholicism began with the Tractarian Movement in Oxford, and supporters sought to move the Anglican Church nearer to its Roman Catholic roots.

The emphasis has been on church worship with keen interest in liturgy, sacraments and especially the Eucharist. Anglican Evangelicalism emerged from the general resurgence in evangelicalism around the same time and is associated with key figures such as Charles Simeon and members of the Clapham Sect (Balleine, 1908). Supporters sought to move the Church of England nearer to its Reformed roots. The emphasis has been on the preaching of scripture that leads to personal conversion and holy living. Between these two wings lies what is termed variously as 'middle of the road', 'traditional' or 'Broad-church' Anglicanism. Although sometimes identified as a separate movement within the Church of England (Jones, 2003), churches in this category are linked mainly by not belonging to either of the two wings, Anglo-catholic or Evangelical. Broad churches in this sense represent congregations that embrace a range of practices and theological stances. Alongside these three traditions have been a number of other influences that have affected parts of the Church of England to varying extents. Most recently, the Charismatic Movement has had a widespread impact on the Church of England, mostly associated with evangelicalism (Scotland, 2003).

Statistics

In numerical terms, the first decade of the twenty-first century saw a continuation in the decline of the Church of England that had characterized the latter half of the previous century. The importance of the data on church attendance was finally recognized by the Church in 2000, when a review headed by the then Bishop of Wakefield, Nigel McCulloch, came up with a new way of assessing attendance and a new strap line for the process: 'Statistics for Mission' (Sturdy, 2000). Since then the Church has invested more resources in its Research and Statistics unit and made its annual returns more freely available online. The 2013 report showed that 'Usual Sunday Attendance' was 784,600 in 2013 and this had been declining by about one per cent a year since 2004 (Research and Statistics, 2014). Other measures such as numbers on the electoral roll, Christmas and Easter attendance, baptisms, and confirmations also declined over the same period. In 2012, the Church added the 'Worshipping Community' measure that took into account other sorts of service, such as those that happened mid-week or away from church buildings (Research and Statistics, 2017). This obviously gave a higher figure, but it is too soon to tell from the available data (to 2016 at the time of writing) if this is also declining. The overall picture of numerical decline is in line with declines in many other traditional churches in Britain and elsewhere in Europe, and with the general decline in religious affiliation in the population.

ISSUES IN THE CHURCH OF ENGLAND FROM 2000

Each December the *Church Times* reviews its output during the year to give an overview of events and topics that made the headlines. These reviews offer a useful insight into the matters that preoccupied readers and the Church at large, and how they were perceived by editors and commentators. Some of the material relates to matters that filled other newspapers at the time and which would have been of interest to the general public. Alongside this are articles related to specifically ecclesiastical matters that pertained mainly to the Church of England or Anglican Communion, but also to other churches and even other religions. What follows in this section distils some of the church-related items mentioned in the 'Review of the Year' sections of the *Church Times* from 2000 to 2013. The list is not exhaustive, but gives an overview of some of the matters that were important at the time.

Church Schools

In 2000, the Archbishops' Council commissioned a review of the Church's role in education, which focused mainly on church schools, but which also included teacher training and other matters related to education. The underlying assumptions were that involvement in the education of children was an important part of the mission of the Church and that it was time to take stock of how this mission should develop in the coming years. This was an opportune time because there were major changes underway in the funding of education generally, which are described in more detail in Chapter 10. The working group was chaired by Lord Dearing who had considerable experience in education reviews in the state sector. The report recommended that the Church should take a bold initiative in expanding its provision of schools, especially in the secondary sector. In the years that followed the publication of the report, the wider events taking place in society led many to question the value of educating children in schools that were shaped by particular religions. Nonetheless, the Church tried to take advantage of the changing educational environment to take greater control over its schools and to expand provision where it could.

Fresh Expressions

The Church of England has long recognized that it needs to move from 'maintenance to mission' (Simmonds, 1995). Declining attendance figures highlight the need to focus energy on gaining new converts rather than propping up the status quo. The report *Mission-shaped church* (Archbishops' Council, 2004) was produced by a group headed by Bishop Graham Cray and published in early 2004. It was enthusiastically embraced by General Synod and widely read in the following years. One of the most influential parts of the report was the commendation of 'Fresh Expressions of Church', a term that came to dominate the mission of the Church over much of the next decade. Drawing on inspiration from the Emerging Church movement (Guest, 2017; Marti & Ganiel, 2014), Fresh Expressions was an attempt to produce worship and structures of belonging that were relevant to an English population for whom church buildings and traditional liturgy were strange, mysterious and totally unrelated to their lives. Examples of Fresh Expressions in the report included café church, cell church, alternative worship communities, and school-based or school-linked congregations.

The Fresh Expressions movement was most at home in Evangelical circles, where it allowed novel experiments in sharing faith. The flowering of the movement was not universally welcomed (Davison & Milbank, 2010; Nelstrop & Percy, 2008), but Rowan Williams spoke of it as perhaps the one thing he would like to be remembered for in the Church of England (Goddard, 2013). One of the key underlying questions about the movement is the extent to which it is a fundamental change in the nature of church and faith rather than the re-packaging of traditional theology in a culturally relevant guise. This aspect of the Church of England was included as part of the 2013 survey (Village, 2015), but does not feature in the analysis here because it was not heard of in 2001.

Marriage and Divorce

This was a key issue at the turn of the century because the Church was in the process of changing its rules and guidelines on the remarriage of divorced people in church. The changes in rules allowing this were passed by Synod in 2002, and the guidelines that followed placed the onus on incumbents to decide who should, and who should not, be allowed to remarry in church. During the next few years, remarriage in church became commonplace and no longer the divisive issue it had been. By 2013, divorced and remarriage was no longer an impediment to being a priest or, indeed, a bishop. In the period between the surveys, the rules on where people could marry changed, and the expansion of wedding venues led to a decline in church weddings (see Chapter 4).

Clergy Training and Terms of Service

Clergy and their formation were in focus during the first decade of the century. The Hind Report (Archbishops' Council, 2003) made a number of recommendations about the way that clergy should be prepared for ministry before and after ordination. Synod also debated the conditions of service of clergy, which were out of step with modern employment practice. Traditionally, incumbents were not considered to be employees as such, and indeed are still paid a stipend rather than a salary. They had security of tenure but at the expense of some rights enjoyed by others in more typical employment. After a long consultation and debate, measures were passed that formalized rules and procedures for disciplining wayward clergy (Church of England, 2003) and introduced 'common tenure' to replace freehold (Church of England, 2009). The financial crash in 2008, combined with the bulge of retiring clergy, meant that the Church's pension fund could not keep up with traditional arrangements, leading an increase in pensionable retirement age from 65 to 68 (Editorial, 2010).

The Ordination of Women as Bishops

In terms of Synod debates, this was the issue that dominated the Church of England in the period between the surveys. For many, the principle of having women bishops was conceded alongside that of having women as priests, but it was not until 2000 that General Synod finally requested the House of Bishops to report on the issues that needed to be addressed before women could be admitted to the episcopate. The report, chaired by the Bishop of Rochester, was produced in 2004 (House of Bishops, 2004), and in 2005 Synod agreed to start the process of removing the legal obstacles to consecrating women bishops. Although this was not difficult in itself, the thorny issue was whether there should be some sort of alternative episcopal oversight or financial compensation for dissenters, as there had been over the issue of women priests. The first draft measure was presented in 2009 and underwent intense scrutiny until a vote in November 2012. This was a notorious moment when the measure failed by six votes to get the necessary two-thirds majority in the House of Laity, to the evident frustration on many inside and outside the Church. Another bishops' working group hastily produced revised proposals that were circulated to dioceses in February 2014 and passed in General Synod in July. Libby Lane was consecrated as Bishop of Stockport in January 2015. The second *Church Times* survey thus coincided with a time when the initial measure had failed the previous autumn and a steering group was in the process of bringing forward a new measure, which would be circulated for approval the following year.

Relationships with the Anglican Communion and with Other Churches

The Anglican Communion membership includes 39 Anglican provinces from diverse countries and cultures. Working out what it means to be 'in communion' has been a major preoccupation for Anglicanism over the last two decades or more. The pressures caused by differing views on sexuality were evident in the 1998 Lambeth Conference, but it was the authorizing of a rite for blessing same-sex unions by the New Westminster diocese in Canada in 2002 and the consecration as bishop of Gene Robinson, an openly gay man, in the USA in 2003 that brought these pressures to a head. Rowan Williams created the Lambeth Commission on Communion in 2003 with Archbishop Robin Eames as chair. The Commission produced the *Windsor Report* in October 2004 (Eames, 2004), which suggested the creation of a covenant document that would be ratified by all provinces and which would define the terms of membership of the Anglican Communion. Not surprisingly it proved an impossible task to find wording that would suit everyone. Drafts were considered by the General Synod in 2008 and 2010 before being circulated around dioceses in 2010 for approval. By 2012, shortly before Rowan Williams left office, it was clear that the covenant would not gain the majority support of the English dioceses, and support in other provinces was patchy at best. When Justin Welby came to office the covenant was quietly shelved and other ways seemed necessary to maintain the fragile Communion.

If finding common ground with other Anglicans was hard enough, doing so with other denominations has been even harder. Methodism emerged from the Church of England in the eighteenth century, and while it developed a very different culture, the theological differences with the Church of England were minimal. Attempts in the 1980s to unify the churches floundered because the Anglo-catholic wing of the Church of England was holding out for closer ties with Rome, and accommodating Methodism, which had women ministers, was seen as a threat to that end. By 2003, women priests was no longer an issue, so the two churches were able to agree a covenant, which committed them to removing the obstacles preventing complete unity. However, these obstacles proved difficult to overcome and though the process was still in motion in 2013 it was far from complete. In November 2014, Synod accepted a report from the Joint Implementation Committee which had suggested ways forward to on issues such as episcopacy and shared ministries.

Talks between the Roman Catholic Church and Anglicans have been going on since 1969 under the auspices of the Anglican–Roman Catholic International Commission (ARCIC). From time to time, the commission has produced reports on a range of matters that highlight the points of common understanding and disagreement. The second phase of discussions was completed in 2006; it included topics such as salvation, communion, authority, and the status of Mary. ARCIC III began in 2011, which was also around the time of that the Roman Catholic Church launched the Ordinariate of Our Lady of Walsingham (Beavan, 2011). This institution was created to allow Church of England clergy and laity who objected to women being priests or bishops to move individually or as congregations to the Roman Church, while retaining their Anglican distinctiveness. As a symbol of disunity within the Church of England it could hardly be bolder, but the numbers that have joined the Ordinariate are relatively small to date and it has not been a runaway success (Thompson, 2016).

The Status of Same-Sex Relationships

If the issue of women bishops was the central focus of Synod during this period, the issue that was most pressing across the Anglican Communion as a whole was what to do about homosexuality. The position of the Church of England had been stated in a motion passed by Synod in 1987 and reiterated in *Issues in Human Sexuality,* a statement issued by the House of Bishops (House of Bishops, 1991). These upheld heterosexual marriage as the ideal and only legitimate context for the expression of sexual activity. While urging congregations to welcome even practicing homophiles (the term used in the original report) this option was specifically barred for clergy. The appointment of Gene Robinson as Bishop of New Hampshire in 2002 and the suggested appointment of Jeffery John as Bishop of Reading in 2003 created turmoil in Anglicanism, prompting the release of a discussion document from the House of Bishops (House of Bishops, 2003). This document was intended to help debate and discussion within the church, rather than defining or redefining the Church's position on sexuality. The powerful reaction of traditionalists across the Church of England and the wider Anglican Communion to the idea of allowing same-sex relationships for clergy made it obvious that consensus was not going to be reached easily if at all. Synod was also pre-occupied with other matters, so in February 2004 it took note of *Some Issues* and commended it for discussion in the Church, but did not do much more. The advent of civil partnerships in England and Wales in 2004 prompted a pastoral statement from the House of Bishops, which did not condemn those who enter into such arrangements and even allowed this for clergy, but on the clear expectation that they remained celibate (House of Bishops, 2005). Meanwhile, the Church had set in motion a 'listening process' along the lines suggested at Lambeth 1998. This process was reviewed in the Pilling Report that drew together responses from across Church and which was published shortly after the second *Church Times* survey (Davies, 2013).

Responding to the World Beyond the Church

The previous sections highlighted some of the numerous issues that pre-occupied those responsible for the governance of the Church of England in the first decade or so of this century. It would be wrong to fail to mention that a large part of what happened at synods, committees and working groups was related to the world that the Church was seeking to serve. A list of topics discussed in General Synod, for instance, would be very long indeed and cover everything from prisons to climate change, refugees to television, international development to terrorism and many more besides. Most readers of the *Church Times* would have views on these topics, some of them strongly held and perhaps at odds with others in the Church. While it would be interesting to explore these views using the surveys, the questionnaires were primarily designed to explore those issues that have been, or are, pressing or central to the life of the Church.

CONCLUSIONS

If you had gone to worship in a parish church in 2001 and returned to the same place in 2013, what would have changed? The answer may be rather little. A service book would probably have been replaced by a service sheet or a service sheet replaced by one that was produced with better technology. The church might have dispensed with paper altogether and moved to having video projectors and a better sound system. The language of Common Worship would be familiar if the previous service had been from the 1980 Alternative Service Book, but a few bits of the service might appear in a different place. If the worship in 2001 had been from the Book of Common Prayer it might have changed rather little, but perhaps it would be read from Common Worship 'Order Two', which retains the form and language of the original service. Those taking the service might be dressed in the same way, unless there had been a marked change in the tradition of the incumbent, and the furnishings would probably be as that had apparently been forever, unless the church happened to have been reordered in the meantime. The person taking the service would be more likely to be a woman, and more likely to be older, than had been the case in 2001. The chances are that the congregation would be smaller than it had been and its average age a little greater, with fewer young adults or children. In this sense, the change was incremental rather than startling.

Look beyond a service at how the Church of England and its members related to society and you might see more evidence of change. Fewer people would ever have been in a parish church so if they did attend a service it would be unfamiliar to them. There would probably be more suspicion of Christians and religious people generally, and less restraint among commentators or comedians in mocking their beliefs. Churchgoers might be finding it harder to express their faith openly in public or to allow their faith to influence the way they were in the workplace, particularly if their faith was at odds with liberal views about sexuality. The Church might, on the other hand, be more valued than it had been for its work with the poor and marginalized: fighting injustice, working to counter the effects of austerity, and being a force for bringing healing and reconciliation.

In the period between 2001 and 2013, the Church had continued to wrestle with the key underlying question that had been facing it for decades: what does it mean to be the Church *of* England when England is leaving behind the Church? How far does this particular church have to reflect the beliefs and values of the society it serves, and how far should it hold onto those beliefs and practices that have long been part of its tradition? This is particularly difficult for a national church because such an institution is more likely than other churches to include a wide range of affiliates. There will be some who rarely if ever take part in Church activities, yet feel this is 'their' church. There will be others who frequently attend worship and who might help to run the Church by doing jobs, serving on committees or taking leadership. In the Church of England, these people come from a wide range of Christian backgrounds, so even within the Church itself there may be very different views of what counts as the 'received tradition'. The chapters that follow are an attempt to understand how far the rank and file of the Church, ordained and lay, held on to traditional beliefs, values and practices, and how far they moved away from them over a period that roughly matched the first decade of the third millennium.

REFERENCES

Archbishops' Council. (2003). *Formation for ministry within a learning church.* London: Church of England.

Archbishops' Council. (2004). *Mission-shaped church: Church planting and Fresh Expressions of Church in a changing context.* London: Church of England.

Atherstone, A. (2014). *Archbishop Justin Welby: Risk-taker and reconciler.* London: Darton Longman & Todd.

Balleine, G. R. (1908). *A history of the Evangelical party in the Church of England.* London: Church Bookroom Press.

Barnett, A. (2015, December 24). David Cameron Christmas message: PM calls Britain a 'Christian country'. *The Independent.* Retrieved from https://www.independent.co.uk/news/uk/politics/david-cameron-christmas-message-pm-to-hail-britains-christian-values-a6785021.html.

Bates, S. (2004). *A church at war: Anglicans and homosexuality.* London: I. B. Tauris.

Bayley, S. (2007, June 24). A decade on…the Dome finally works. *The Observer.* Retrieved from https://www.theguardian.com/uk/2007/jun/24/dome.architecture.

Beavan, E. (2011, January 21). Ordinary time begins for ex-Anglicans. *Church Times*, p. 5.

Brown, A., & Woodhead, L. (2016). *That was the church, that was: How the Church of England lost the English people.* London: Bloomsbury Continuum.

Bruce, S. (2002). *God is dead: Secularization in the West*. Oxford: Blackwell.

Cameron, D. (2010). Big Society speech. Retrieved July 25, 2018, from https://www.gov.uk/government/speeches/big-society-speech.

Cantle, T. (2001). *Community cohesion: A report of the independent review team*. London: Home Office.

Church of England. (2003). *Clergy discipline measure*. Retrieved August 2, 2018, from https://www.legislation.gov.uk/ukcm/2003/3/contents.

Church of England. (2009). *Ecclesiastical offices (terms of service) measure 2009*. Retrieved August 2, 2018, from https://www.legislation.gov.uk/ukcm/2009/1/section/3.

Crockett, A., & Voas, D. (2003). A divergence of views: Attitude change and the religious crisis over homosexuality. *Sociological Research Online, 8*(4). http://www.socresonline.org.uk/8/4/crockett.html.

Davie, G. (1994). *Religion in Britain since 1945: Believing without belonging*. Oxford and Cambridge, MA: Blackwell.

Davie, G. (2015). *Religion in Britain: A persistent paradox* (2nd ed.). Oxford: Wiley.

Davies, M. (2013, December 6). Pilling report backs blessings but no new doctrine on gays. *Church Times*, pp. 3–4.

Davison, A., & Milbank, A. (2010). *For the parish: A critique of Fresh Expressions*. London: SCM Press.

Dawkins, R. (2012, December 11). Richard Dawkins: Census shows that Christianity in Britain is 'on the way out'. *The Daily Telegraph*. Retrieved from https://www.telegraph.co.uk/news/religion/9738031/Richard-Dawkins-Census-shows-that-Christianity-in-Britain-is-on-the-way-out.html.

Eames, R. (2004). *The Windsor report*. London: The Lambeth Commission on Communion.

Editorial. (2010, July 16). Clergy pensions: Pension age to be 68, and accrual period 41½ years. *Church Times*, p. 28.

Francis, L. J., Robbins, M., & Astley, J. (2005). *Fragmented faith? Exposing the fault-lines in the Church of England*. Milton Keynes: Paternoster Press.

Gill, R. (2002). *Changing worlds*. London: T&T Clark.

Goddard, A. (2013). *Rowan Williams: His legacy*. Oxford: Lion.

Guest, M. (2017). The Emerging Church in transatlantic perspective. *Journal for the Scientific Study of Religion, 56*(1), 41–51. https://doi.org/10.1111/jssr.12326.

Harden, R. (2008, February 15). Lambeth endures protests and Page 3 girls in sharia row. *Church Times*, p. 2.

Higton, M. (2004). *Difficult Gospel: The theology of Rowan Williams*. London: SCM Press.

House of Bishops. (1991). *Issues in human sexuality: A statement by the House of Bishops of the General Synod of the Church of England*. London: Church of England.

House of Bishops. (2003). *Some issues in human sexuality: A guide to the debate*. London: Church of England.

House of Bishops. (2004). *Women bishops in the Church of England?* London: Church of England.

House of Bishops. (2005). *Civil partnerships*. London: Church of England.

Hylson-Smith, K. (1989). *Evangelicals in the Church of England 1734–1984*. Edinburgh: T & T Clark.

Hylson-Smith, K. (1993). *High churchmanship in the Church of England from the sixteenth century to the late twentieth century*. Edinburgh: T&T Clark.

Jones, T. E. (2003). *The Broad Church: A biography of a movement*. Lanham, MD: Lexington Books.

Loopstra, R., Reeves, A., Taylor-Robinson, D., Barr, B., McKee, M., & Stuckler, D. (2015). Austerity, sanctions, and the rise of food banks in the UK. *British Medical Journal (Clinical research ed), 350*(h1775). https://doi.org/10.1136/bmj.h1775.

Marti, G., & Ganiel, G. (2014). *The deconstructed church: Understanding Emerging Christianity*. New York: Oxford University Press.

Nelstrop, L., & Percy, M. (Eds.). (2008). *Evaluating Fresh Expressions*. Norwich: Canterbury Press.

Nockles, P. B. (1994). *The Oxford Movement in context: Anglican high churchmanship, 1760–1857*. Cambridge: Cambridge University Press.

Park, A., & Rhead, R. (2013). Personal relationships: Changing attitudes towards sex, marriage and parenthood. In A. Park, C. Bryson, E. Clery, J. Curtice, & M. Phillips (Eds.), *British Social Attitudes* (Vol. 30, pp. 1–32). London: NatCen Social Research.

Pigott, R. (2013). British Airways Christian employee Nadia Eweida wins case. Retrieved July 25, 2018, from https://www.bbc.co.uk/news/uk-21025332.

Research and Statistics. (2014). *Statistics for mission 2013*. London: Archbishops' Council.

Research and Statistics. (2016). *Parish finance statistics 2014*. London: Archbishops' Council.

Research and Statistics. (2017). *Statistics for mission 2016*. London: Archbishops' Council.

Scotland, N. (2003). Evangelicalism and the Charismatic Movement (UK). In C. G. Bartholomew, R. Parry, & A. V. West (Eds.), *The futures of evangelicalism: Issues and prospects* (pp. 271–301). Leicester: Inter-Varsity Press.

Scotland, N. (2004). *Evangelical Anglicans in a revolutionary age, 1789–1901*. Carlisle: Paternoster.

Simmonds, P. (1995). *From maintenance to mission: Towards the conversion of England too.* Cambridge: Grove Books.

Sturdy, G. (2000, September 15). New-style head-count is almost in place. *Church Times*, p. 6.

Thompson, D. (2016, August 26). Britain's ordinariate is in peril: Here is how to save it. *Catholic Herald*, pp. 20–23.

Village, A. (2015). Who goes there? Attendance at Fresh Expressions of Church in relation to psychological type preferences among readers of the Church Times. *Practical Theology, 8*(2), 112–129. https://doi.org/10.1179/17560 74815y.0000000007.

Williams, R. (2002). *Statement at first press conference.* Retrieved 2 August, 2018, from http://aoc2013.brix.fatbeehive.com/articles.php/1809/statement-at-first-press-conference.

CHAPTER 2

The Surveys and the Analysis

SURVEYING OPINIONS IN THE CHURCH OF ENGLAND

The *Church Times* is the main weekly newspaper of the Church of England. It was founded by the printer George Palmer in 1863 and was a family-run business until it was taken over by the charitable trust Hymns Ancient & Modern in 1989. Originally aimed at promoting Anglo-catholicism, it broadened its appeal from the 1950s and it now reports on a wide range of opinion and news from across the Anglican spectrum. It does still tend to attract more readers from the Anglo-catholic or Broad-church traditions, possibly because the other weekly, *The Church of England Newspaper*, is aimed at a more Evangelical readership. The *Church Times* circulation was around 33,000 in 2001, but this had fallen to around 23,000 by 2013, the year of its 150th anniversary. Despite this decline, it is still read by a broad spectrum of members of the Church of England, both clergy and laity. Using *Church Times* readers as a proxy for the Church at large is possible, but it requires some justification and caution in how the results are analysed and interpreted.

Although *Church Times* readers are not representative of the whole of the Church of England, they may be one of the best ways of gauging changes in opinion. Getting a representative sample of opinion in the Church of England is not easy. For a start, the boundaries of the Church are ill-defined and it is not clear who does and does not belong. The nearest thing to a membership list is the church electoral roll maintained

© The Author(s) 2018
A. Village, *The Church of England
in the First Decade of the 21st Century*,
https://doi.org/10.1007/978-3-030-04528-9_2

by Parochial Church Councils, which is open to any baptized person over the age of sixteen who declares themselves to be a member of the Church of England. Some people who hardly ever go to church can be on the list, and some regular worshippers are not, so sampling people on electoral rolls may not be representative, even if it was possible to do so. Sampling even regular worshippers is notoriously difficult to do because of the reluctance of many to take part in surveys and the low return rate of questionnaires taken home from services. Some studies try to overcome this by getting everyone in church on a particular Sunday to complete a questionnaire during services. A notable example in the Church of England was a survey of all congregations in the Southwark Diocese in 2010–2012, which yielded over 30,000 questionnaires (Francis & Lankshear, 2015a, 2015b; Lankshear, Francis, & Ipgrave, 2015). The survey took a great deal of preparation and organization and was possible only with support from the diocesan hierarchy and parishes. The questionnaire had to be sufficiently short to be completed in about 15 minutes, and even then, people who were not at the church that week were missed and not everyone who was present returned a completed survey. Despite this, the results gave a good insight into a limited spectrum of issues from one particular diocese. The problem in generalizing the results to the whole Church is that Southwark lies south of the Thames in London and is a very unusual diocese in terms of its population density and ethnic diversity. Congregational surveys are the best method we have for assessing attitudes, but doing them across the whole denomination is time-consuming and expensive, and they do not always give the level of detail that researchers need.

Sampling clergy is somewhat easier because there are fewer of them, and you can target them individually if you have access to their contact details. This was done in the Church Growth study run by the Church of England in 2013 (Church Growth Research Programme, 2013). Questionnaires were sent to 3735 incumbents employed by the Church at the time, and around 1700 (46%) were returned (Voas & Watt, 2014). The age and sex profiles were roughly similar to those reported for the Church nationally, but it is not possible to be sure that even this sample was truly representative of the Church as a whole. The main problem with sampling *only* clergy is that we know that their views do not always match those of the laity, so it may be misleading to use them as a proxy for the whole of the Church of England.

Although the people sampled in the *Church Times* surveys are not wholly representative of the Church of England, they do cover a wide range of opinion emanating from different wings of the Church. Filling out questionnaires is not easy for some, and it requires a certain level of commitment, time-availability and literacy. Some sections of the Church are almost certainly under-represented among *Church Times* readers, such as Evangelicals, younger people and those who lack higher levels of education. Even so, such groups were not entirely absent in the data-sets, and provided the *range* of opinion expressed covers the likely range in the Church as a whole, it is possible to allow for the fact that some groups are under- or over-represented in the sample. One way would be to weight statistically averages according to the proportions of different traditions, men and women, education levels, age groups and so on in the Church of England. Unfortunately, we have no way of knowing what those proportions are, so the best way is to report opinion separately for the three main traditions (Anglo-catholic, Broad church and Evangelical) and to use statistical methods to control for the different profiles between surveys.

The details of the statistical methods used are given in Appendix 2.1. The main points to note here are that the data are presented in two main ways. First, all the responses from both surveys are analysed to make comparisons between groups such as men and women, clergy and laity, those with degrees and those without, and so on. The results control for the different profiles of the two surveys and allow testing of differences between groups assuming all other factors are held constant. So, for example, we can see if clergy have different views from laity allowing for the fact that there was a higher proportion of men among clergy than among laity, and there was a higher proportion of clergy in the first survey two than in the second one. This means that we can judge the difference between groups in a statistically rigorous manner and draw conclusions about views among different sections of the Church. Second, differences between the 2001 and 2013 surveys are compared graphically within each of the three main church traditions: Anglo-catholic, Broad church and Evangelical. For each tradition, figures are calculated by age cohort (identified by decade of birth) and survey. This allows for the different age and tradition profiles of each survey and shows how far opinions are related to when a person was born or to changes in opinion between the two surveys.

The Two *Church Times* Surveys

It is unlikely, as we have seen, that the survey profiles accurately reflect the profile of the Church of England at large. This is because *Church Times* readers are not necessarily typical of the Church of England, and because readers may not have been equally likely to reply to the survey. The profile of the two survey samples was different, but again, we do not know for certain if this reflected changes in the *Church Times* readership (which might have reflected changes in the Church of England as a whole) or whether this was simply due to the way the samples were gathered. Despite these caveats, it is likely that two samples of the same population (*Church Times* readers) taken a decade or so apart will tell us something about changes in the Church of England between the surveys. Full details of the profiles for respondents in each survey are given in Appendix 2.2. This chapter will concentrate on looking at changes in the profiles between the two surveys and asking whether this tells us anything about the direction of the Church at large. In comparing profiles, it is better to separate out laity and clergy because their profiles are quite different and changes will be driven by different factors.

The 2001 Survey

In 2001, when *Church Times* circulation was around 33,000, a four-page insert questionnaire was included in two editions at the end of March and beginning of April. (For more details, see Francis, Robbins, & Astley, 2005, pp. 12–14.) Despite the relatively large number of questions, over 9000 questionnaires were returned, representing a response rate of 27%. Not all were fully completed or compatible with the second survey sample, some were from outside England, and some were people who attended only once a month at most. When these were removed, the overall sample for the first survey used in this study was 6989, of which 25% were ordained and 75% were lay people. This is obviously a much higher proportion of clergy than in the Church at large at the time. The best comparable estimates are from the Church of England statistics unit, which in the 2012 edition of *Ministry Statistics* reported there were 17,256 clergy (including chaplains and 'active retired' clergy) in 2002. In 2002, there were also reckoned to be 766,000 adults attending on a 'usual Sunday', so this would mean around 2.2% of the adult

Church of England were clergy.[1] This suggests clergy may have been ten times more likely to read the *Church Times* and then complete the survey than were lay people.

The 2013 Survey

In 2013, the *Church Times* circulation was around 23,000, which included a fully online edition. The second survey therefore included both a four-page questionnaire in the print edition and a separate online version. Overall, there were 4909 replies (2775 paper and 2152 online), representing a response rate of 21%, which was slightly lower than in 2001. Restricting the sample to Anglicans from England who attended at least twice a month and who had completed sufficient items in the questionnaire reduced the sample for the second survey to 3695. Of these, 40% were ordained, a significantly higher proportion than in 2001. The reason for the difference is not clear, but it was probably due either to changes in the readership of the newspaper or to differences in the likelihood of clergy versus laity returning the survey. There was a higher proportion of clergy among the online returns (42% compared with 38% for the paper version), but this would not of itself explain the greater proportion of clergy in the second survey. Contrary to what you might expect, figures for the Church of England suggest that between 2002 and 2012 the total number of licensed clergy went up from 17,256 to 18,623, mainly due to increases in the numbers of self-supporting or active retired clergy. Over the same period, the adult Usual Sunday Attendance (uSa) had dropped from 766,000 to 680,200. Expressed as a proportion of the adult uSa, clergy numbers had increased from 2.2% in 2002 to 2.7% in 2012. These figures are only a very rough index, but they do indicate that there may actually be more clergy per head of

---

[1] The clergy data are from Table 1 of *Ministry Statistics 2012* (Research and Statistics, 2013) which includes figures for 'stipendiary' and 'self-supporting' clergy as well as 'chaplains and other ordained ministers' and 'active retired ordained' for the years 2002, 2007, and 2012. Figures under these headings were summed to estimate the total clergy numbers. The Usual Sunday Attendance is a figure available from *Church Statistics* and *Statistics for Mission* published on the Church of England Research and Statistics web page https://www.churchofengland.org/more/policy-and-thinking/research-and-statistics.

Church of England worshippers now than at the turn of the century. An increase in the proportion of clergy in the *Church Times* surveys seems to be in line with the overall trend in the Church, but the size of that increase was much larger than the national figures would predict.

LAITY IN THE SURVEYS

The profile of the lay people in the two surveys is shown in Appendix 2.2.[2] The data show that the majority of respondents were women (55%). In most congregations in the Church of England, women outnumber men by about 2 to 1, so we would expect about 67% of a representative sample to be women and about 33% would be men (Levitt, 2003). The greater preponderance of women is evident across many churches and thought to reflect the fact that women generally tend to be more religious than men, at least in terms of affiliating to religion or attending worship. In the *Church Times* surveys, 43% of laity responses were from men in 2001 and 49% in 2013. This is a higher proportion of men than found in congregations generally, perhaps because men are either more likely than women to read the *Church Times* or more likely to complete a questionnaire.

In the *Church Times* surveys, age was measured to the nearest decade, which is sufficient to observe the main trends in terms of difference between groups and over time. The age profile in Appendix 2.2 shows the laity in the sample to be middle-aged or older, with half in their 50s or 60s and a third being 70 or older. The nearest comparable data from the Church of England are from the diversity monitoring exercise in 2007 (roughly halfway between the two *Church Times* surveys), which sampled a large number of parishes across the whole Church (Research and Statistics, 2009). The report was mainly about ethnic diversity, but contained information of the age of adult attenders that suggests around half were 65 or older, and a fifth were aged 55–64.[3] This suggests around 18–25% would be under 50, which is slightly higher than the

[2] The samples from 2013 might have included some who also completed the 2001 survey. Respondents were asked in 2013 if they had completed the 2001 survey, but only around 10% said they had.

[3] Unfortunately, the national survey used age bands that are not directly comparable with the *Church Times* surveys, so the proportion in each decade group was hard to ascertain.

Table 2.1 Age profiles of laity by sex, location and church tradition (both surveys combined)

	Number	Percent aged		
		<50	*50–69*	*70+*
Men	3362	18	50	32
Women	4099	17	49	34
Rural	2794	13	52	35
Suburban	2144	20	45	35
Urban	2523	19	52	29
Anglo-catholic	3217	17	47	37
Broad church	3138	16	53	32
Evangelical	1106	23	50	27

17% for the *Church Times* surveys, but suggests the latter are not wholly unrepresentative in terms of age.

The data in Table 2.1 compare the proportions in three age groups (under 50, 50–69, and 70 or older) according to sex, location and church tradition.[4] In general, they confirm what we might suspect to be the case: the oldest sector of the Church of England is likely to be women from non-Evangelical churches in rural areas, and the youngest is likely to be Evangelical men from urban or suburban areas. There were fewer younger people in rural areas than elsewhere, and the disparity was most evident among the under fifties, with this group comprising just 13% of those from rural areas, compared with 19 or 20% from other areas. Examining the three main traditions in the Church showed that Evangelicals tended to be younger, on average than either those classed as Broad church or Anglo-catholic. For laity, 23% of Evangelicals were under fifty compared with 16 or 17% of other traditions.

The majority of the laity in the sample were married (61%), with 18% being single and 13% widowed. National Census data for 2001 and 2011 suggest that around 50% of the adult population in England and Wales are married, around 30% are single, and around 8% are widowed (ONS, 2014). The difference in the *Church Times* sample is partly a matter of the older age profile, but there also seemed to be fewer single and more

---

[4] Church tradition was assessed on the survey using a single question that asked respondents to locate themselves on a widely used 7-point scale ranging from Anglo-catholic at one end to Evangelical at the other (Randall, 2005; Village, 2012). Those scoring 1–2 were treated as Anglo-catholic, those scoring 3–5 as Broad church and those scoring 6–7 as Evangelical.

married people than you would expect for people who were mostly over fifty. In the *Church Times* sample, 4% were divorced, which is lower than the national figures for people over fifty. Civil partnerships were not in place in 2001, but 31 people (1% of the sample) ticked this option in 2013, which was a much higher proportion that the 0.2% recorded in the National Census in 2011.

In terms of other demographics, there was a roughly equally split between rural, suburban and urban areas, around 60% were graduates, 35% were in full- or part-time work, and 55% were retired. Asked about their present or most recent work, 71% rated this as 'professional' and only 4% as 'manual'. Household incomes probably reflect the high proportion of retired people in the sample, with 34% recording under £20k a year, 42% £20–39k and 23% £40k or more. Church tradition was mainly Anglo-catholic (43%) or Broad church (42%) rather than Evangelical (12%).

The profile that emerges from these figures is of a predominately older group of people, many of whom are retired, and who tend to be well educated and have (or had) professional jobs. In this sense, they are probably not that different from the majority of people you would find in church in mainly Anglo-catholic or Broad-church congregations on a typical Sunday. The opinions and attitudes of this group of people are likely to be a microcosm of the Church at large.

Comparing Laity Between 2001 and 2013

There are a number of differences apparent between the profiles of the two surveys, some of which might reflect national trends. For example, there were slightly fewer married and more single people in 2013 compared with 2001, household incomes were higher, and Internet access rose from 55 to 85%. Some caution is needed in comparing the two surveys because only the 2013 survey had an online version. So, for example, the proportion of men increased from 43 to 49%, but a significantly higher proportion of men completed the 2013 online version (49%) compared with women (40%). The best comparison of changes in the sex ratio is thus to restrict analysis to paper surveys, where the proportion of men was 43% (of 5239) in 2001 and 45% (of 1243) in 2013, which was not a statistically significant change. Whatever the reasons for the rather high proportion of men in the samples, the evidence suggests that there was no major shift in the ratio of men to women among laity between the first and second surveys.

Age profiles are important information for churches because they allow them to forecast more accurately changes in numbers over the coming decades. If numbers are stable but most members are elderly, it might be a sign there is a steep decline just around the corner. This was certainly the conclusion of the 1998 Church Attendance survey (Brierley, 2000), which predicted that many mainstream denominations might be all but extinct within a generation. What might undermine this conclusion is the possibility that age profiles are stable because people are likely to join at any age, rather than mainly when they are young. So having few younger adults might not be a problem if recruitment of those in middle age replaces those who die in old age.

The overall picture of change is apparent from frequency histograms showing the percentage of laity in each age group in the samples from 2001 and 2013 (Fig. 2.1). This shows there was a substantial difference between the two surveys indicating a significantly ageing profile. Although the proportion of respondents in their 60s remained constant at 29%, the proportion in their 40s or 50s declined by 18% while the proportion in their 70s or older increased by an equivalent amount. This trend almost certainly reflects what is happening in the Church at large, but long-term comparable figures are hard to come by.

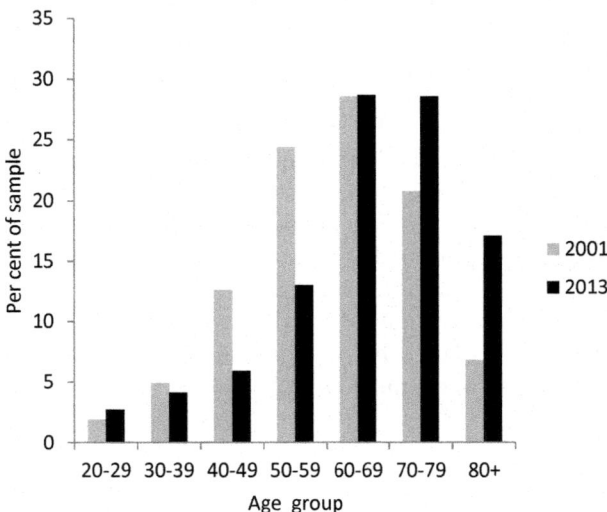

Fig. 2.1 Age profiles of laity in 2001 and 2013

CLERGY IN THE SURVEYS

Clergy profiles are bound to be different from those of laity because of the way the Church selects people for ordination. In general, ordinands tend to be people who have previously been to university and who have evidenced high levels of commitment to their local parish or benefice. Although the Church of England was for a time discouraging young adults from being ordained (they were often told to go and 'get some more experience of life'), it is now encouraging younger people to explore vocation to ordained ministry.[5] At the other end of age spectrum, only 7% of the 6804 candidates recommended for training between 2002 and 2012 were 60 or older (Research and Statistics, 2013, Table 13), and the normal age for ceasing active ministry is 70. Clergy in the sample were younger, on average, than laity, even though the sample included retired as well as non-retired clergy. Across both *Church Times* surveys, 21% of clergy were under fifty and 28% were seventy or older, compared with 17 and 33%, respectively, for laity. For non-retired clergy, 34% of the sample were under fifty, 62% were in their fifties or sixties, and 4% were seventy or older.

The data in Table 2.2 compare the proportions of clergy in three age groups (<50, 50–69, and 70+) according to sex, location and church tradition. There was a far higher proportion of men aged seventy or older than was the case for women, reflecting the fact that women were not ordained to the priesthood until 1994. If we compare just stipendiary clergy, there was no difference in age between men and women, with around 42% being under fifty and around 58% being in their fifties or sixties. As with the laity, there were fewer younger clergy in rural areas than elsewhere. The disparity for clergy was even greater (15% under fifty in rural areas compared with 24 or 25% elsewhere) and held true for just stipendiary clergy (34% under fifty in rural areas compared with 46% elsewhere). As with laity, Evangelicals tended to be younger, on average, than either Anglo-catholics or Broad church: 29% of Evangelical clergy were under fifty compared with 18 or 21% of the other traditions.

[5] In 2012, 22% of recommended candidates were under the age of 30, compared to 15% in both 2002 and 2007 (Research and Statistics, 2013, Figure 20).

Table 2.2 Age profiles
of clergy by sex, location
and church tradition
(both surveys combined)

	Number	Percent aged		
		<50	*50–69*	*70+*
Men	2513	21	48	32
Women	710	22	62	16
Rural	1213	15	55	30
Suburban	987	25	47	28
Urban	1023	24	50	27
Anglo-catholic	1484	18	50	32
Broad church	1132	21	53	26
Evangelical	607	29	51	28

Comparing Clergy Between 2001 and 2013

Women were not ordained as deacons in the Church of England until 1987 and not as priests until 1994, so there remains an overwhelming preponderance of men among clergy. Among clergy in the *Church Times* survey, there was no significant difference in method of completing the survey in 2013 (47% of 1084 clergymen completed online versus 49% of 389 clergywomen), so the overall sex ratio for each survey could legitimately be compared. The proportion of women was 18% (of 1750) in 2001 and 26% (of 1473) in 2013, which was a statistically significant increase (as we might expect). If we look at just parochial stipendiary clergy in the survey, the proportion of women was 13% in 2001 and 22% 2013, which is remarkably close to equivalent figure from the official statistics. Church of England data for 2001 showed 9352 stipendiary clergy, of which 13% were women (Church of England, 2003). By 2013, there were 8120 stipendiary clergy, of which 25% were women (Research and Statistics, 2015). The sex ratio of clergy in the Church of England has been followed with some interest because one would expect that once the prohibition on women priests was removed it would gradually change to reflect the ratio of men to women among the laity. Looking at the 2016 cohort of ordinations suggests that there are roughly 60% men (Research and Statistics, 2017, Table 4), so there is still some way to go before it can be said that men and women in congregations are equally likely to become ordained.

The age profile change of clergy between the surveys once again indicates an ageing population (Fig. 2.2). The major decline was among

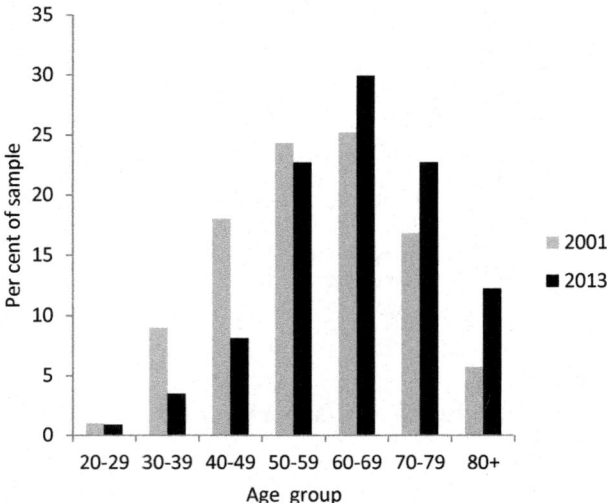

Fig. 2.2   Age profiles of clergy in 2001 and 2013

those in their 30s or 40s (15%) and the major increase among those in their 70s or older (13%). The bulge in retirements of clergy has been long recognized, and the data here show this continued in the period between the two surveys. Taking just stipendiary clergy, the proportion under 50 declined from 51 to 27%, while the proportion in their 50s or 60s increased from 48 to 73%, a massive change in just a decade or so. This ageing profile of clergy reflects the figures available from the Church of England nationally, which reported for 2012 that 64% of stipendiary clergy were in their 50s or 60s (Research and Statistics, 2013, Table 4).

The overall age profile across both surveys showed a high preponderance of clergy in their 70s or older who will necessarily be retired from stipendiary ministry, but who are very likely to still be taking services. For some, this might be just a few times a year, but many in their 70s and early 80s may be helping out parishes on a regular basis. A large number of parishes are heavily supported, if not maintained, by retired clergy who may take Sunday services or occasional offices, and offer pastoral care. In 2012, there were 5700 'active retired' clergy in the Church of England, equivalent to around 20% of licensed minsters.

In terms of other demographics, the clergy in the sample were roughly equally split between rural, suburban and urban areas, just over 80% were graduates, and their church tradition was mainly Anglo-catholic or Broad church rather than Evangelical (Appendix 2.2). Compared with the laity, clergy were similarly distributed between rural and urban areas, more likely to have degrees, and slightly more likely to align themselves with either the Catholic or Evangelical wings of the church, rather than the Broad-church tradition.

Appendix 2.1

This appendix is aimed at readers who may be relatively unfamiliar with the methods used to assess attitudes and analyse survey data. It also explains in detail how to interpret the graphs used throughout the rest of the book.

Comparing Attitudes Between Groups and Between Surveys

One of the best ways of comparing attitudes or beliefs in large samples such as the one used here is to employ Likert items, named after Rensis Likert, an American social scientist who first developed them in the 1930s. Likert items are statements that project a certain attitude or belief: 'Hell exists', 'The Church should do more for young people', 'Abortion is wrong' and so on. Respondents are asked to indicate their agreement or disagreement with the statement on a scale which has a number of different responses. The *Church Times* had a five-point scale: 'Agree Strongly', 'Agree', 'Not Certain', 'Disagree' and 'Disagree Strongly'. People were asked to circle one for each statement. Psychologists often code the answers numerically and combine answers to produce so-called summated rating scales that give a score for a particular general attitude (see, e.g., Coolican, 2014; Oppenheim, 2008; Vogel & Wanke, 2016). In this study, the responses to individual items are used, and to make reporting easier, they have been recoded so that the percentage of people endorsing a statement (i.e. answering either 'Strongly Agree' or 'Agree') is the main result used throughout.

The variations pointed out in this chapter between the profiles of clergy and laity and between the 2001 and 2013 surveys have consequences for how we go about measuring differences in opinions between various groups or over time. If we want to compare clergy with laity, for example, we could take a simple overall average score for a given item across both surveys. We might then assume that any difference we find reflects the consequence of ordination on attitudes. However, this does not allow for the fact that laity are mainly women and clergy are mainly men, or for the fact that there were relatively more clergy in the second survey than in the first one. There is a danger that what appears to be a difference between clergy and lay people is actually variation related to sex or time, rather than to ordination. In cross-sectional studies of this nature (where we sample a slice of the population at a particular time), this sort of problem is quite common. Even if we had a random sample of lay people and a random sample of clergy, there would be systematic differences in the samples in terms of age, education and gender because in a random sample we would find more men than women (because male clergy outnumber female clergy) and the men would probably be older, on average, than the women (because there are many more retired male clergy than retired female clergy). However, we can overcome these problems mathematically by using multiple regression techniques that test differences between groups while holding all other factors equal. Although the computations are complex when there are many different groups, they are easy with modern computers and the method allows us to compare scores for different groups after controlling for some of the other factors that were measured in the survey.

What is tested is how likely or unlikely it is that the difference observed in a sample represents a difference present in the whole population. For this study, the population being sampled is the whole of the *Church Times* readership. So the test is whether or not the overall difference in average attitude scores between groups (say men and women) is a real difference or simply a random effect. If the probability of it being just a random effect is less than 1 in 20, we assume it is a genuine difference, and this is what is meant by 'statistically significant'. We can attach different levels of confidence to the test: if we find a 1 in 100 (1%) probability rather than a 1 in 20 (5%), we can be five times more confident that any difference we observe is a genuine difference. There are two things worth bearing in mind when looking at the figures reporting estimated means for different groups (such as Fig. 3.1). The first is that the scale of horizontal axis, which shows the percentage agreement with the item, varies between items. This is because agreement varied considerably between items and using the same scale each time can obscure what is going on. The downside of not using full 100% scale throughout is that differences can appear large when they are only a few per cent. For this reason, the graphs also have the actual percentage value by the bars. The second thing to bear in mind is that the sample sizes are large, so even small differences are likely to be statistically significant. Statistical significance shows how likely it is that the difference is due to chance, rather than necessarily the size of the difference. Probabilities are shown on the graphs, and those reported as $p < .05$ usually refer to differences that are statistically significant but mostly trivial in size.

The differences between groups (men versus women, laity versus clergy, church traditions and so on) were tested on the total returns for both surveys (10,684) using the generalized linear modelling procedures in the statistical software package SPSS (IBM_SPSS, 2013).[6] The model was set up to test the differences between given groups assuming all other factors were equal. So, for example, there might be a difference in the level of agreement with a test item between men and women overall, but if we allow statistically for the difference between the sexes in average age, education level and whether or not they were ordained, we might find that difference disappears. The different overall scores for men and women in this case could be explained by factors other than simply sex. However, if the difference persists after adding the statistical controls, it might be because men and women have different opinions, irrespective of their background and experience. It could also be that the difference is still due to other factors that were not measured in the survey but which were related to sex (e.g., opinion might be driven by personality, and men and women might have different personality profiles). Measuring as many relevant factors as possible and controlling for their effects in the analysis is the best way of identifying those factors which are most fundamental in shaping opinions.

To examine changes between surveys, it was clear that each tradition needed to be treated separately because patterns of change sometimes

---

[6]A binary logistic model was applied using the SPSS generalized linear models (GENLIN) procedure. Dependent variables were coded 0=not endorsed and 1=endorsed, and all independent variables were entered simultaneously as main effects. Means reported are estimated marginal means expressed as percentages.

varied markedly between them. The underlying question was whether people born in a particular decade were retaining their attitudes between surveys, or whether attitudes were changing within as well as between cohorts. The best way to explore this was to plot average scores for each attitude by church tradition, by birth cohort and by survey. These graphs indicate if attitudes vary between those who were Anglo-catholics, Broad church or Evangelicals, whether younger people differed between older people, and whether attitudes shifted between 2001 and 2013 within people born around the same time.

In longer-term studies, it is possible to plot attitudes of birth cohorts throughout their lives, and this has been done for some attitudes in the British Social Attitudes Survey (Park & Rhead, 2013). In many cases, generations retain attitudes through life, suggesting that long-term attitudinal shifts occur because attitudes change from one generation to the next. However, it could also be possible that both processes are at work: each succeeding generation tends to be more liberal (or conservative), and each generation changes as it ages. In the graphs used in this book, difference between cohorts is indicated by the slopes of the lines, while difference within cohorts over time is indicated by difference between the lines for each survey. However, the separation of points for samples of the same cohort (i.e. for people born in the 1970s, 1960s and so on) could be due to the fact that the cohorts aged a decade between the surveys, and not because opinions changed for other reasons. To ensure that the graphs indicated genuine shifts in cohort opinions, rather than the changes we might expect as the cohort aged, the points for the second survey were corrected to allow for age effects.[7] In this way, we can say with more confidence that a difference in the average score of the same cohort between surveys represents a genuine shift of opinion.

To illustrate the effects of correction, Fig. 2.3 shows the percentage of Anglo-catholics who agreed that they could influence their church's decision-making. This is something that seems to vary with age, increasing from early life, peaking in midlife and declining thereafter. This pattern is evident in both the 2001 (solid circles) and the 2013 (open circles)

---

[7]To make the correction, the average change in scores between two age groups was subtracted from the 2013 survey score for that cohort. So, for example, if 30-year-olds scored 3% higher than 40-year-olds in 2001 and 6% higher in 2013, the average change between these age groups (4.5%) was subtracted from the 2013 score for 40-year-olds to give an 'age-corrected' estimate that indicated a genuine shift in opinion rather than the effect of ageing.

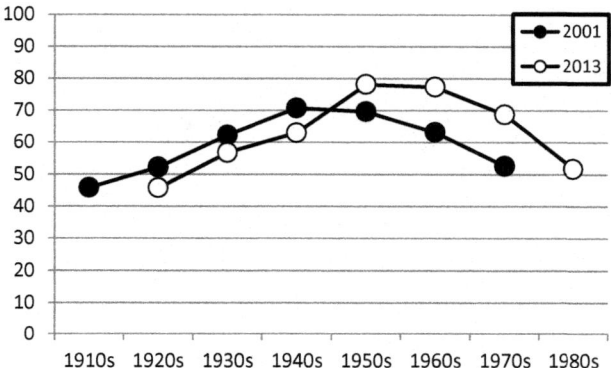

Fig. 2.3 Example of a cohort graph uncorrected for age-related changes

surveys. This means, for example, that people born in the 1970s, who were in their 20s–30s when the first survey took place, would be expected to increase in agreement somewhat in the second survey, when they were in their 40s. What seems to be higher agreement for this cohort in the second survey might simply be the normal effect of ageing. Similarly, the 1930s cohort, who were in their 60s–70s in 2001, might be expected to have lower scores in 2013 because they were then in their 80s.

When we correct the 2013 survey for the average age-related changes across both surveys, we have a better picture of sifts in cohort opinion over the decade. The corrected results are given for the 1920s–1970s cohorts, because these are ones where the same cohort was measured in both surveys. Figure 2.4 suggests opinion was pretty much as expected from the age-related change, with perhaps some increase in the percentage over and above simple ageing for those born in the 1950s and 1960s. This adjustment makes relatively little difference, unless there is a marked age effect, as is the case here.

The second example (Fig. 2.5) shows the percentage of Anglo-catholics who supported the ordination of practicing homosexuals as priests in 2001 (solid circles) and 2013 (open circles), according to the decade in which they were born and after correcting for age effects. In this case, we see that in both surveys, younger people (born in the 1960s or 1970s) were more supportive of this idea than people born earlier in the century: the slope of both lines is upwards. However, if we look within cohorts born in any particular decade, opinion became more

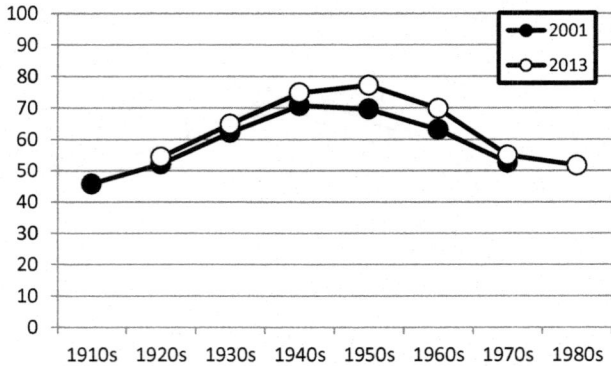

Fig. 2.4 Example of a cohort graph corrected for age-related changes

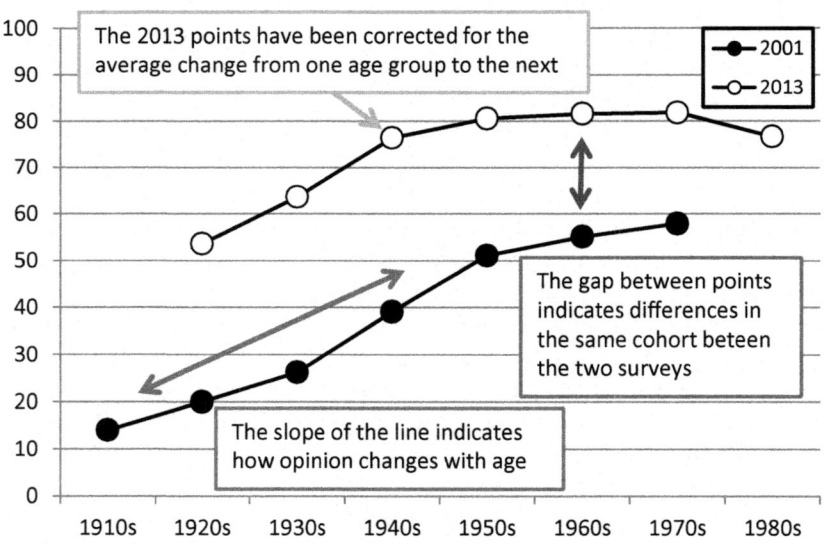

Fig. 2.5 Explanation of a cohort graph corrected for age-related changes

supportive of this idea between the 2001 and 2013 survey, even after allowing for the effects ageing on each cohort. So the shift in opinion in this case is occurring both because of generational change and because of changes within generations over time.

APPENDIX 2.2

Profiles of the two surveys for laity and clergy

		Laity			Clergy		
		2001	2013	Total	2001	2013	Total
	N =	5239	2222	7461	1750	1473	3223
		%	%	%	%	%	%
Sex	Men	43	49	45	82	74	78
	Women	57	51	55	18	26	22
Age group	<50	19	13	17	28	13	21
	50s and 60s	53	42	50	50	53	51
	70+	28	46	33	23	35	28
Marital status	Single	18	20	18	16	13	14
	Married	63	55	61	72	70	71
	Living with partner	1	2	1	1	1	1
	Widowed	11	16	13	4	7	5
	Separated	1	1	1	1	1	1
	Divorced	4	4	4	3	4	3
	Divorced and remarried	2	2	2	3	4	3
	Civil partnership	0	1	0	0	2	0
Location	Rural	37	38	37	37	38	38
	Suburban	26	35	29	29	33	31
	Urban	37	27	34	34	29	32
Education	No degree	36	41	38	11	23	17
	Degree	64	59	62	89	77	83
Work status	In full-time work	25	18	22	54	38	47
	In part-time work	14	12	13	7	9	8
	Homemaker	8	4	7	2	1	1
	Unemployed	1	1	1	1	1	1
	Student	1	3	2	0	1	1
	Retired	51	64	55	37	50	43
Type of work	Manual	4	4	4	1	1	1
	Non-manual	26	22	25	3	5	4
	Professional	70	74	71	96	94	95
Household income	<£20k	39	24	34	49	15	33
	£20–39k	42	43	42	39	58	48
	>£39k	19	33	23	12	27	19
Internet access	None	45	15	36	34	6	21
	Work and/or home	55	85	64	67	94	79
Tradition	Anglo-catholic	44	40	43	48	44	46
	Broad church	40	48	42	32	39	35
	Evangelical	16	12	15	20	17	19

REFERENCES

Brierley, P. (2000). *The tide is running out*. London: Christian Research.

Church Growth Research Programme. (2013). *From anecdote to evidence*. London: The Church Commissioners for England.

Church of England. (2003). *Church statistics 2001*. London: Church House Publishing.

Coolican, H. (2014). *Research methods and statistics in psychology* (6th ed.). Hove: Psychology Press.

Francis, L., & Lankshear, D. W. (2015a). Inside Southwark Cathedral: A study in the congregation's motivational style. *Journal of Beliefs & Values, 36*(3), 276–284. https://doi.org/10.1080/13617672.2015.1095543.

Francis, L. J., & Lankshear, D. W. (2015b). Introducing the Congregational Bonding Social Capital scale: A study among Anglican churchgoers in south London. *Journal of Beliefs & Values, 36*(2), 224–230. https://doi.org/10.10 80/13617672.2015.1041786.

Francis, L. J., Robbins, M., & Astley, J. (2005). *Fragmented faith? Exposing the fault-lines in the Church of England*. Milton Keynes: Paternoster Press.

IBM_SPSS. (2013). *IBM SPSS 22 Advanced statistics*. Chicago: IBM Corporation.

Lankshear, D. W., Francis, L. J., & Ipgrave, M. (2015). The cathedral alongside parish churches: Comparing congregations. In L. J. Francis (Ed.), *Anglican cathedrals in modern life: The science of cathedral studies* (pp. 95–110). New York: Palgrave Macmillan. https://doi.org/10.1057/9781137559319_5.

Levitt, M. (2003). Where are the men and boys? The gender imbalance in the Church of England. *Journal of Contemporary Religion, 18*(1), 61–75. https://doi.org/10.1080/13537900305488.

ONS. (2014). *How have living arrangements and marital status in England and Wales changed since 2001?* London: Office for National Statistics.

Oppenheim, A. N. (2008). *Questionnaire design, interviewing and attitude measurement*. London: Continuum.

Park, A., & Rhead, R. (2013). Personal relationships: Changing attitudes towards sex, marriage and parenthood. In A. Park, C. Bryson, E. Clery, J. Curtice, & M. Phillips (Eds.), *British Social Attitudes* (Vol. 30, pp. 1–32). London: NatCen Social Research.

Randall, K. (2005). *Evangelicals etcetera: Conflict and conviction in the Church of England's parties*. Aldershot: Ashgate.

Research and Statistics. (2009). *Celebrating diversity in the Church of England*. London: Archbishops' Council.

Research and Statistics. (2013). *Statistics for mission 2012: Ministry*. London: Archbishops' Council.

Research and Statistics. (2015). *Ministry statistics 2012 to 2015*. London: Archbishops' Council.

Research and Statistics. (2017). *Ministry statistics 2016.* London: Archbishops' Council.

Village, A. (2012). English Anglicanism: Construct validity of a scale of Anglo-catholic versus evangelical self-identification. In F.-V. Anthony & H.-G. Ziebertz (Eds.), *Religious identity and national heritage: Empirical-theological perspectives* (pp. 93–122). Leiden: Brill. https://doi.org/10.1163/9789004228788_007.

Voas, D., & Watt, L. (2014). Numerical change in church attendance: National, local and individual factors. Retrieved October 31, 2016, from http://www.churchgrowthresearch.org.uk/UserFiles/File/Voas_report_technical_version.pdf.

Vogel, T., & Wanke, M. (2016). *Attitudes and attitude change* (2nd ed.). London: Routledge.

CHAPTER 3

Basic Beliefs

Introduction

The Church of England emerged in the sixteenth century as a result of the split between Henry VIII and the church in Rome over his divorce of Catherine of Aragon. The Reformation was well underway on the Continent, and this was the wider context that set the tone for the English Reformation, where beliefs and doctrines were central to defining the identity of the new church. This is nowhere more clearly seen than in the 39 Articles of Religion, found at the back of the Book of Common Prayer. The preface shows what they were intended to do:

> Agreed upon by the Archbishops and Bishops of both Provinces and the whole clergy in the Convocation holden at London in the year 1562 for the avoiding of diversities of opinions and for the establishing of consent touching true religion.

It is very unlikely that any member of the Church of England today, clergy or lay, could quote all of the Articles, or even know what is in most of them. Any that could do so might be considered a little strange, as are some of the Articles themselves. They emerged at a time of controversy with Roman Catholicism, and so contain specific admonitions that relate to the world in which they arose. Article 22 of Purgatory says that this 'Romish Doctrine' is a 'fond thing vainly invented, and grounded upon

© The Author(s) 2018
A. Village, *The Church of England in the First Decade of the 21st Century*,
https://doi.org/10.1007/978-3-030-04528-9_3

no warranty of Scripture, but rather repugnant to the Word of God'. The central place of scripture is evident, and when the articles point to the creeds, the historic statements of Christian faith, it does so because it sees them as supported by the Bible: 'The Three Creeds, *Nicene* Creed, *Athanasius's* Creed, and that which is commonly called the *Apostles'* Creed, ought thoroughly to be received and believed: for they may be proved by most certain warrants of holy Scripture' (Article 8).

The creeds are likely to be much more familiar to churchgoers than the Articles: the Apostles Creed is part of morning and evening prayer, and the Nicene Creed is repeated week in week out at the Eucharist. They were themselves shaped by the controversies of their times: in the case of the Nicene Creed, it was the fourth-century disputes over the nature of Jesus, so while the Father Almighty gets a brief mention at the beginning, and the Holy Spirit a brief mention near the end, it is the origins, incarnation and future of Jesus that are most clearly spelt out. The virginity of Mary, the resurrection, Jesus' ascent into heaven, and the future judgement are key ideas that have seeped into the soul of Anglicanism over the last five centuries. What these things actually mean is not always clear, though the Articles did try to explicate a few key issues. Article 3 affirms that Christ died and was buried, but also that he went down to hell, which is not part of the Nicene Creed but occurs in the Apostle's Creed in the term 'descended to the dead'. Article 4 makes it clear that resurrection means resurrection of the body:

> Christ did truly rise again from death, and took again his body, with flesh, bones, and all things appertaining to the perfection of Man's nature; wherewith he ascended into Heaven, and there sitteth, until he return to judge all Men at the last day.

If the founding fathers hoped that the Articles of Religion would indeed mean the end of diversities of opinions and the establishment of consent touching true religion, they were sadly mistaken. There has probably never been a time when the Church of England was without controversy over matters of doctrine and belief. Inevitably, these debates spread beyond the confines of churches and beliefs that may once have been widely held in the English population changed over the course of the twentieth century. Just what these changes were and how they related to changes in religious affiliation have kept sociologists of religion busy for some years. Grace Davie's work on religion in Britain has been important in shaping the way that we understand the relationship of belief and religious affiliation, and the relationship of beliefs among churchgoers to beliefs among the general population. The original edition of *Religion in Britain* was published in the mid-1990s (Davie, 1994) and looked at data for church attendance and belief among the population from the end of the Second World War. She noted that two rather contradictory trends emerged from the analysis: first, there had been sharp declines in the rates of attendance at churches (especially the Church of England); second, the proportion of the population that believed in the existence of God had remained relatively high (see also, Clements, 2016, p. 14). The subtitle of the book 'Believing without belonging' captured the imagination of academics and clerics, becoming something of a catchphrase, though it is sometimes misunderstood because both terms in the phrase need to be defined carefully. 'Believing' may embrace a wide range of faith positions, and 'Not belonging' may not necessarily refer to people who never attend or who would not consider themselves a member of the Church. Davie's argument was not that traditional orthodox beliefs of the kinds expressed in the Articles, and Creeds were still common, but rather that some sort of religious beliefs were present, albeit often amorphous and sometimes far from orthodox. Britain was not a nation of atheists or a nation of non-attending orthodox believers; instead, it was a nation where religious beliefs remained, but most people did not often attend worship services. The subtitle of the revised second edition, 'A Persistent Paradox' (Davie, 2015), reflects the ongoing importance of religion, despite the continuing decline of many mainstream churches. The second edition was able to draw on the results of the 2001 and 2011 National Censuses (which roughly spanned the period of the *Church Times* surveys), both of which included a question asking about religious affiliation. The high proportion of the English population that self-identified as Christians (about 72% in 2001 and 59% in 2011[1]) shocked some secularists and demanded explanation in terms of understanding why so many people seemed willing to identify as Christians, yet were unwilling to be part of the religious life of the national church.

By then, Davie had coined the term 'vicarious religion' (Davie, 2015, pp. 81–88) to describe the way that churches may enact rituals and hold traditional beliefs on behalf of a wider segment of the population who,

---

[1] These figures are for England and Wales, the average for just England was slightly higher (ONS, 2012).

implicitly at least, are aware of this arrangement. Davie points out that churchgoers, generally, and clergy, in particular, are expected to maintain beliefs and moral standards that the rest of the population seem able to abandon without opprobrium. If this is true, then it is interesting to ask just how far *Church Times* readers hold orthodox or traditional views, and whether belief of this sort is showing signs of eroding. It certainly seems to be the case that religious affiliation is generally declining (witness the changes in the National Census figures and continuing declines in mainstream church attendance) and that this is beginning to show in belief in God. A survey in 2017 found that just 29% of adults in the UK believed there is a God (YouGov/Times, 2017). It is not very useful to ask if *Church Times* readers believe in God,[2] but understanding how some of the core creedal and traditional beliefs are distributed in the sample may indicate what it is that the Church of England believes vicariously for the nation. There are grounds for thinking that this does matter both to the Church and the population at large, as a look at some examples from recent history will show.

Liberalism in the Church of England

Many of the doctrinal disputes within the Church of England first came to prominence with the advent of modern science and biblical historical-criticism in the nineteenth century. Discoveries and conjecture about the origins of scripture and the origins of life (especially human life) inevitably raised questions about the veracity and plausibility of foundational Christian narratives and doctrines. What started as the musings of a few liberal intellectuals was soon seen as a threat to the existence of the Church that had to be countered. The tracts produced by the early founders of the Oxford Movement were an attempt to re-assert traditional beliefs in the face of a rising tide of what seemed to be damaging heresies and a move to a secular liberal state (Hylson-Smith, 1993; Nockles, 1994).

Within Anglicanism, the liberal movement was given huge impetus by *Essays and Reviews* (Parker, 1860), a collection of seven articles published a year after Darwin's *Origin of Species*. These essays, notably one by the Oxford scholar Benjamin Jowett, drew on the latest critical biblical

---

[2]There were such questions in the 2001 survey, and 98% believed that God exists, 85% that God is a personal being and 14% that God is an impersonal power.

scholarship in order to promote a more rational approach to religion and to understanding the Bible. They were widely read across the Church of England (with more copies sold in two years than *Origins* sold in ten) and provoked strong counter-reactions from both Anglo-catholics and Evangelicals (Chapman, 2011; Wellings, 2003). The ideas continued to be promoted despite this opposition, and the appointment of Fredrick Temple (one of the essayists) as Archbishop of Canterbury encouraged the formation of the 'Churchmen's Union' in 1898 (Nichols, 1993). The journal *Modern Churchman* was founded in 1911 as a forum for liberal Anglican thinking and continues in that role under its current title of *Modern Believing* (Clatworthy, 2014).

Although the Oxford Movement arose as a reaction against liberalism, towards the end of the nineteenth century some Anglo-catholics were beginning to embrace more liberal theology (Ward, 1964), as exemplified by *Lux Mundi*, a collection of essays edited by Charles Gore (1889). Gore's notion of 'Liberal Catholicism' was influential through to the early twentieth century, when Randall Davidson was Archbishop of Canterbury, and evolved into the more Modernist approach exemplified by the edited collection *Essays Catholic & Critical* (Selwyn, 1926). Although not all Anglo-catholics embrace liberal theology, the association between sections of Anglo-catholicism and liberalism is a persistent feature of this tradition within the Church of England.

From early in the twentieth century, men with liberal ideas were being put forward for high office and, as noted earlier, some sections of the wider Church and English population tended to see this as a bridge too far. Controversies over basic doctrines such as the incarnation or resurrection have surfaced with the appointment of bishops (e.g. Hensley Henson in 1917 and David Jenkins in 1984) and the publication of books by bishops such as *Honest to God* (Robinson, 1963). The 'Jenkins affair' (Dyson, 1985) may have marked a watershed in the influence of liberalism in the Church of England. Here was an academic who was seeped in what were by then well-trodden liberal ideas on core miracles of the Christian faith. Such ideas were fully at home in university theology departments, but when he was appointed as a bishop and said in an interview that the resurrection was more than 'a conjuring trick with bones' he seemed to be disparaging the core belief expressed in Article 4. The resulting furore may have made it less likely that outspoken liberals would be appointed as bishops thereafter, but the task of trying to re-configure Christianity in rational terms continues to the present day, despite the changing fortunes of liberalism within the Church of England (Adams, 2007; Burgess, 2005). This doctrinal aspect of liberalism relates to beliefs about nature of God, miracles, the nature of scripture, the afterlife and universalism. Although the radical scepticism of the 1960s and 1970s led to a counter-resurgence of more traditional or orthodox belief, the liberal theological movement has left the Church of England with a wide spectrum of beliefs and no clear consensus in many areas of doctrine (Hannaford, 2000).

In the period between the *Church Times* surveys, the main debates about doctrine have been about moral or social issues such as the ordination of women or homosexuality. There has been little public controversy over core doctrines, which may reflect a greater acceptance of plurality in beliefs among laity and clergy, or perhaps the fact that other issues have been more pressing. In these circumstances, we might expect some erosion of core doctrines if these require the need to accept miraculous events that are hard to reconcile with a modern world view. On the other hand, a willingness to allow members to believe what they will might allow liberals to be more liberal and conservatives to be more conservative.

The 2013 *Church Times* surveys repeated 11 items related to basic beliefs about core doctrines, plurality, miracles and the Bible that were also present in the 2001 survey. Results for some of these 11 items were similar, so the presentation is of those that were most typical of opinions in particular categories, with summary mentions of other items as necessary.

Exploring the Data

Jesus Rose Physically from the Dead

The bodily resurrection of Jesus is seen by many as the central miracle on which the Christian faith rests, so we would expect a high level of assent to this statement, and indeed, across both surveys there was an 87% endorsement. Those who dissented may have rejected any notion of an actual resurrection or, more likely, would consider the resurrection to be a spiritual rather than physical event. You might imagine that belief in a *bodily* resurrection is waning in the Church of England as people become more sophisticated and scientifically minded. In fact, there was a very slight overall increase in this belief between the surveys (86–88%). There was no difference between clergy and laity, nor did it depend on where people lived (Fig. 3.1). A slightly higher proportion of men than

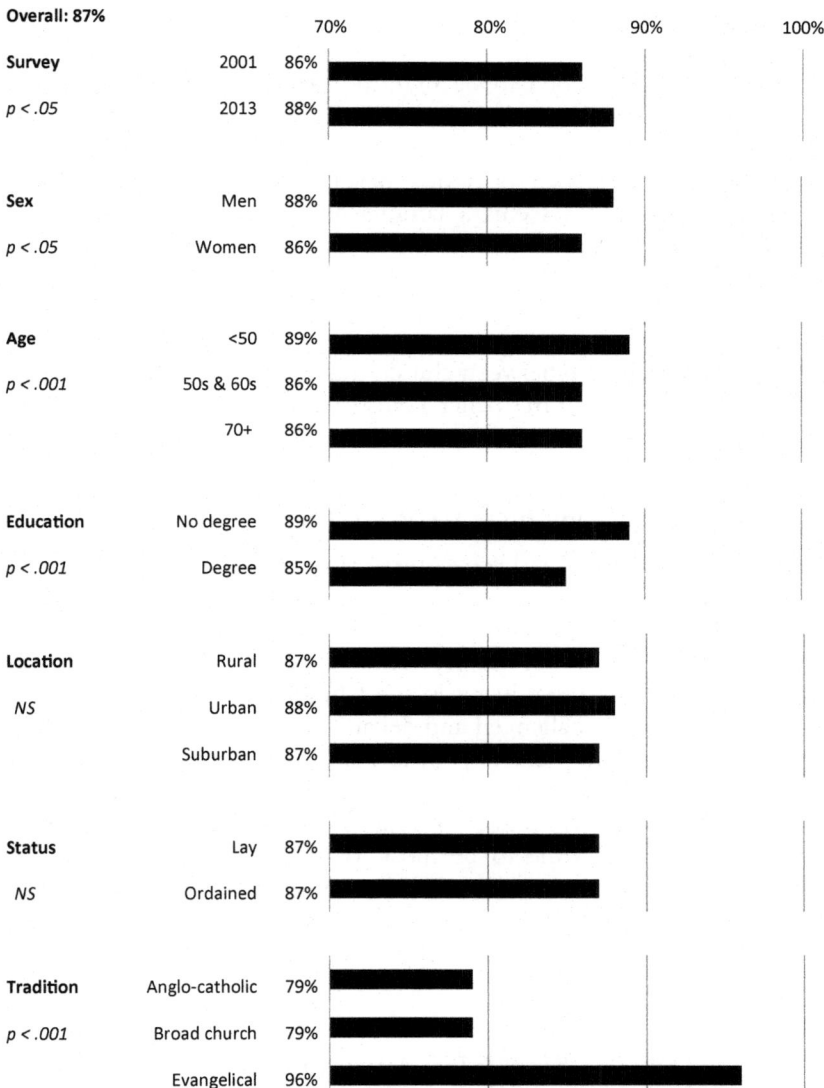

Fig. 3.1 Jesus rose physically from the dead: estimated means

women accepted this belief, but the main differences were by age, education and tradition.

Those under 50 tended to be slightly more accepting of this belief than older people, and this trend was apparent in the cohort analyses, especially among younger cohorts in Anglo-catholic and Broad church traditions, where levels of orthodox belief increased slightly between surveys (Fig. 3.2). This seems a counter-intuitive result if such belief was simply about plausibility in relation to the supposedly 'scientific' worldview of contemporary Britain. Clearly, other factors are important. Graduates were less likely than non-graduates to accept this belief, though even in this group acceptance was well above 80%. The most marked differences were between church traditions, with nearly all (96%) of Evangelicals accepting this belief, compared with 79% in the other two traditions.

Jesus' Birth Was a Virgin Birth

Another doctrine that has been controversial in the past is the virgin birth, and this item was also on both questionnaires. Overall across both surveys, 73% of participants endorsed this item, significantly less than the 87% for belief in the bodily resurrection. This probably reflects the history of the debate of these issues in the Church of England, where the virgin birth has been challenged and debated for much longer. Although assent to this belief was generally lower than for the bodily resurrection, the patterns across different groups and between cohorts were virtually identical, so there is no need to reproduce the figures in detail. You might expect this doctrine to be most frequently held among Anglo-catholics, but the liberal roots of this tradition have had more influence here than the Roman Catholic ones. Among Anglo-catholics, 63% endorsed this belief, compared with 59% of Broad church and 90% of Evangelicals.

There Is Life After Death

Life after death is a belief that is central to Christianity (the resurrection of Jesus is the foretaste of the resurrection of all believers), so again it is unsurprising that overall endorsement of this item was 93% and there was little variation between groups or between the two

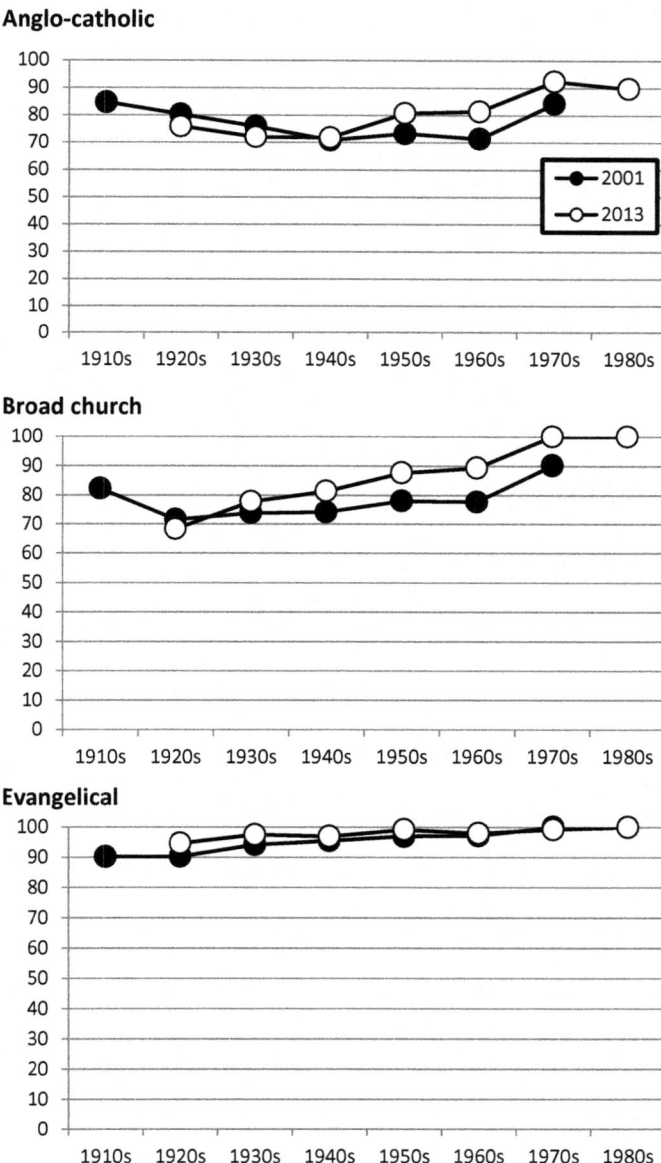

Fig. 3.2 Jesus rose physically from the dead: cohort changes

surveys. Clergy were more likely to hold this view than were laity (95% versus 91%), and Evangelicals more likely (97%) than the other two traditions (89%). Life after death has featured in surveys of the general population, where it seems to be believed by just under half the population (see Clements, 2016, pp. 48–52). Interestingly, the European Values Survey allows Anglicans to be identified, and here the figure is only slightly higher for Church affiliates than for the population as a whole (48% versus 44% for the 2008 survey). If these figures are comparable to the average results of the two *Church Times* surveys, then those who identify as Church of England in the general population would seem to be much less likely than *Church Times* readers to believe in life after death (48% versus 93%).

Hell Really Exists

The questionnaires contained two items: 'Heaven really exists' and 'Hell really exists'. In common with other surveys, there was a strong disparity between the replies to these items, with heaven being more readily accepted (88% overall) than hell (53% overall). The idea of a place of eternal punishment and suffering seems much harder to reconcile with a loving God than a place of eternal rest and peace. This difference reflects national polling data for the whole population (see Clements, 2016, pp. 52–61), where various surveys suggest more people believe in heaven (around 50%) than in hell (around 30%). The generally higher belief among a purely religious sample than the population generally is exactly what we would expect. There were similar differences between groups to those seen in the previous two items, with greater endorsement by men, by those under 50, by those with no degrees and by Evangelicals (Fig. 3.3). Again, the disparity between Evangelicals and the rest of the Church was the most marked of all the comparisons. In general, there was little change within cohorts between the two surveys (Fig. 3.4), though in most cases there was a slight decline, which was reflected in the overall difference between the surveys as belief in hell declined from 55% in 2001 to 51% in 2013. This decline in 'traditional' belief is in contrast to the slight increase in the previous two items. The overall figure for heaven was unchanged between surveys.

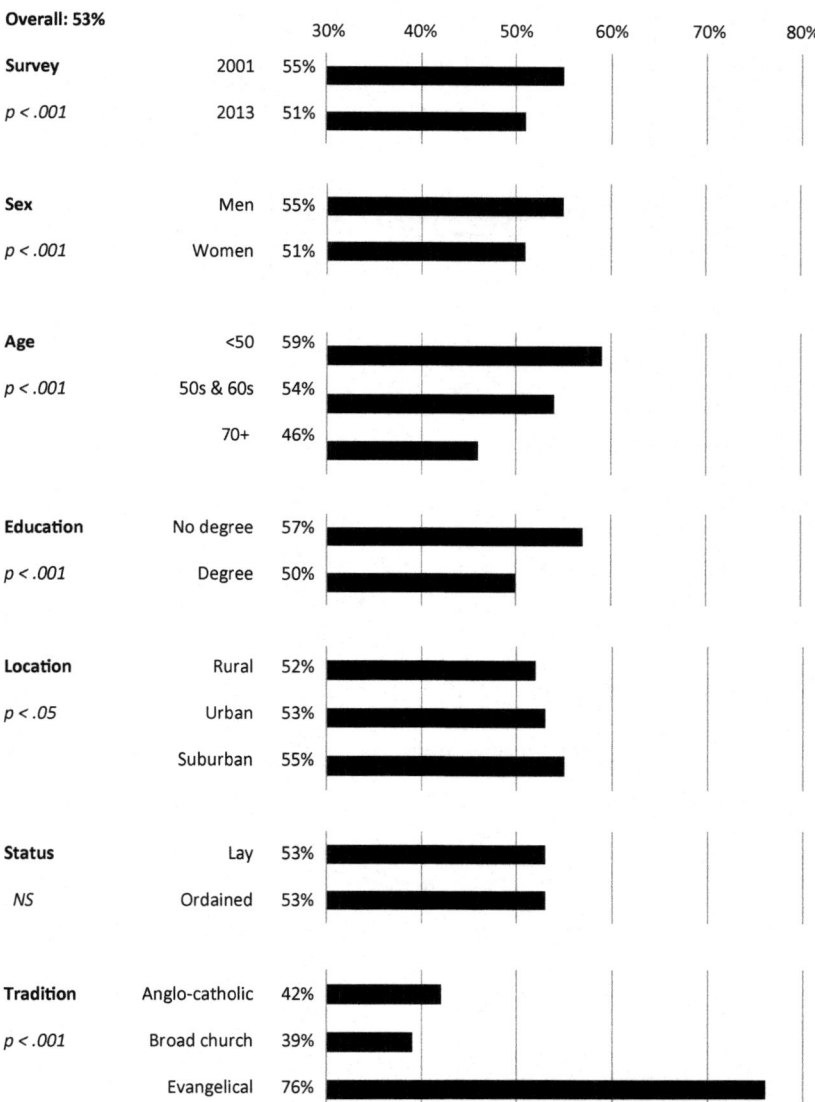

Fig. 3.3 Hell really exists: estimated means

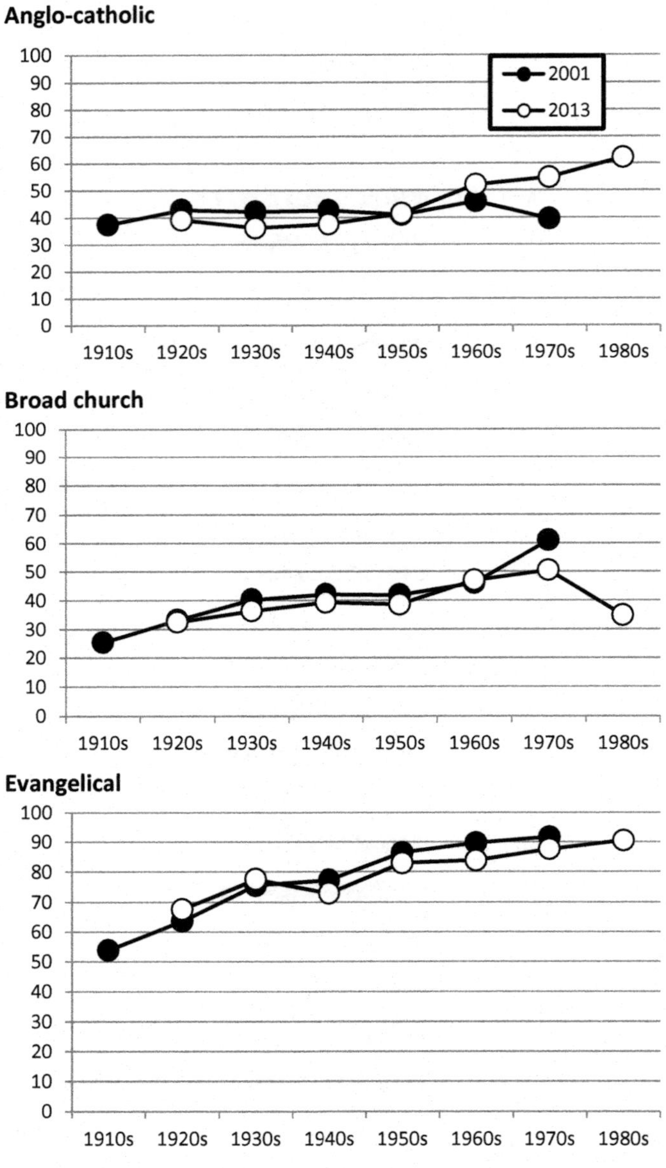

Anglo-catholic

Broad church

Evangelical

Fig. 3.4   Hell really exists: cohort changes

Christianity Is the Only True Religion

The idea that Christianity is one religion among many and that what it teaches does not exhaust all there is to say about God would seem to fit with the growing multiculturalism in Britain since the Second World War. Two items in the surveys addressed the issue of pluralism from opposite directions, both were slightly extreme in phrasing because a bland statement that, for example, sees value in some other religions is likely to get universal assent. What is more decisive is whether someone is willing to place other religions on an equal footing to their own ('All religions are of equal value') or whether they see their religion as the only one that offers truth ('Christianity is the only true religion'). Agreement with the idea that Christianity is the only true religion was much higher (55% across both surveys), than agreement that all religions are of equal value (10% across both surveys), which suggests that opinion was divided on the value of other religions: on the one hand, very few saw all religions as *equally* valid, but on the other hand, nearly half might recognize religious truths in other religions.

In terms of seeing Christianity as the only true religion, this was more likely among men, among the over 70s, among those with no degrees and among Evangelicals (Fig. 3.5). There was a slight decline in agreement between surveys (56–53%), but the cohort analysis suggested a more complicated picture (Fig. 3.6). Among Anglo-catholics (and to some extent the Broad church), agreement increased with age in 2001, but the opposite was true in 2013, suggesting those born prior to the 1950s had become slightly more plural, and those born after the 1950s slightly less plural, between the surveys. Among Evangelicals, there was little change between surveys, with younger people being even more exclusive in this matter than their older peers.

Very few people were willing to give equal value to all religions, but there were some marked differences between groups (Fig. 3.7). Agreement was higher among women, the under fifties, those without degrees, lay people and Anglo-catholics. The surprising result here was that graduates and clergy seemed to take a less plural view (unlike the case with the previous item), which may be because a sentiment that might want to find some value in other religions needs to be balanced against a naïve pluralism that simply accepts at face value any claims that are made by other religions. Agreement with this item increased between the surveys and cohort analysis (not shown) indicated that this was because of small changes across all Anglo-catholic and Broad-church cohorts.

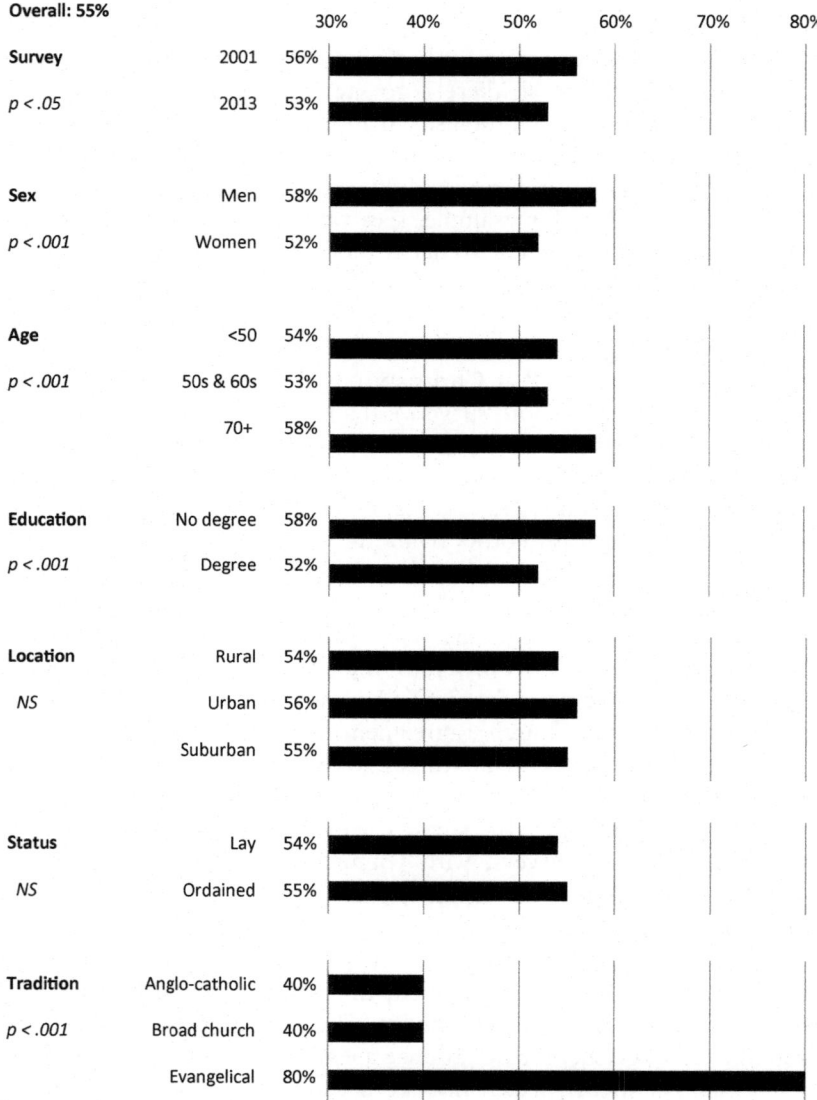

Fig. 3.5   Christianity is the only true religion: estimated means

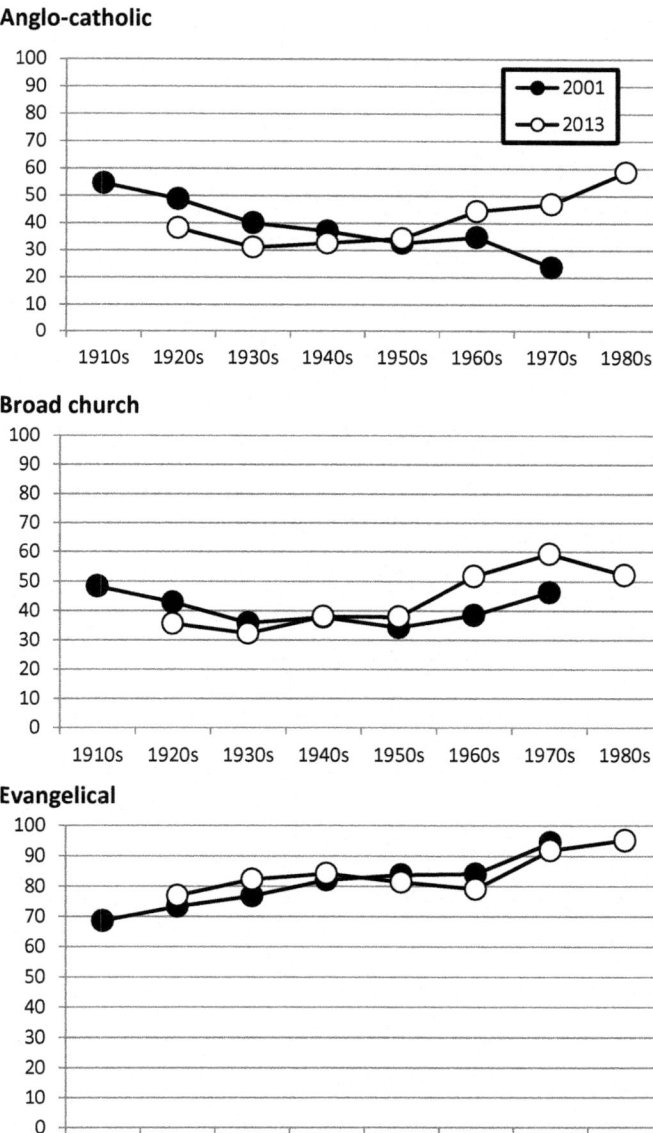

Fig. 3.6 Christianity is the only true religion: cohort changes

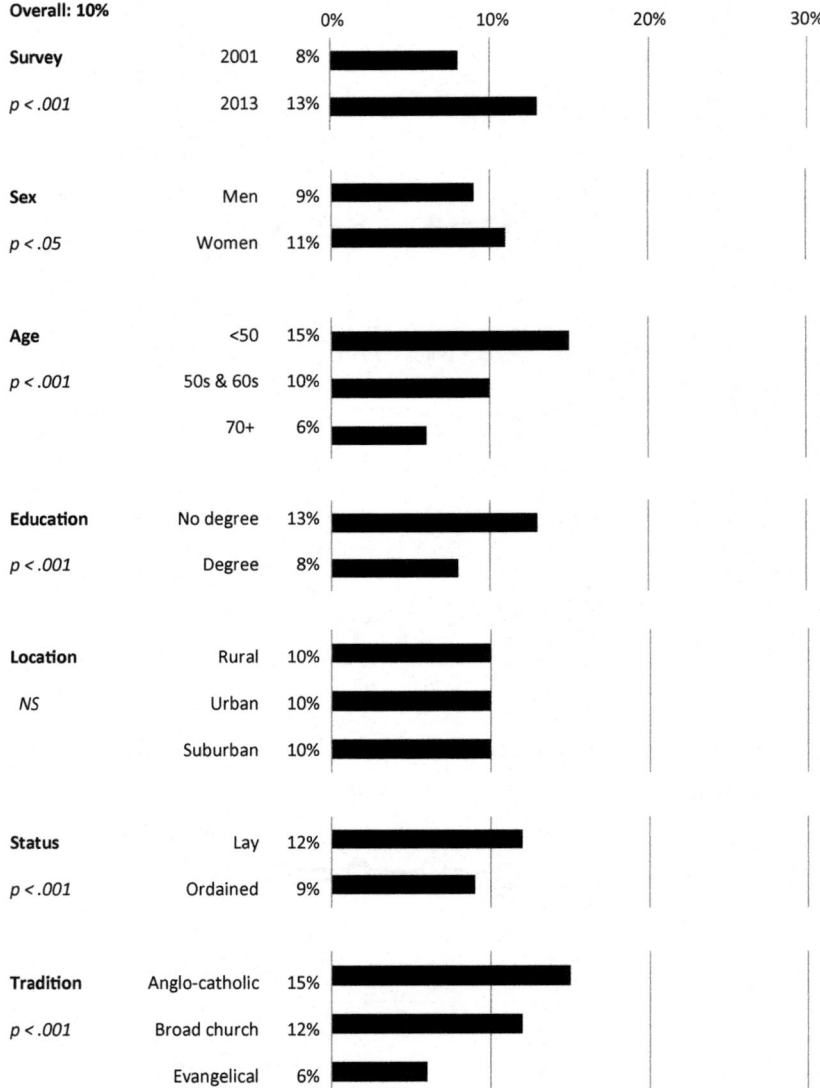

Fig. 3.7 All religions are of equal value: estimated means

All Living Things Evolved

The issue of evolution and its relationship to religion has been hotly debated in the USA for over a century, and rejection of evolution is still higher there than in most Western countries (Miller, Scott, & Okamoto, 2006). In England, belief about evolution is a less central issue for many Christians, and many more are willing to accept that it happened, albeit perhaps under the control or influence of God (Lawes, 2009). Creationists have a range of sometimes sophisticated beliefs about evolution, and a single item of this kind cannot capture all the subtleties of what it means for a religious person to accept or reject the idea that living things have their origins in the evolution of one life form into another. Nonetheless, the overall level of response to this single item (72% endorsement) does seem to cohere with the results from a more detailed study of this topic that Sylvia Baker and I have done in churches in England (Village & Baker, 2018). That study, which oversampled those with creationist beliefs, found that 67% of 544 people from the Church of England accepted the idea of evolution, compared with 17% of 1462 people from Evangelical or Pentecostal denominations.[3]

The differences between groups in the *Church Times* surveys also reflected the results of the more detailed study of beliefs about evolution, with no difference between the sexes, greater acceptance among the over 50s than among the under 50s, and greater acceptance among those with degrees than those without (Fig. 3.8). The age difference seems odd until you look at age cohorts by church tradition (Fig. 3.9), where it seemed that it was mainly younger Evangelicals who were less likely to accept evolution than their older counterparts. Location had no effect, but unlike the other items this was a case where clergy were different from laity, with a greater likelihood of accepting evolution. Once again it was church tradition that showed the greatest disparity, with only 50% of Evangelicals agreeing that all living things evolved, compared with 80% of those in the other two traditions.

This was an item that showed significant change between surveys: 64% agreement in 2001 increasing to 78% agreement in 2013. The cohort

[3]In the paper, we were looking at rejection of evolution, and the figure reported for 'not rejecting' included some who were uncertain, and Anglicans were grouped with Methodists. Figures presented here are recalculated from the data set, using just Church of England participants.

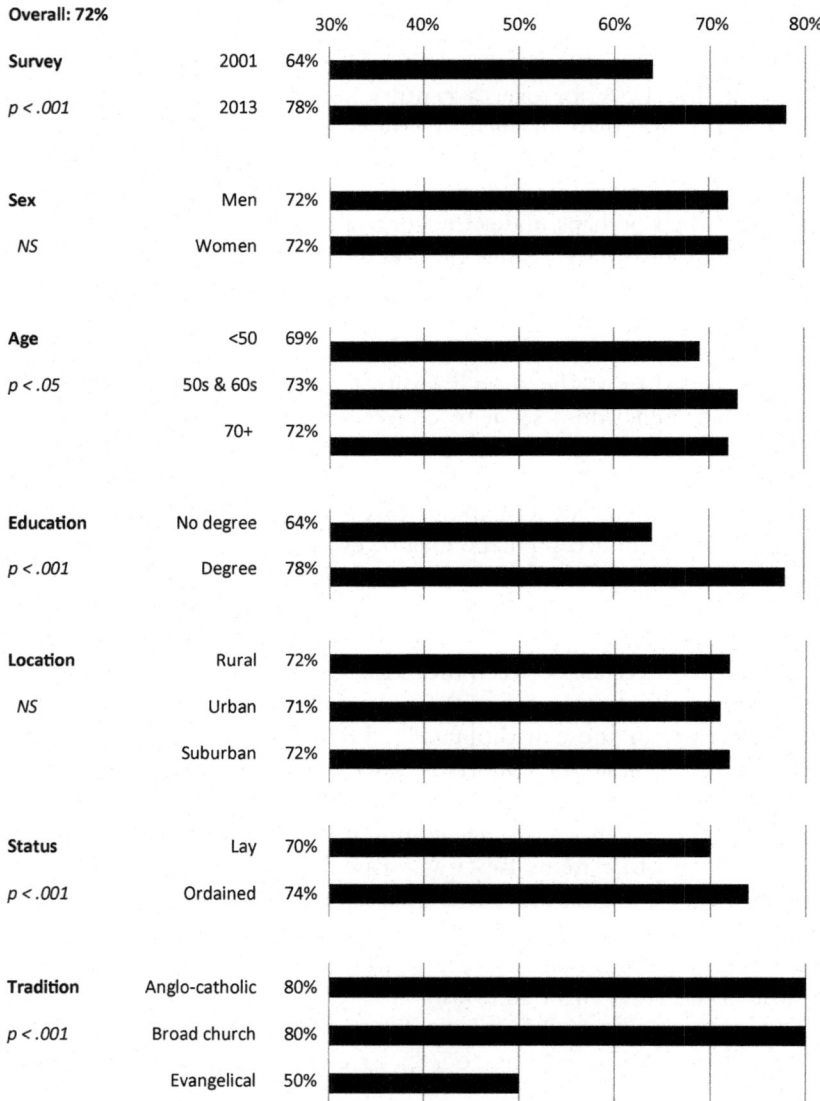

Fig. 3.8 All living things evolved: estimated means

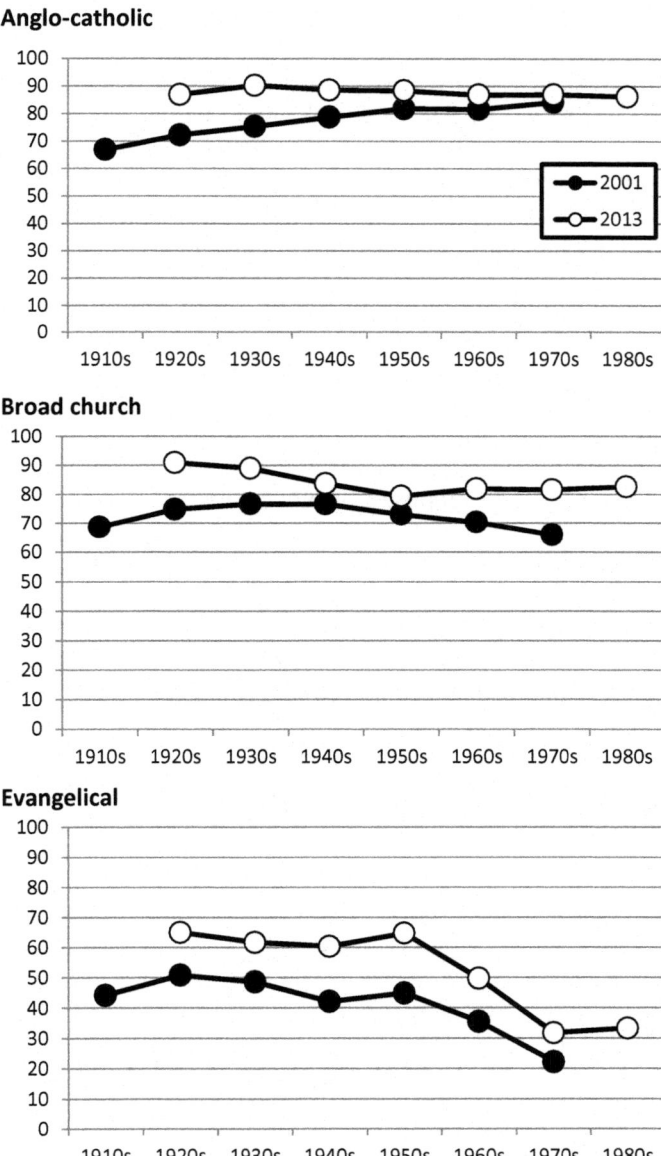

Fig. 3.9 All living things evolved: cohort changes

analysis showed that this was a change within most birth cohorts in all traditions (Fig. 3.9); in each case, cohorts became more accepting over the period between the surveys. There was a lot of attention given to evolution in 2009, which was the 200th anniversary of Charles Darwin's birth and the 150th anniversary of the publication of *The Origin of Species*. Perhaps, the discussions about evolution, which often related to whether it is compatible with religious belief, encouraged greater acceptance of the idea among some Anglicans.

The Bible Contains Some Human Errors

The belief that the Bible is without error has long been a cornerstone of Evangelical identity in the USA (ICBI, 1978). In Britain, it is a less widely accepted belief, even among some Evangelicals, but nonetheless it remains an important assertion for some. The item used in the *Church Times* surveys asserts the opposite of biblical inerrancy, and it is a good indicator of more liberal rather than more conservative beliefs about the Bible. The 2013 survey contained twelve items of a scale which I devised to measure more accurately liberal versus conservative beliefs about the Bible among Church of England lay people (Village, 2007), and which has proved useful in studying Bible beliefs among other samples of churchgoers (Village, 2012, 2016). The Bible scale includes this item on biblical inerrancy, which correlates well with other items in the scale,[4] and which was also present in the 2001 survey. Those who agree with this item tend to have more liberal views that see the Bible as containing inspired truth about God, and as being important for believers, but which do not necessarily see it as being authoritative on all matters. Liberal views also accept that the Bible is a mixture of literal and symbolic truth, that it may be wrong about some things, and that it stands alongside other sources, including the writings of other faiths, in offering humans knowledge about God. Conservative views of the Bible see it as the inspired word of God that is authoritative in all matters of faith and conduct and that gives humans exclusive knowledge about God. Although conservatives accept the idea of symbolic meanings, they are much more inclined to interpret literally and reject the idea that the

---

[4]The scale is coded so that conservative items score high, so this item is reverse coded when used in the scale since it implies a more liberal belief about the Bible. In the 2013 survey sample, it was correlated at $r = .68$ with the scale as a whole.

Bible contains mistakes or errors. These two views are not wholly distinct, and most members of the Church of England lie on a continuum between liberal and conservative beliefs about the Bible (Village, 2005, 2007, 2016).

The *Church Times* readers seem to be generally on the liberal end of this continuum, with 68% across the two surveys agreeing that the Bible does contain some human errors. The most liberal views were among the over 50s rather than the under 50s, among those with degrees, among the clergy and among Anglo-catholics (Fig. 3.10). The importance of Bible beliefs for Evangelicals is evident in these results, with only 41% agreeing compared with 76% among the Broad-church and 80% of Anglo-catholics. The differences between groups are similar to those in Fig. 3.9 for the item on evolution, and this is hardly surprising because it is likely that belief about the Bible is a key factor driving belief about evolution.

The cohort analysis showed again that the age effect arose mainly because biblical inerrancy is a belief held most strongly among younger Evangelicals and, to a lesser extent, among younger cohorts in Broad churches (Fig. 3.11). Interestingly, though, it seems that this belief may have waned between the surveys among Evangelicals born in the 1940s to 1960s, and this was the main reason for the overall change (66% accepting some errors in 2001 compared with 70% in 2013).

CONCLUSIONS

In general, the survey results reflected the sorts of trends that we might expect across the different groups in the Church of England, though some myths may need to be expelled. Younger people are not necessarily more liberal than older people, and in terms of some core beliefs (resurrection, virgin birth, heaven and hell), they were more traditional than older people. They were perhaps more plural in outlook, but this could be shifting, particularly among younger Anglo-catholics, where the idea of Christianity being the only true religion was more popular in 2013 than it had been in 2001. Clergy are not necessarily more liberal than lay people, and in some areas (life after death and the existence of heaven), they were, if anything, more traditional. In terms of pluralism, clergy were equally likely as laity to assert Christianity as the only true religion, but less likely to see all religions as of equal value. The lack of any significant differences between rural and urban areas across any of these

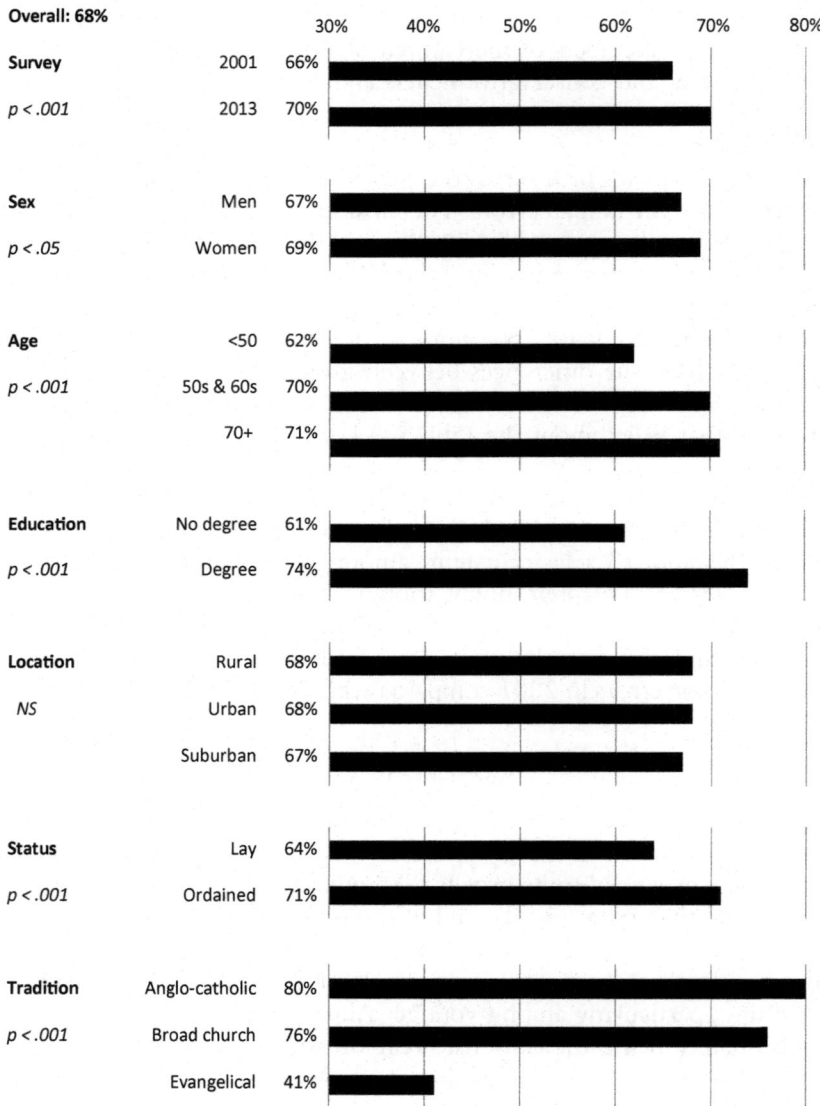

Fig. 3.10 The Bible contains some human errors: estimated means

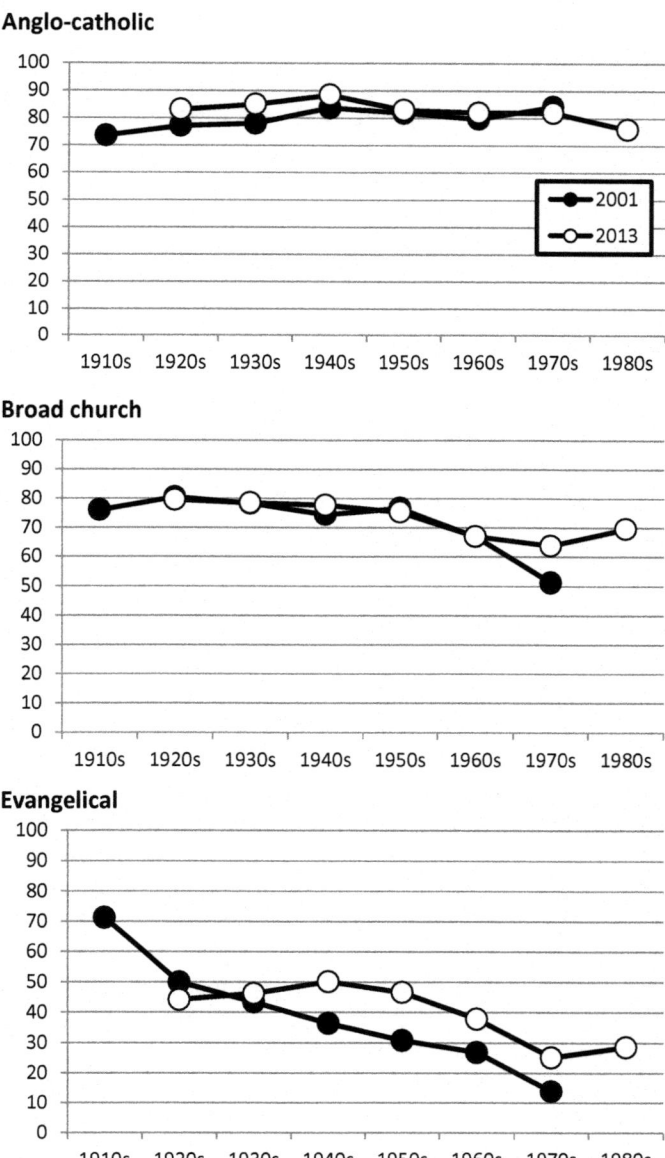

Fig. 3.11 The Bible contains some human errors: cohort changes

measures is also worth noting; cities and towns are not hotbeds of liberal thinking, and nor are rural areas bastions of doctrinal conservatism.

Other differences were more predictable and in line with what we might expect, such as the liberalism of Anglo-catholics and conservatism of Evangelicals, or the greater liberalism of graduates than non-graduates. Differences between men and women were slight, and where they did occur it tended to be women that took a more liberal view.

What of changes between the surveys? Here, the picture was mixed and depended on the type of belief. Core doctrines related to life after death, resurrection, virgin birth and the existence of heaven changed very little overall and were accepted by nearly everyone. The exception was belief in the virgin birth, which was lower among those from Anglo-catholic or Broad-church backgrounds. Belief in hell declined very slightly across most cohorts. The most marked change was in the growth of acceptance of evolution, which was not because of greater acceptance by younger people, but rather because of changing attitudes across all birth cohorts in all traditions. This could not be explained solely by shifts in beliefs about the Bible, which were minor in most traditions, but may instead reflect a growing willingness to accept the widespread scientific consensus that supports evolution. Interestingly, the main change in Bible belief was among Evangelicals, who seemed less tied to biblical inerrancy than they were in 2001.

What does this say in terms of the role of the Church of England as a vicarious deposit of traditional beliefs for the nation? Overall it suggests that both clergy and lay members are holding onto the core beliefs that the founding fathers tried to articulate in some of the Articles of religion. Where belief has eroded (such as belief in hell) it was already fairly low by the start of the century, but even now it is still more prevalent in this sample than in the population as a whole. Despite the prevailing mood of religious pluralism, it seems Church of England members will not go very far along the line of accepting equality of worth, and not completely along the line of accepting truth from other religions. When it comes to issues that might be seen as more peripheral, such as evolution, the trend is to go with ideas that allow the Bible to be interpreted less literally and therefore reduce the conflict between scientific and religious explanations of our origins. Evangelicals in the Church of England certainly remain the group that is most strongly hefted to traditional beliefs, but there are signs of some changes in those beliefs that do not undermine the core tenants of the faith.

If this picture is generally true of the Church of England, then it might mean it is well-placed hold a vicarious role for religious belief in England. There is not a wholesale abandonment of core doctrines, but movements in some beliefs that perhaps allow the Church to be seen as more plausible in some quarters. The assumption behind the idea of vicarious religion is that the large numbers of people who might affiliate as Christian, but who do not attend any particular church, may want church people to hold beliefs that they themselves do not. While this may be true, the prevalence of 'orthodox' beliefs in the general population might be more widespread than we imagine. There is little solid evidence, since most national surveys ask rather general questions about religion or the existence of God. However, a week after the 2011 National Census, Ipsos MORI conducted a poll for the Richard Dawkins Foundation for Reason and Science (UK) that was an attempt to show that the 59% affiliation to Christianity recorded in the census was meaningless in terms of what people actually believed about the faith. The study was based on a nationally representative sample of those who said they answered (or would have answered) 'Christian' to the question 'What is your religion?' (Ipsos MORI, 2012). Although Dawkins interpreted the results as proving what he set out to prove (Dawkins, 2012), a more detailed examination suggests just the opposite. Even in this sample, where attendance at church was very low, some 32% believed in the *bodily* resurrection of Jesus, and 39% believed that Jesus was resurrected in some way. The adult population of England and Wales at the time was 44,105,545. If 59% affiliated as Christian, then that would equate over eight million people accepting the bodily resurrection and over 31 million accepting that some sort of resurrection happened. While not every affiliating Christian seemed to hold to this core doctrine, a very large number did. It may be that these are the people who are content that the Church of England remains one of the places where such belief is nurtured and preserved.

References

Adams, M. M. (2007). A shameless defence of a liberal church. *Modern Believing, 48*(1), 25–37. https://doi.org/10.3828/mb.48.1.25.

Burgess, N. (2005). Geoffrey Fisher's ghost—The 'liberal conspiracy' in the Church of England. *Modern Believing, 46*(3), 63–70. https://doi.org/10.3828/mb.46.3.63.

Chapman, M. D. (2011). Essays and reviews: 150 years on. *Modern Believing*, *52*(2), 14–22. https://doi.org/10.3828/mb.52.2.14.

Clatworthy, J. (2014). Editorial: [Liberal theology, with some background on the beginning of what became Modern Church]. *Modern Believing*, *55*(4), v–xxi. https://doi.org/10.3828/mb.2014.31.

Clements, B. (2016). *Surveying Christian beliefs and religious debates in post-war Britain*. New York: Palgrave Macmillan.

Davie, G. (1994). *Religion in Britain since 1945: Believing without belonging*. Oxford and Cambridge, MA: Blackwell.

Davie, G. (2015). *Religion in Britain: A persistent paradox* (2nd ed.). Oxford: Wiley.

Dawkins, R. (2012, December 11). Richard Dawkins: Census shows that Christianity in Britain is 'on the way out'. *The Daily Telegraph*. Retrieved from https://www.telegraph.co.uk/news/religion/9738031/Richard-Dawkins-Census-shows-that-Christianity-in-Britain-is-on-the-way-out.html.

Dyson, A. (1985). The bishop of Durham and all that. *Modern Churchman*, *27*(3), 1–2. https://doi.org/10.3828/mc.27.3.1.

Gore, C. (Ed.). (1889). *Lux Mundi: A series of studies in the religion of the incarnation*. London: John Murray.

Hannaford, R. (2000). The legacy of liberal Anglican theology. *Theology*, *103*(812), 89–97. https://doi.org/10.1177/0040571x0010300203.

Hylson-Smith, K. (1993). *High churchmanship in the Church of England from the sixteenth century to the late twentieth century*. Edinburgh: T&T Clark.

ICBI. (1978). *Chicago Statement on Biblical Inerrancy*. Retrieved December 6, 2017, from http://www.bible-researcher.com/chicago1.html.

Ipsos MORI. (2012). *Religious and social attitudes of UK Christians in 2011*. Retrieved June 14, 2018, from https://www.ipsos-mori.com/researchpublications/researcharchive/2921/Religious-and-Social-Attitudes-of-UK-Christians-in-2011.aspx.

Lawes, C. (2009). *Faith and Darwin: Harmony, conflict, or confusion?* London: Theos.

Miller, J. D., Scott, E. C., & Okamoto, S. (2006). Public acceptance of evolution. *Science, 313*(5788), 765–766. https://doi.org/10.1126/science.1126746.

Nichols, A. (1993). *The panther and the hind: A theological history of Anglicanism*. Edinburgh: T&T Clark.

Nockles, P. B. (1994). *The Oxford Movement in context: Anglican high churchmanship, 1760–1857*. Cambridge: Cambridge University Press.

ONS. (2012). *Religion in England and Wales 2011*. London: Office for National Statistics.

Parker, J. W. (Ed.). (1860). *Essays and reviews*. London: Parker.

Robinson, J. A. T. (1963). *Honest to God*. London: SCM Press.

Selwyn, E. G. (1926). *Essays Catholic & critical*. London: Society for Promoting Christian Knowledge.

Village, A. (2005). Assessing belief about the Bible: A study among Anglican laity. *Review of Religious Research, 46*(3), 243–254. https://doi.org/10.2307/3512554.

Village, A. (2007). *The Bible and lay people: An empirical approach to ordinary hermeneutics*. Aldershot and Burlington, VT: Ashgate.

Village, A. (2012). Biblical literalism among Anglican clergy: What is the role of psychological type? *Mental Health, Religion & Culture, 15*(9), 955–968. https://doi.org/10.1080/13674676.2012.681482.

Village, A. (2016). Biblical conservatism and psychological type. *Journal of Empirical Theology, 29*(2), 137–159. https://doi.org/10.1163/15709256-12341340.

Village, A., & Baker, S. (2018). Rejecting Darwinian evolution: The effects of education, church tradition, and individual theological stance among UK churchgoers. *Review of Religious Research*. https://doi.org/10.1007/s13644-018-0335-8.

Ward, W. R. (1964). Oxford and the origins of liberal Catholicism in the Church of England. *Studies in Church History, 1*, 233–252. https://doi.org/10.1017/s0424208400004368.

Wellings, M. (2003). *Evangelicals embattled: Responses of evangelicals in the Church of England to ritualism, Darwinism, and theological liberalism 1890–1930*. Carlisle: Paternoster Press.

YouGov/Times. (2017). *Religion survey*. Retrieved June 14, 2018, from https://d25d2506sfb94s.cloudfront.net/cumulus_uploads/document/uz340ezwgn/TimesResults_171212_Religion_w.pdf.

CHAPTER 4

Marriage and Divorce

INTRODUCTION

The place of marriage in society has undergone profound changes in the UK and elsewhere over the last 70 years or more. Traditional Christian views about cohabitation and divorce have, by and large, given way to more liberal attitudes that have removed the stigma and made it much more likely that couples will live together before marriage, never marry at all, and, if they do, be willing to end their marriage by divorce. The Church of England has had to come to terms with these changes by balancing the need to affirm traditional beliefs and practices with the need to evolve in order to proclaim a faith that is meaningful and relevant to contemporary people. This chapter explores how rank and file members of the Church responded to the changing mores of English society in the first decade of the twentieth century. It begins by drawing on national and church statistics to describe these changes, and by noting some of the key teaching documents that were issued by the Church of England in the decades prior to and during the survey period. The data that are then reported refer to items that assess beliefs related to a number of specific issues that were particularly pertinent for the Church in this period.

© The Author(s) 2018
A. Village, *The Church of England
in the First Decade of the 21st Century*,
https://doi.org/10.1007/978-3-030-04528-9_4

Attitudes to Marriage and Divorce in British Society

The progress of change in society at large has been monitored in a range of statistical and survey data, which show how both attitudes and practice have evolved alongside changes in legislation. The frequency of marriage is best expressed as the number of men or women who marry in a given year against the number of each sex who are eligible to do so. Data from the Office for National Statistics show that the general marriage rate (marriages per year per 1000 eligible people) was at historically high levels in the mid-twentieth century (ONS, 2014b). This was partly because of a growth in civil marriages from the 1950s, which peaked in the 1970s after the reforms in the law allowed large numbers of people to divorce and remarry who had previously found this impossible (Haskey, 2015). The marriage rate then fell from 67 for men and 52 for women in 1975 to 27 for men and 24 for women in 2001, the year of the first *Church Times* survey Despite a slight easing of the rate of decline between the two surveys, by 2015 the figures were their lowest ever at 22 for men and 20 for women (ONS, 2018b). The same data source also shows that not only was marriage becoming less frequent, but also that a lower proportion was through religious ceremonies. In 1991, 51% of marriages were solemnized in this way, but this fell to 36% in 2001 and to 30% by 2012. This was partly because the law changed in 1994 to allow weddings to take place in a range of locations besides churches and registry offices. The proportion of all marriages that took place in the Church of England (and the Church in Wales) fell from 34% in 1991, to 24% in 2001, and to 22% in 2012. The net effect would be that many parish churches would have experienced a rapid decline the number of weddings in the decades leading up to 2001, and a steady decline thereafter.

Cohabitation is not so easily measured in the general population, and it is only relatively recently that there have been reliable figures. The difficultly in measuring cohabitation is partly due to the difficultly in defining what it is. For some, it could mean a brief period of living together, for others it is a temporary interlude prior to marriage, and for yet others it may mean a long-term relationship that has all the appearance of a marriage, but which is not technically solemnized. There is currently no legal status for 'common law' marriage in England and Wales, and even if couples have lived together for many years and have children they lack the legal rights and responsibilities of married couples or couples in civil partnerships (Fairbairn, 2018). What the data for Britain do show

(Beaujouan & Bhrolcháin, 2014) is that fewer than 1% of adults under 50 in Britain were cohabitating at any one time in the 1960s, but this had risen to over 60% by the first decade of the twenty-first century. To some extent, then, the rise in cohabitation has offset the decline in marriages, so that the proportion of men and women who have been in at least one partnership (marriage or cohabitation) by the age of 40 remains at about 90%. Nonetheless, the shift has had profound consequences, not least for the number of children born outside of marriage, which was less than 10% in the 1960s, rose to over 40% by 2001, and to 47% by 2013 (Haskey, 2014; ONS, 2014a). The stigma associated with cohabitation and illegitimacy has declined markedly and continued to do so in the period between the *Church Times* surveys. In 2006, 67% of the population agreed that there is 'little social difference between marriage and living together', and this rose to 77% by 2014 (NatCen, 2018).

The changing attitudes and practices around marriage and cohabitation are also reflected in how society views the breakdown of marriage. Divorce or annulment of marriages has always been possible in England, but it was only from the middle of the nineteenth century that access to divorce became possible through the courts rather than Parliament, and it was not until the Divorce Reform Act of 1969 that divorce was possible on the grounds of 'irretrievable breakdown' (Burton, 2015). The latter could be evidenced by the fact of separation, removing the necessity of one party having to prove the fault of the other. Nonetheless, divorce remains an essentially litigious process and, despite subsequent attempts to reform the law to make divorce easier, it can still be protracted, painful, and expensive. It may partly be the difficulties surrounding divorce that have made people less willing to enter into marriage in the first place. Although religious opposition is often cited by some as the main reason why divorce reforms have been so slow and tortuous, the Church has not in general tried to block changes for the population as a whole, and in some cases has been at the forefront of urging reform (Burton, 2015).

The divorce rate was already increasing in England and Wales prior to the changes in divorce laws in the early 1970s, and the laws were reflecting changes in attitudes that began some decades earlier. In the 1960s there were about 3 divorces per 1000 married men and women; this rose to about 11 by the end of the 1970s and reached a peak in 1993 of 14 (ONS, 2017). Since then the trend has been for a decline, with the rate falling between the *Church Times* surveys from 13 in 2001 to 10 in 2013. The decline may reflect the fact that younger people are likely to cohabit rather than marry, and a cohabiting relationship breakdown is not recorded in the divorce figures. There may also have been some changes to attitudes towards divorce: the British Social Attitudes survey included an item 'Do you agree or disagree that divorce is usually the best solution when a couple can't seem to work out their marriage problems?' in 1994, 2002 and 2012 (NatCen, 2018). The percentage agreeing or strongly agreeing in those years was 55, 61 and 53% respectively, suggesting there may have been a slight hardening of attitudes in the period between the two *Church Times* surveys. In 2008, the same British Social Attitudes survey found that 27% felt that divorce was never wrong, 68% that it was sometimes wrong and 5% that it was always wrong.

These changing patterns along with increased lone parenthood and diversity in sexual behaviour and sexual partnership have formed what some sociologists have termed 'the second demographic transition' (Haskey, 2014; Lesthaeghe, 2014), which seems to be a feature of a number of societies in different parts of the world. The first transition refers to the declines in mortality (especially child mortality) and fertility that have accompanied industrial and economic development. Characteristics of the second transition are said to include falling proportions of married people in the population, rising age of first marriages, increasing cohabitation and divorce, decline in remarriage rates, and increasing fertility outside marriages (see Lesthaeghe, 2014, Table 1). While this may not be a necessary transition that all societies go through, it does describe well the background against which the *Church Times* surveys took place. The decades prior to the first survey in 2001 had been ones of rapid change in terms of declining rates of marriage, increasing rates of cohabitation and divorce, and rapid changes in attitudes among society generally and among the young in particular. To interpret the results of the survey items related to marriage, sex and divorce, it is first necessary to review the way in which the Church of England responded to the changes in society just described.

Response in the Church of England

As the established church, the Church of England has had to confront the issue of marriage and divorce from a slightly different context to some other denominations. Historically couples have had the right to marry in the parish church where they lived[1] or a parish church where they usually worshipped and had joined the church's electoral roll. Church of England clergy act on behalf of civil registrars, so anyone who is legally entitled to be married could be married by a parish priest, and that marriage should take place in the parish church. This means clergy are more or less obliged to marry couples irrespective of their living arrangements prior to the wedding, so confronting the rise in cohabitation may have seemed more a matter of going with the flow rather than trying in vain to stop the flood. While some incumbents are at pains to highlight Christian values and expectations about chastity outside marriage, others will not make this an issue either for prospective wedding couples or for congregants. As more and more of the couples who asked to be married in parish churches were already living together, the Board of Social Responsibility examined how the Church should respond to cohabitation as part of a wider report on family life produced in the early 1990s (Church of England, 1995). The report shows the way in which the Church has had to balance the desire to affirm heterosexual marriage as the ideal form of partnership and context for sexual relationships, with the desire to affirm signs of this ideal in those couples living together in a committed relationship outside marriage:

> The Christian practice of lifelong, monogamous marriage lies at the heart of the Church's understanding of how the love of God is made manifest in the sexual companionship of a man and a woman. The increasing popularity of cohabitation, among Christians and non-Christians, is no reason to modify this belief. On the contrary, it is an opportunity and a challenge to the Church to articulate its doctrine of marriage in ways so compelling, and to engage in a practice of marriage so life-enhancing, that the institution of marriage regains its centrality. (p. 118)

This stance reflects the attitude of many clergy and their congregations, who try to deal positively with the reality that confronts them in a society where cohabitation may be seen as a good thing to do before

[1] Technically, this may not have been the case in law. The Bill that gave rise to this notion (Lord Hardwicke's Act 1753) was made to prevent 'clandestine' marriages in the eighteenth century, and it stipulated that those who lived in a particular parish must be married in the parish church. It did not say that parish residents had a right to be married there, but this is how it came to be been widely understood (Doe, 1996).

deciding whether or not to get married, and marriage becomes something of an afterthought once a house has been found or the children have arrived. Some clergy may encourage couples to live chaste lives before the wedding, but in most parishes this is increasingly unlikely to be even mentioned as part of marriage preparation. This is not to say that sex outside marriage is universally accepted, and it has continued to be an issue within the Church of England (Paveley, 2011). Just before the first *Church Times* survey the House of Bishops published teaching guidelines on marriage (House of Bishops, 1999) which included an appendix headed 'What does the Church have to say to a couple who are living together without being married?' It is addressed to cohabiting couples, mentions the different kinds of relationships outside marriage and stresses the willingness of the Church to help couples who may be thinking about marriage but who feel negatively about it. For couples who are 'living naturally among [your] friends as husband and wife' the document says 'Even so, the Church would encourage you to make a public stand that is implied in your way of life...' The appendix ends with:

> In any case, the strength of your relationship and its potential for service to the community depend upon your enjoying a full and confident relationship with God and his people. The worshipping community, which is ready to welcome you in celebrating and learning of God's love, is the proper supportive context for the personal relationship at the centre of your life to flourish.

The tone is one of welcome and acceptance, while not going so far as to suggest cohabitation is sufficient or viable alternative to marriage. Over the next decade or so there were more radical calls to accept cohabitation within a wider revised framework that included a different understanding of family, marriage and relationships (Dormor, 2004). These have not yet resulted in an official change in the theology or guidelines relating to marriage and cohabitation, though the issue of same-sex relationships has brought the issue of heterosexual relationships into focus in a slightly different context.

The need to deal with the changing patterns of divorce was even more pressing and urgent for the Church because practice had generally been to not marry divorcees in church, though Canon law did not unequivocally forbid this (Doe, 1996). Compared with other parts of the Anglican Communion, the Church of England was slow in deciding how to deal with the issue. Convocation resolutions in Canterbury and York in 1937–1938 (reaffirmed in Canterbury in 1957) specifically forbade the use of the marriage service for any divorced person whose former partner was still alive. The 1965 Matrimonial Cause Acts had also specifically given clergy the right to refuse to do so, but this meant the situation was somewhat unclear because it implied the divorcees could be married if the parish priest gave permission. After General Synod agreed in 1981 that there could be circumstances in which a divorced person may be married in church during the lifetime of a former spouse, the House of Bishops issued guidance as to what those circumstances might be (House of Bishops, 1985). The rules were partly about the nature of the previous relationship, and partly about whether the person wishing to remarry had been the cause of the breakdown, or whether or not they had a mature understanding of their part in the breakdown. These things are hard to prescribe, and practice varied widely across different dioceses. Ministers were usually required to consult their bishop for advice, some of whom would always advise against. The final decision was, technically, with the minister, but it would be hard to ignore the advice of a bishop, so some bishops made it clear they preferred not to be asked.

The period leading up to the first *Church Times* survey saw a number of cases in which the anomalies of the system were apparent (Armstrong, 2015). Clergy have long been expected to show higher standards than their parishioners in these sorts of matters and divorcees were generally refused permission to train for ordination prior to the 1990s. However, existing clergy could sometimes remain in post after they divorced, so divorcee per se was not a bar to ministry. Divorcees were eventually allowed to go forward for ordination following the Clergy (Ordination) Measure in 1990, again not as right but after some scrutiny of the circumstances around the breakdown of their marriage and only after their bishop had completed a faculty (Church of England, 2017). Prohibitions for bishops remained in place until 2010, when the House of Bishops decided to relax the rules on the consecration of those who were divorced or married to spouses who had been divorced and whose previous partner was still alive.

Current practice for remarriage in church after divorce is based on a motion passed by General Synod in 2002, which places the responsibility for deciding which divorcees can marry in church upon incumbents.

Bishops can be consulted, but the guidelines make it clear that it is up to local parish priests to act as the gatekeepers and arbiters in these matters (House of Bishops, 2002). The period leading up to this motion, which was when the first *Church Times* survey took place, was one of intense and sometimes acrimonious debate in some circles of the Church of England, so it was natural to include items related to this subject in the questionnaire. The period between the two *Church Times* surveys was one in which this practice became commonplace, and in some parishes it may not even be raised as an issue when couples apply to be married. Figures collated by the Office for National Statistics show that in the Church of England in 2001 about 12% of marriages were between couples where one or both partners had previously been divorced. This figure rose to 17% by 2004, following the changes in Church rules, declined slightly to 16% by 2007 and has remained at this level since then (ONS, 2018a). Divorced and remarried priests also became more common, though there are no reliable figures for this. When Nicholas Holtam became Bishop of Salisbury in 2011 he was the first in England who was married to a divorcee, and in 2014 Jonathan Baker became the first bishop to remarry after divorce. So at the time of the second *Church Times* survey having divorced and remarried bishops was a recent innovation, whereas this had been the case for priests for some years.

The changing pattern of interest in these matters can be traced through the number of mentions they had in the *Church Times* from the 1960s (Fig. 4.1).[2] This showed a strong peak in articles related to remarriage and divorce around the early 1980s, when the issue was being debated in Synod prior to allowing the possibility of divorcees being remarried in church. A second peak is apparent in the late 1990s, when the issue was about divorced clergy and the report *Something to Celebrate* was also being discussed. The report accounts for the corresponding peak in articles related to cohabitation. Since then, in the period of the *Church Times* surveys at the start of the twenty-first century, both issues have been less prominent in the newspaper. This is the context in which opinions of readers were being assessed.

---

[2] The search items for cohabitation were 'cohabit*', 'sex outside marriage', 'trial marriage' and 'living in sin'. For divorce and remarriage they were 'divorce' and 'remarriage'.

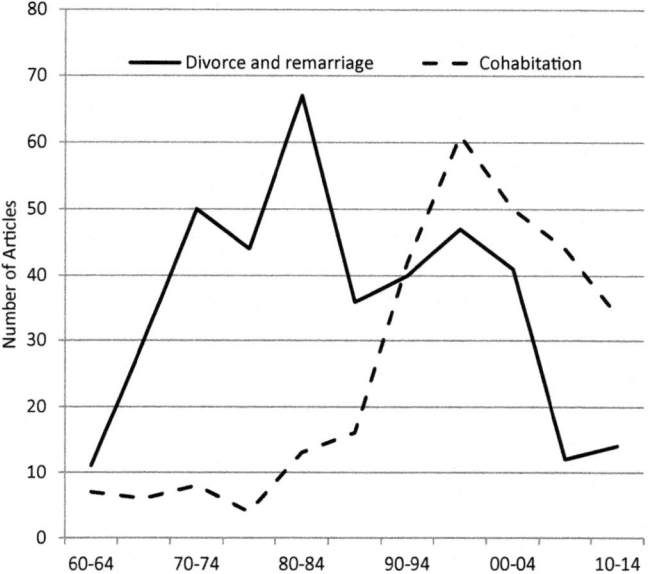

Fig. 4.1 Number of *Church Times* articles related to divorce and remarriage or cohabitation in five-year periods

EXPLORING THE DATA

It Is Wrong for Men and Women to Have Sex Before Marriage

The issue of sex outside marriage and cohabitation was explored in the questionnaires by three related items that were shaped partly by the way the issues have been framed in wider sociological studies. The first, 'It is wrong for men and women to have sex before marriage', is about heterosexual sex outside marriage, and it reflects a question asked in the British Social Attitude surveys since the 1980s (Park & Rhead, 2013). It implies that this is sex between couples who intended to marry, and does not therefore cover casual sexual relationships, or those where couples have no intentions to marry. There might have been some advantages in updating the wording to fit present-day circumstances, but these were outweighed by the value of being able to compare *Church Times* data with national trends. The second item 'It is all right for a couple to live together without intending to be married' is about long-term cohabitation, and the significance of marriage itself. The third 'It is a good idea for couples who intend to get married to live together first' is about short-term cohabitation, or 'trial marriage', and implies that this might be something that should be positively encouraged, rather than grudgingly accepted as the norm. Attitudes to all three items are likely to be strongly correlated, and that was indeed the case in these data, where differences between groups and patterns of change were broadly similar. The data presented are for the first item, with the other two being mentioned to indicate overall levels of endorsement and any differences in trends.

Overall, across the two surveys, 42% of *Church Times* readers agreed that sex before marriage was wrong. There were no significant differences in attitudes by location or between laity and clergy, but there were some marked differences between other categories (Fig. 4.2). Men were more likely to agree it was wrong than were women (44% versus 40%) and there was a similar difference between those without degrees (44%) and those with degrees (40%). There was a marked difference between the three age groups, with only a third of the under 50s feeling this was wrong compared with over half of those in the 70+ group. The difference between Evangelicals and other traditions was the most striking, with 70% agreeing it was wrong compared with only 27–30% of non-Evangelicals.

There was a marked shift between the surveys: 51% agreed that sex before marriage was wrong in 2001, but this had fallen to 33% by 2013, a dramatic change in opinion that is evident in the cohort graphs (Fig. 4.3). There are a number of interesting trends evident in the graphs, which suggest that the change in attitudes may have affected birth cohorts differently. In 2001, there was a strong age-related effect which was most obvious among the Anglo-catholic and Broad-church traditions: in the first survey opposition to sex before marriage increased with age for those born before or during the war. This trend was less obvious among Evangelicals, who tended generally to be more opposed. The post-war 'baby boomer' generations tended to be more accepting of sex before marriage, though in each tradition there was a suggestion that later cohorts born in the 60s and 70s may have been more conservative on this matter. The most striking change by 2013 is among the older birth cohorts where, after adjusting for age effects, it seemed there was a widespread shift towards more liberal attitudes in this area. This was not apparent in the post-war cohorts, where attitudes were similar to those in 2001 or, if anything a little more conservative. The net effect is that the

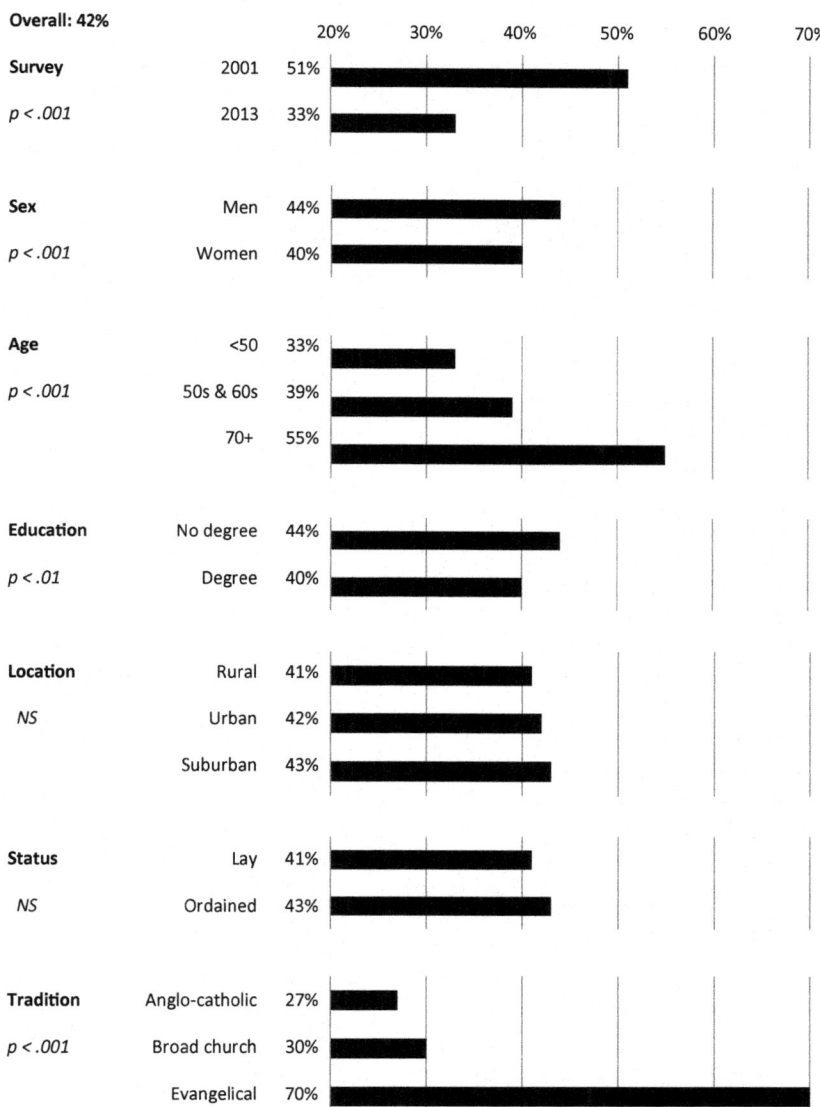

Fig. 4.2 It is wrong for men and women to have sex before marriage: estimated means

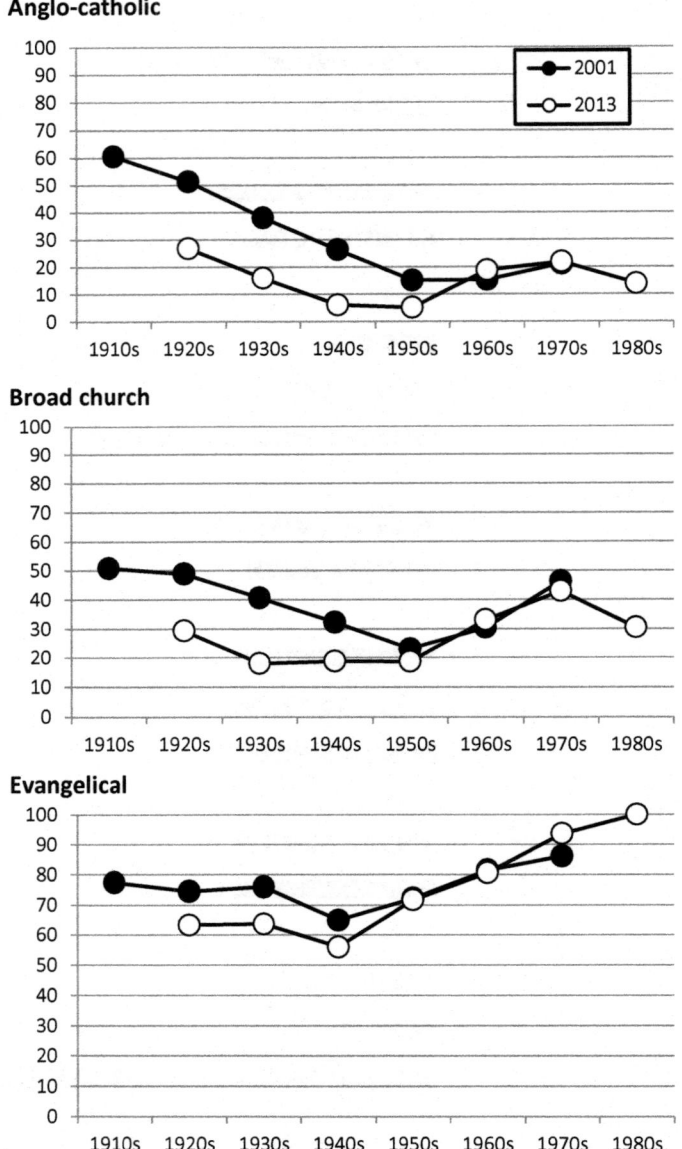

Fig. 4.3 It is wrong for men and women to have sex before marriage: cohort changes

age effect noted in the overall analysis seems to have been driven largely by the situation at the turn of the century, when younger respondents were more liberal on this matter. By 2013, the age effect was less obvious, and if anything it looks as if it may have been reversed. Among Evangelicals, for example, younger cohorts were much more likely to agree sex before marriage is wrong than were the older cohorts.

The item on long-term cohabitation was phrased in the opposite direction, and overall only 24% agreed that it is all right for a couple to live together without intending to be married. As with the previous items, there were no differences by location or ordination status, and in this case there was also no difference between men and women. As with sex before marriage, more conservative views were apparent among older people, those without degrees, and Evangelicals. Agreement increased from 19% in 2001 to 30% in 2013, and there was a similar trend for older cohorts to show more liberal shifts than those born after the 1950s.

The third item on trial marriage was also phased in a liberal direction, and overall even fewer (18%) agreed that it is a good idea for couples who intend to get married to live together first. For this item, the differences of age and tradition were the same as before, but clergy were less likely than laity to support this idea (16% versus 20%). The cohort analysis showed a slightly different effect, with liberal shifts across all cohorts for non-Evangelicals, so that the age differences apparent in 2001 were unchanged in 2013 (Fig. 4.4). Evangelicals still seem uniformly opposed to trial marriage whereas among Anglo-catholics there is some minority support, slightly more so among those born after the 1950s.

I Am in Favour of Divorced People Being Remarried in Church

The issue of divorce was explored in the *Church Times* surveys by looking at specific church-related issues rather than asking about general attitudes towards the matter. The first item, 'I am in favor of divorced people being remarried in church', was endorsed by 70% of the respondents across the two surveys, and this level of support was found in most groups (Fig. 4.5). For this item there were no overall differences between men and women, or by location. Younger people were generally more in favour, as were those with degrees and clergy (73%) compared to laity (66%). The trend by tradition was slightly different than we have seen hitherto: in this issue it was those from the Broad-church who were more accepting (76%) than either Anglo-catholics (67%) or Evangelicals (65%).

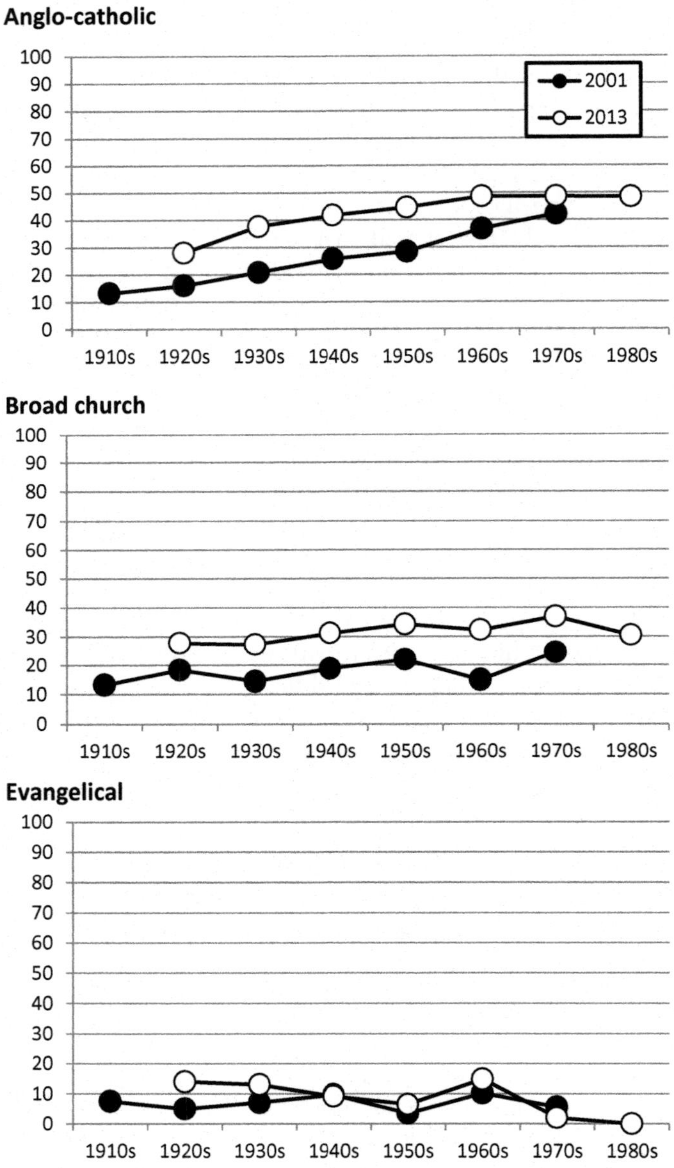

Anglo-catholic

Broad church

Evangelical

Fig. 4.4 It is a good idea for couples who intend to get married to live together first: cohort changes

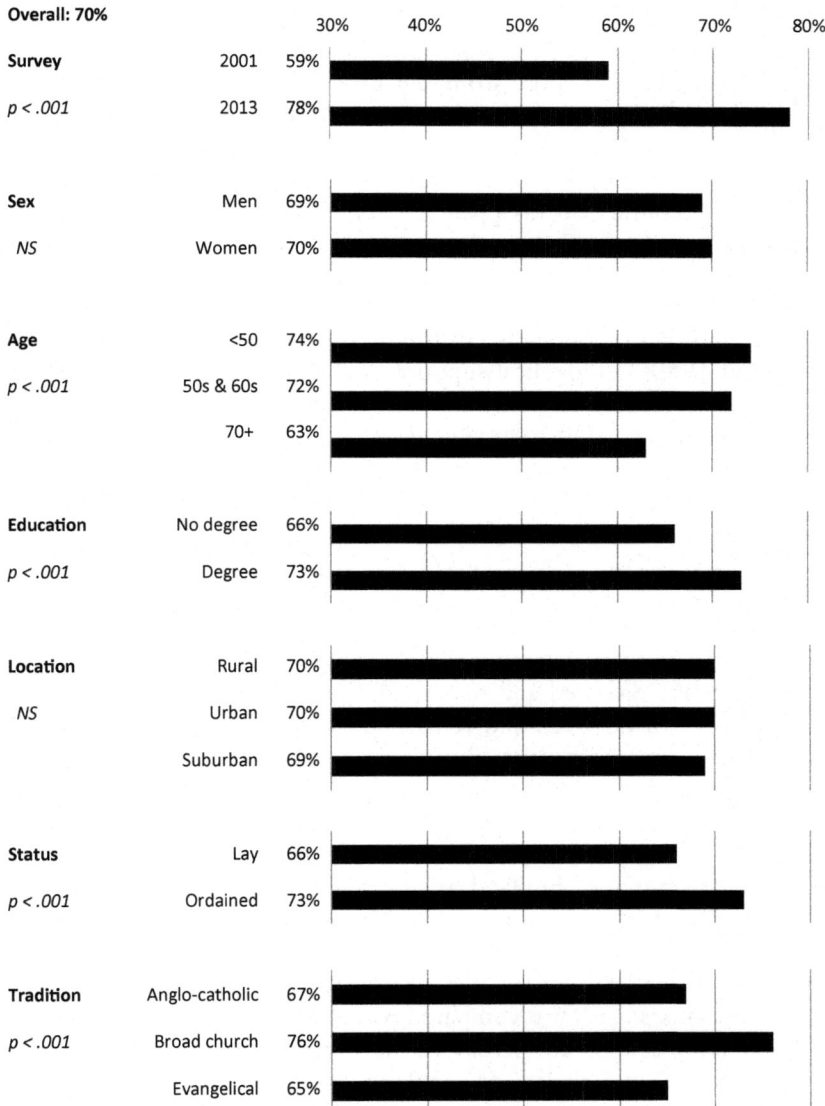

Fig. 4.5 I am in favour of divorced people being remarried in church: estimated means

The cohort analysis of this item showed similarities to the previous items, though again there were slightly different patterns in different traditions (Fig. 4.6). For those from the Broad church acceptance of the remarriage of divorcees was already over 50% for all cohorts in 2001, and there was increased acceptance across the board by 2013, when the figure was above 80% in most cases and any suggestion of older cohorts being less accepting had disappeared. For Anglo-catholics, there was a marked age effect in 2001, with the oldest cohorts being half as likely to agree as the youngest. By 2013, the pre-war cohorts had shifted to a more liberal position (with at least 70% agreement), but there was some suggestion of more conservatism on this issue for those born in the 1970s and 1980s. Evangelical support in 2001 ranged from 40 to 60% between cohorts, with those born in the 1940s being the most in favour. There was a marked shift to greater acceptance in these cohorts by 2013 though, as with Anglo-catholics, a suggestion of more conservative views for those born in the 1970s and 1980s.

I Am in Favour of Divorced and Remarried Bishops

The other two items on divorce also concentrated on an issue specific to the Church, and that is whether clergy should be allowed to continue in office if they are divorced and remarried. There were two separate items 'I am in favor of divorced and remarried priests' and 'I am in favor of divorced and remarried bishops', presented one after the other in both questionnaires. As with other items separating priests and bishops, the results are typically very similar, but there is always slightly less acceptance for bishops than for priests. This reflects the way change comes about in the Church of England, with change coming first to the priesthood and then to the episcopate. Here I present the results for bishops and draw comparison with priests where necessary.

Overall, across the two surveys, 58% were in favour of divorced and remarried bishops. This was compared with 65% for priests, and this level of difference was apparent across all the various groups in the analysis. It seems that about 5 to 10% of people in each survey would expect that bishops were more restricted in this area than priests. There were differences between groups in most categories, apart from location, with identical results for rural, suburban, and urban areas and similar attitudes among men and women (Fig. 4.7). The other differences were similar to those found for the item on divorce and remarriage in church: greater

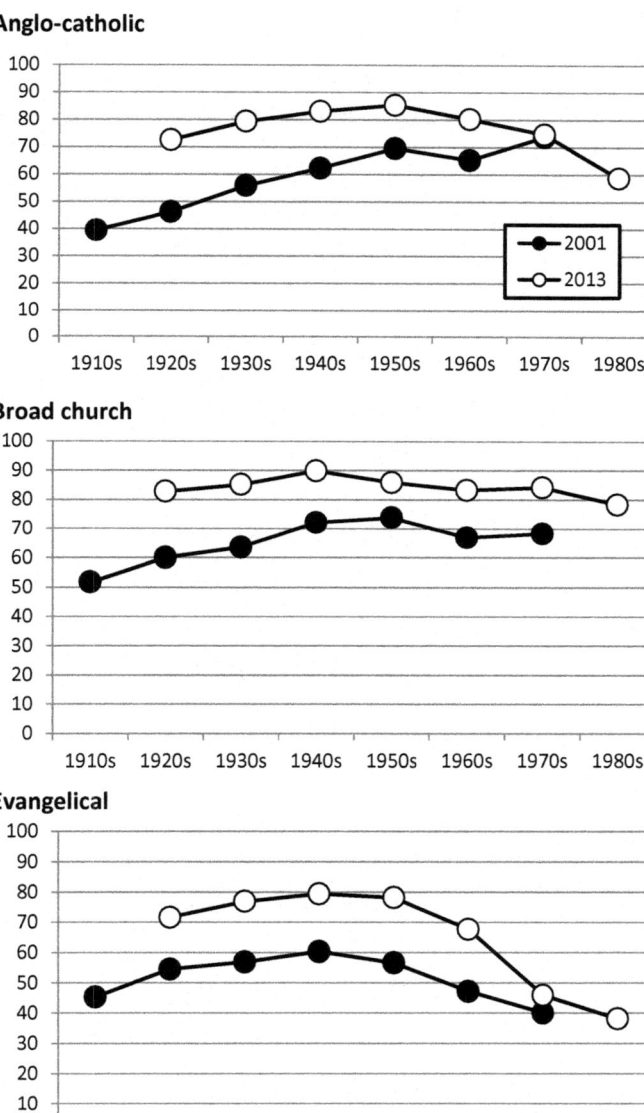

Fig. 4.6 I am in favour of divorced people being remarried in church: cohort changes

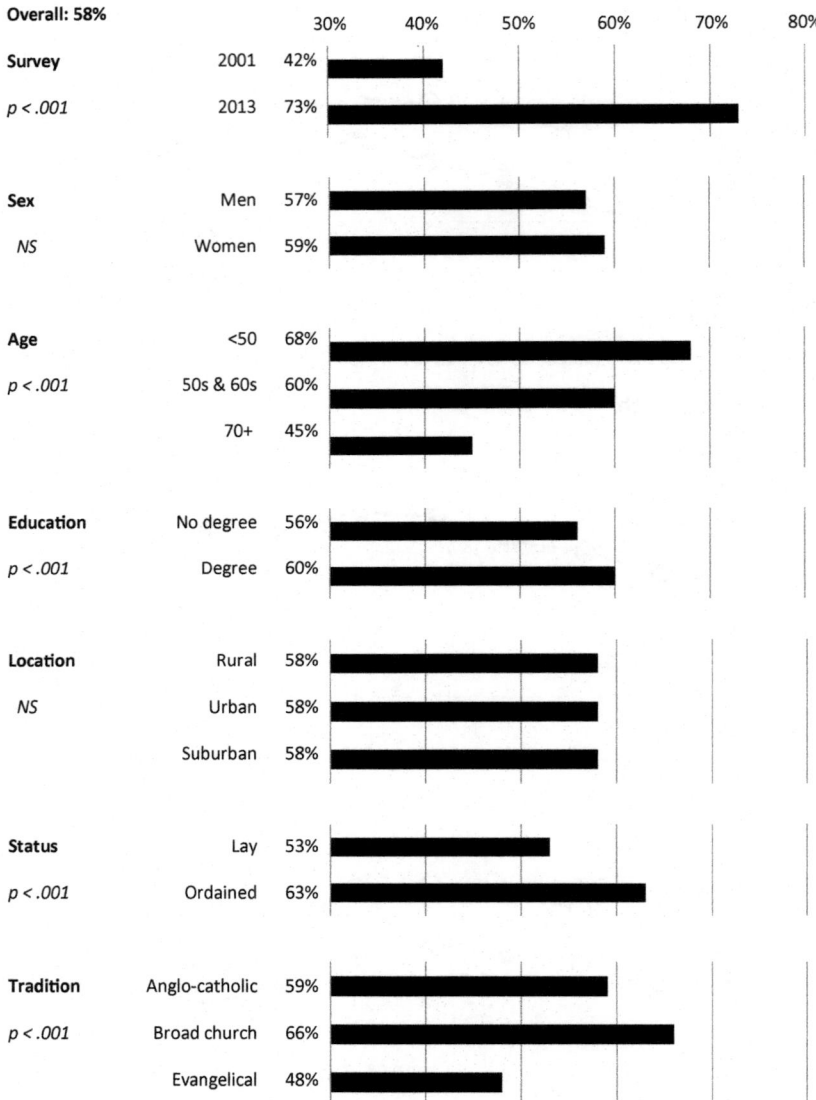

Fig. 4.7 I am in favour of divorced and remarried bishops: estimated means

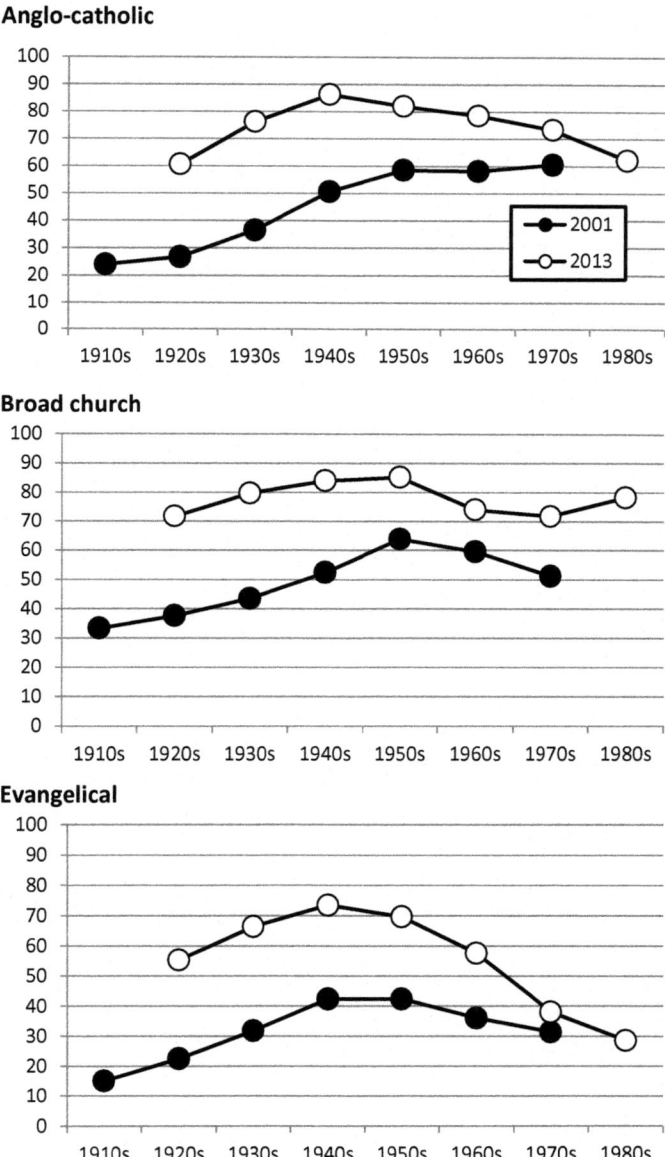

Fig. 4.8 I am in favour of divorced and remarried bishops: cohort changes

acceptance among the under 50s, those with degrees, clergy, and those from the Broad church.

The change between surveys was even more marked than for remarriage in church, going from 42% endorsement in 2001 to 73% in 2013. The cohort analysis showed that this change was the result of changes in all cohorts in all traditions, with the biggest changes being among those born in the 1920s to 1940s (Fig. 4.8). Younger cohorts had been generally more in favour in 2001, and they seemed to have changed slightly less dramatically, so that in non-Evangelical traditions there was less evidence of an age effect by 2013. Among Evangelicals in 2013 there was a trend for less favour among the younger cohorts. These patterns were repeated in the data for priests, but all figures were shifted upwards by about 5%.

Conclusions

Although there were subtle and sometimes important differences in attitudes towards the various facets of cohabitation and marriage measured by the surveys, the overall picture was of consistent variations across different groups and rapid changes in opinions between the surveys. If doctrinal issues shaped the battlegrounds in the Church of England in the nineteenth and early twentieth centuries, it was in the areas of social and moral issues were most rapidly changing at the start of the twenty-first century. The matters examined in this chapter were under deepest scrutiny in the decades that preceded the first *Church Times* survey, but they were still undergoing some change in the first decade of this century, and to some extent the theological and practical issues have not yet been finally settled. The documents that have emerged from Church of England in the last few years still maintain the ideal of marriage as a public declaration of a lifelong, exclusive commitment in which sex is given its proper context and purpose (House of Bishops, 1991, 2003). Working out what that means for clergy and laity in parishes across the country is a trickier question. The data presented in this chapter revealed a number of important things about the beliefs and attitudes of those clergy and laity.

First are the varying levels of support for different kinds of 'less than ideal' behaviour related to marriage. In general, there was more support for the remarrying of divorcees in church, or for having divorced and remarried clergy, than there was for sex before marriage. Sex before marriage was itself more generally acceptable than permanent cohabitation or trial marriage. These differences might have been affected by the particular phrasing of these items ('A good idea...' suggests a positive support, whereas 'All right for...' suggests a more passive tolerance, and 'It is wrong...' a positive rejection), but it might also be that respondents had particular reasons for being more tolerant in some areas than in others. For example, some people remained against the idea of people living together as a means of 'testing' a relationship but may have been more supportive of cohabitation that was a natural expression of love and commitment, even if marriage was not even being considered. A couple that applies to remarry in church after a divorce is probably trying to move beyond passed failures and ask God's help for a new relationship. If the official documents of the Church espouse a desire to hold to ideals while accepting those who fall short, this sentiment seems to be echoed in the opinions of many in the Church of England.

The second important point that emerged from the data is the pattern of variations across the different groups in the Church. These 'fault lines' were noticed in the first analysis of the 2001 survey data (Francis, Robbins, & Astley, 2005), and the 2013 survey confirmed many of these. When it came to sex outside marriage and matters of cohabitation, Evangelicals were strongly and consistently more conservative than either of the other two traditions. On divorce items, Evangelicals were also more conservative but here the pattern was for those in the Broad church to be the most accepting of change while Anglo-catholics were less so, especially over marrying divorcees in church. Another difference was between the conservatism of older people and the more liberal views of younger people. This is what we might expect, and it was especially noticeable in the 2001 survey. The consistently more liberal views of those with degrees are also in line with the way that education can lead to a loosening of traditional values or beliefs. Other differences were less obvious or less consistent, as with those between the sexes, between clergy and laity, or between those living in rural or urban environments. These 'fault-lines' show the way in which debates about social and moral issues in the Church of England can highlight the diversity of opinion.

The third and crucial point is the pattern of change between the two surveys, and the way in which this change is taking place within the Church. In these areas, there have been decisive shifts of opinion on matters such divorce and remarriage, and sex before marriage. The pattern of these changes across birth cohorts suggests that the main reason for change in this period was a change in attitudes across the board, rather than because older people held onto traditional beliefs but were being replaced by more liberal younger generations. If anything, older birth cohorts showed more liberalization than the more recent birth cohorts. The effect of this change is that by 2013 the difference between older and younger people was far less obvious, and sometimes difficult to predict. In some cases, the direction of difference may even have reversed, with younger people being more conservative than their older counterparts. I will return to this issue in the concluding chapter, where the trends seen in this area of church life are discussed in the context of other shifts in opinions and attitudes.

The direction of travel is much as we might expect from the debates of these issues in the periods before and during the survey period. Opinion has followed the more liberal treatment of those who cohabit before marriage or those whose marriages end in divorce. This was probably occasioned in the Church of England by the sheer numbers of those who fell into these categories in the 1980s and 1990s, such that it would be difficult for clergy or laity to avoid mixing with cohabiting couples or divorcees in church. What becomes commonplace will often become acceptable, and this seems to be reflected both in the issues debated in Synod, and in the opinions expressed in the *Church Times* surveys. For many, the battles of the past have been set aside and people have simply got on with the accommodating the changed reality of everyday life. At the start of the century, the issues of marriage and divorce became overshadowed by issues of sexuality, and it is tempting to imagine that they are no longer important issues. They do, however, represent an area in which biblical and traditional church teaching points to quite different practice and values from those that prevail in British society at the moment. The danger of affirming ideals while simultaneously affirming those who fall short of them is that the ideals can become hollow entities that do not actually make any difference to people's lives.

REFERENCES

Armstrong, N. (2015). Divorce and the English clergy c. 1970–1990. *Twentieth Century British History, 26*(2), 298–320. https://doi.org/10.1093/tcbh/hwu062.

Beaujouan, É., & Bhrolcháin, M. N. (2014). Cohabitation and marriage in Britain since the 1970s. In R. Probert (Ed.), *Cohabitation and non-marital births in England and Wales, 1600–2012* (pp. 192–213). London, UK: Palgrave Macmillan.

Burton, F. (2015). *Family law* (2nd ed.). London: Routledge.

Church of England. (1995). *Something to celebrate: Valuing families in church and society*. London: Church House Publishing.

Church of England. (2017). *Sending candidates to BAP*. London: Church of England.

Doe, C. N. (1996). *The legal framework of the Church of England: A critical study in a comparative context*. Oxford: Clarendon Press.

Dormor, D. J. (2004). *Just cohabiting? The church, sex, and getting married*. London: Darton, Longman & Todd.

Fairbairn, C. (2018). *"Common law marriage" and cohabitation*. London: House of Commons Library.

Francis, L. J., Robbins, M., & Astley, J. (2005). *Fragmented faith? Exposing the fault-lines in the Church of England*. Milton Keynes: Paternoster Press.

Haskey, J. (2014). Cohabitation and births outside marriage after 1970: A rapidly evolving phenomenon. In R. Probert (Ed.), *Cohabitation and non-marital births in England and Wales, 1600–2012* (pp. 158–191). London, UK: Palgrave Macmillan.

Haskey, J. (2015). Marriage rites: Trends in marriages by manner of solemnisation and denomination in England and Wales 1841–2012. In J. Miles, P. Mody, & R. Probert (Eds.), *Marriage rites and rights* (pp. 19–56). Oxford: Hart Publishing.

House of Bishops. (1985). *Marriage discipline, GS 669*. London: Church of England.

House of Bishops. (1991). *Issues in human sexuality: A statement by the House of Bishops of the General Synod of the Church of England*. London: Church of England.

House of Bishops. (1999). *Marriage: A teaching document*. London: Church of England.

House of Bishops. (2002). *Marriage in church after divorce: Advice to clergy*. London: Church of England.

House of Bishops. (2003). *Some issues in human sexuality: A guide to the debate*. London: Church of England.

Lesthaeghe, R. (2014). The second demographic transition: A concise overview of its development. *Proceedings of the National Academy of Sciences of the United States of America, 111*(51), 18112–18115. https://doi.org/10.1073/pnas.1420441111.

NatCen. (2018). *British social attitudes information system*. Retrieved June 18, 2018, from National Centre for Social Research www.britsocat.com/.

ONS. (2014a). *Live births in England and Wales by characteristics of mother 1: 2013*. London: Office for National Statistics.

ONS. (2014b). *Marriage summary statistics 2012*. Retrieved June 15, 2018, from https://www.ons.gov.uk/peoplepopulationandcommunity/birthsdeaths andmarriages/marriagecohabitationandcivilpartnerships/datasets/marriage summarystatisticsprovisional.

ONS. (2017). *Divorces in England and Wales: 2016*. London: Office for National Statistics.

ONS. (2018a). *Church of England marriages by previous marital status, England, 2001 to 2015*. Retrieved August 15, 2018, from https://www.ons.gov.uk/ peoplepopulationandcommunity/birthsdeathsandmarriages/marriagecohabi- tationandcivilpartnerships/adhocs/008887churchofenglandmarriagesbyprevi- ousmaritalstatusengland2001to2015.

ONS. (2018b). *Marriages in England and Wales: 2015*. London: Office for National Statistics.

Park, A., & Rhead, R. (2013). Personal relationships: Changing attitudes towards sex, marriage and parenthood. In A. Park, C. Bryson, E. Clery, J. Curtice, & M. Phillips (Eds.), *British Social Attitudes* (Vol. 30, pp. 1–32). London: NatCen Social Research.

Paveley, R. (2011, February 2). Just cohabiting? *Church Times*, pp. 21–22.

CHAPTER 5

Women in Leadership

INTRODUCTION

Chapter 4 noted the profound changes in attitudes towards marriage and cohabitation that had taken place in the UK in the decades leading up to the first *Church Times* survey in 2001. These changes are intimately linked with the changing lives of women over the same period because they came about in no small part as a result of women taking greater control of their fertility and their roles in society. These trends are evident in national statistics and in surveys of attitudes towards the role of women in relation to childcare and working beyond the home. They form the context in which the Church of England had to come to terms with the status of women in terms of priesthood and leadership, something which has been an ongoing process for many decades. This chapter first looks briefly at some of the changes in British society at the end of the twentieth and beginning of the twenty-first century that set the context for the ordination of the first women priests in 1994 and the consecration of the first women as bishops 21 years later. It then looks briefly at how the Church responded in terms of the process that led to the ordination of women as priests and then as bishops. The *Church Times* surveys each had two items related to the ordination of women which are examined in the next section. In 2001, the Church of England had been ordaining women priests for seven years but there were no women bishops. In 2013, the measure to allow the consecration of women

© The Author(s) 2018
A. Village, *The Church of England
in the First Decade of the 21st Century*,
https://doi.org/10.1007/978-3-030-04528-9_5

bishops had still not passed through General Synod, but things were about to change.

Gender Roles in British Society

The statistic that probably most clearly sums up the changes in gender roles in the UK over the last fifty years is the employment rate for men and women (i.e. the percentage of those aged 16–64 who are in employment). Since the 1960s, this has fallen in men (from 92% in 1971 to 76% in 2013) and risen in women (from 53 to 67% over the same period). The change has been facilitated by legal changes that have promoted equal treatment on pay and equality of opportunity for men and women, as well as the introduction of statutory maternity support. Other measures have used the benefit system to encourage lone parents (who are mainly women) to return to work, and to increase the state pension age of women to bring it into line with that of men. Although women are almost as likely to be working as men, there is still a gap in favour of men which is most evident among 20–40 year olds, the age when some women start families and do not work outside the home (ONS, 2013).

The similarity of employment rates between the genders disguises differences in the type of work that men and women do, which accounts for the ongoing gender pay gap. A crucial difference is that women do fewer hours, on average than men, partly because many mothers with dependent children mix part-time work outside the home with looking after their families. Men tend to work in higher skilled jobs, and women tend to predominate in caring professions and the leisure industry. The differences can be subtle: for example, roughly equal proportions of men and women work in professional occupations, but men dominate in high-paying jobs such as those in the digital industries, whereas women dominate in lower paying professions such as nursing (ONS, 2018). These sorts of factors help to explain why there is still considerable disparity between men and women in many sections of society, despite laws that are designed to prevent this. This may partly be due to the persistence of traditional attitudes and to women still doing the lion's share of domestic work in the home.

A report based on the 2012 British Social Attitudes survey was entitled 'Gender roles: An incomplete revolution?', which seems to encapsulate neatly the extent of change and the lingering attitudes that prevent women from achieving complete equality with men. A number of items have been included in surveys since the 1980s and most show that attitudes had already shifted towards more gender equality by the turn of the century (Park, Bryson, Clery, Curtice, & Phillips, 2013, Table A.2). In 1984, 43% agreed it was a man's job to earn money and a woman's job to look after the family, but this had fallen to 17% by 2002 and to 13% by 2012. This is largely because successive generational cohorts have more egalitarian attitudes, so in 2012 there was a marked difference in response between the under 25s (4%) and those over 66 (28%). In relation to child rearing, there remained some doubts about the effect of mothers working: in 1989, 46% agreed a pre-school child is likely to suffer if his or her mother works, and this fell only slightly to 38% in 2002 and 30% in 2012. For several decades attitudes have been in favour of women being encouraged to work, but there is a minority opinion that prefers to see them in traditional roles, particularly for mothers of young children. Behaviours have been slower to change, as evidenced by the fact that even in 2012 women spent substantially more time than men doing household work, and six out of ten felt they did more than their fair share.

This is the society in which the Church of England operated during the first decade of the twenty-first century. Women had made great inroads into the labour market and, in strict legal terms, could operate without being discriminated against by virtue of their sex. More deep-seated social structures made the reality of complete equality more difficult to achieve, and the difference was most apparent in the under-representation of women in the more high-skilled and managerial jobs. Britain had already had its first female Prime Minister, Margaret Thatcher, but when she was in power in the 1980s less than 10% of MPs were women. This rose to just under 20% by 2001, but was still less than 25% in 2013 (Keen & Cracknell, 2018). In 2001, 6% of directorships of FTSE 100 companies were held by women, with the figure for executive directorships being only 2% (Singh & Vinnicombe, 2001). By 2013, these figures had risen a little (17 and 6% respectively), but the disparity was still huge (Sealy & Vinnicombe, 2013). Despite the inroads women made into more senior jobs, when it came to the most senior and highest paid jobs women were still in a tiny minority.

Researchers who have studied the nature and causes of gender role attitudes have noted the distinction between what they term 'hostile sexism' and 'benevolent sexism' (Glick et al., 2000). The former is what is often associated with gender stereotyping and aggressive prejudice.

In men, this is manifest as rejection of attempts by women to usurp the role of men; in women this is manifest as assumptions about men being powerful and arrogant. Benevolent sexism can be more insidious but no less important in upholding traditional gender stereotypes and roles. In men, benevolent sexism is manifest as attitudes that are protective, affectionate but ultimately patronizing of women, who are assumed to be the 'weaker' sex. In women, benevolent sexism is manifest as attitudes that accept men's role as protectors and providers, but which might also assume they are incapable of being nurturing or emotionally intelligent (Glick & Fiske, 1996, 1999). Unsurprisingly, men are more likely than women to display hostile sexism, but benevolent sexism can be equally present in both sexes. Factors such as education or religion can influence these attitudes, with education tending to reduce both forms, but religion sometimes leading to more benevolent (but not more hostile) sexism (Glick, Lameiras, & Rodriguez Castro, 2002). These sorts of studies show that women can be excluded from some roles in society not simply by the aggressive attitudes of men who feel threatened by the opposite sex encroaching on 'their' territory, but also by the apparently more benign attitudes of men and women who may think that they have the best interests of women at heart when they seek to keep them in roles to which they are traditionally thought to be most suited. Both of these factors were at play in the struggle of women trying to enter the priesthood in the Church of England.

Response in the Church of England

The Church of England, like every other institution, has had to learn how to respond to social change and to accustom itself to being organized in ways that reflect the aspirations and expectations of its members. Like some other institutions, it has been slow to change in terms of gender status and roles, resisting the pressure to treat men and women equally, especially in terms of leadership. Unlike most other institutions this reluctance is driven not just by the inertia of tradition or the inability to shed long-held habits and stereotypes. Alongside what some would see as no more than sinful misogyny is also a deeper and more fundamental question about the extent to which traditional gender roles are in some way divinely ordained and therefore not to be left aside lightly. While this might seem to some like using theological arguments to bolster sexism, it has probably been a key factor that kept the Church of England out of step with rest of society in this area. Ultimately, the Church had to decide if its long-held traditional practice of allowing only men to serve as deacons, priests or bishops was something modelled on historical social norms, and which could therefore change as those social norms change, or whether those traditional norms were absolute, divine prescriptions of the way things should be.

The story of how the Church of England moved from having only male priests and bishops to opening those roles to both sexes has been told several times by historians and reflected upon by theologians at great length (Avis, 2003; Gill, 1994; House of Bishops, 1988; Percy, 2017; Petre, 1994), so only a brief outline is needed here to set the scene. The changes in England were in no small part driven by changes that happened in Anglican Churches elsewhere in the world, starting in 1944 when the then Bishop of Hong Kong, Ronald Hall, ordained Florence Tim Oi Li as a priest, giving her authority to minister the holy Sacraments. This was an act of expediency in order to meet the needs of a congregation isolated by war and otherwise unable to receive the ministrations of a priest. Although this ordination was not subsequently recognized by the 1948 Lambeth Conference (the gathering of bishops from across the Anglican Communion), it nonetheless marked a turning point: a possibility had been raised that would not go away. The fact that this had taken place in Hong Kong emphasized the fact that Anglican provinces are able to act independently, a reality that proved crucial to the way in which change came about. The 1968 Lambeth Conference was divided over the issue, but resolved that there were no conclusive arguments for or against ordaining women, and it therefore asked each province to review the issue independently. The aim was to report to the Anglican Consultative Council (ACC), a newly formed body consisting of clerical and lay representatives from across the communion. In the event, the ACC issued a statement in 1971, before it had heard from all the provinces, that effectively gave the green light for bishops to ordain women, provided they had the permission of their province. In same year, Hong Kong ordained two women, and five years later the Episcopal Church in America sanctioned the ordination of women. In the decade that followed women were ordained in provinces such as Canada (1976), New Zealand (1977), and Kenya (1983).

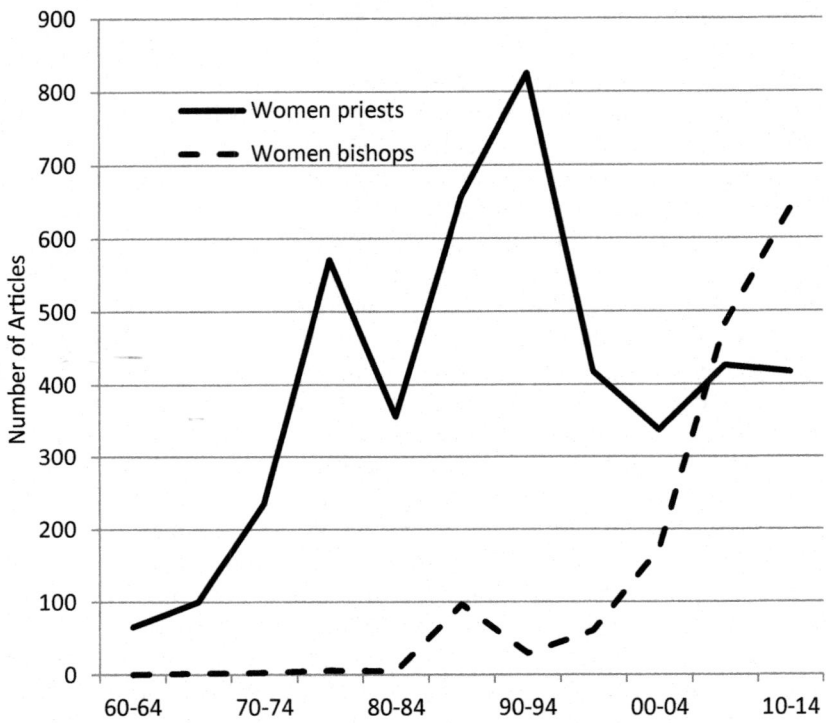

Fig. 5.1 Number of *Church Times* articles related to women's ordination in 5-year periods

The Church of England was caught up in this movement, and the issue was being actively discussed by dioceses in the early 1970s, prior to a debate in General Synod in 1975. That resulted in mixed signals and confusion: a Synod motion stating there were no fundamental theological objections to the ordination of women was passed, but there was no clarity on whether to remove the legal barriers. In the end, it was left to the House of Bishops to decide when the time was right to allow the ordination of women to actually happen. An attempt to allow this was defeated in Synod in 1978, setting the scene for a long protracted struggle that would not finally end until the Synod revisited the issue in 1992. The pattern of intense interest in the mid-1970s and early 1990s is revealed in the analysis of *Church Times* articles on the subject of women's ordination (Fig. 5.1),[1] which peaked in 1970–1975 and 1990–1995, with the 1980s being what some have described as the 'wilderness years' (Petre, 1994).

Over the course of this protracted debate, there were many arguments brought by either side to bolster their case for promoting or resisting change. Supporters for change pointed to fundamental ideas of equality expressed, for example, in Genesis 1:27 or Galatians 3:28. More pragmatic arguments stressed the idea that the ordering of ministry was a secondary matter, not one driven by immutable theology or doctrine, and that national churches such as the Church of England should follow the norms and practices of the societies that they serve. The opposition also drew on fundamental ideas, which fell broadly into two sorts. One related to the maleness of Jesus, and therefore the need for those who 'represented' Jesus at the Eucharist to be male; the other related to the idea that leadership in the Church should be the prerogative of men. More pragmatic arguments were to do with whether the Anglican Church had the authority to act unilaterally to change such a fundamental ordinance without the agreement of the Catholic or Orthodox churches. Generally speaking, Anglo-catholics trended to stress the latter argument, strongly resisting change on the grounds that it would destroy any lingering possibility of union with Rome in the years ahead. Evangelicals were unconcerned about links with Rome and unconvinced by arguments related to sacramental ministry, but some felt the biblical model of male headship should be retained even if this was changing in society at large.

The move to ordain women in 1992 was not at all a sign of unanimity and, alongside changes that paved the way for women priests, the House of Bishops agreed a position that would allow 'two integrities' to coexist in the Church of England. To retain traditionalists, the legislation specified that Parochial Church Councils could pass resolutions indicating that they would not accept a woman ministering at communion ('Resolution A') or a women as incumbent ('Resolution B'). Such parishes could be placed under the oversight of a 'Provincial Episcopal Visitor', that is, a so-called flying bishop who would not ordain women

[1] The figures for women priests counted all articles that contained the phrases 'ordination of women'; 'women's ordination'; 'women priests'; 'women as priests'. The figures of women bishops counted all articles that contained the phrases 'consecration of women'; 'women's consecration'; 'women bishops'; 'women as bishops'.

and who could be invited by a diocesan bishop to offer pastoral care and sacramental ministry to Resolution A/B parishes. Provision was also made for financial compensation for clergy who felt unable to remain in the Church of England because of the change, and about 430 took advantage of this scheme. While the notion of 'two integrities' may have prevented individual parishes from trying to leave the Church of England, it did not stop several hundred clergy leaving over the next few years. It also failed to appease many who voted for change, and who felt that the arrangements lacked any theological integrity, conceded too much to a minority who should fall in line with the majority decision, and led to a damaging ambiguity about the ministry of women (Furlong, 1998; Percy, 2017).

The ambiguity was nowhere more obvious than in the issue of women bishops, still not allowed even though women could be priests. The first woman to be made an Anglican bishop was Barbara Harris in the USA in 1989, so it was hardly surprising that in the Church of England attention soon turned to women in the episcopate (Kuhrt, 2001). This is apparent from the analysis of *Church Times* articles (Fig. 5.1) where interest began to increase rapidly after 2000, even as articles on women as priests declined. The objections to women as bishops are partly the same as the objection to them being priests, but once they are priests, it seems hard to justify why they cannot become bishops. This is where the issue of women in leadership becomes more crucial, something that conservative Evangelicals felt more keenly than conservative Anglo-catholics. The debates continued until 2014 when Synod finally passed the measure that allowed women to be consecrated as bishops: the first was Libby Lane, consecrated in at York minister in 2015. Once again provision was made for parishes to ask to receive pastoral support from male bishops but this time there was no financial compensation offered to those clergy who felt they could not remain in post after the change.

Several things stand out for this story that may be relevant to the survey data. The first is that this has been a tortuous journey that has not always proceeded in predictable steps. Many commentators from early in the previous century predicted it would happen, but few would have foreseen the twists and turns of the plot. These stemmed partly from the way that opinions were divided between different traditions in the Church and partly because of the fine balance of votes in the different houses of the General Synod. The fault lines between the different traditions were apparent in the 2001 survey, though clergy and laity showed similar levels of support (Francis, Robbins, & Astley, 2005). One question to explore is how these fault lines changed, if at all, by 2013. The second is the importance of attitudes, rather than substantial theological beliefs, in shaping changes in this area. Although theological barriers to women's ordination were effectively dismissed as early as 1975, it would be two decades before attitudes had shifted sufficiently to enable the majority view to be enacted. Was this shift possible because younger, less traditional people are beginning to dominate in the Church, or was it due to changing views across the age spectrum? A third issue is the timing of the changes in relation to the *Church Times* surveys: how did opinion on these issues develop between the two surveys as women priests became commonplace and women bishops were an imminent possibility?

Exploring the Data

I Am in Favour of the Ordination of Women as Priests

By 2001 the Church of England had settled into the reality of having women priests, even if that settling meant the continuing of two integrities. Those who strongly opposed the change had probably already left the church, and opposers that did stay comprised only a small proportion of those entering the priesthood. Not surprisingly then, there was widespread support in the sample surveyed: 87% across both surveys in favour of women's ordination. There were some small but statistically significant differences between some of the groups (Fig. 5.2). Women were more likely to be in favour than were men (90% versus 83%), even after allowing for the fact that women clergy, by definition, are going to be in favour (though a few who were deacons were not). The difference between clergy and laity was largely due to women clergy, and ordained men were similar to laymen, especially in 2013. The greater support from younger people is in line with trends in wider society for support of changing gender roles, as is the greater support from those with degrees than those without. The figures for church tradition reflect to some extent what observers noted from the history of the debate: greatest

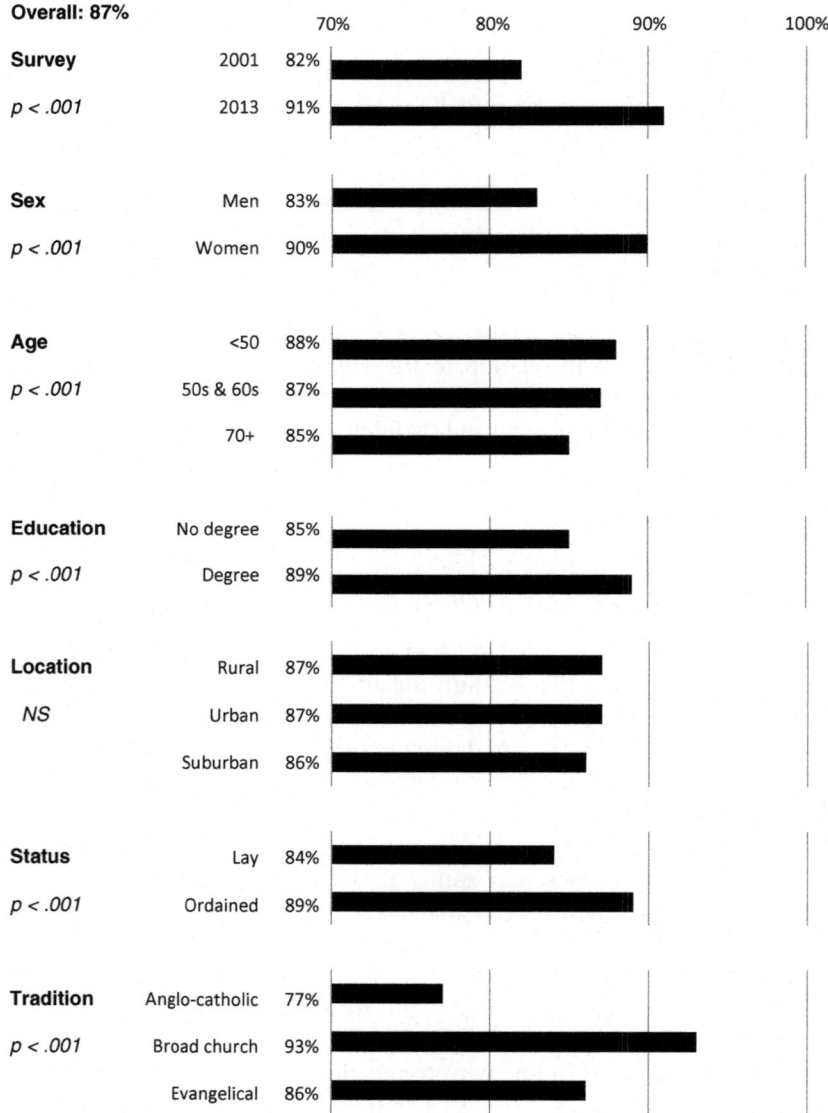

Fig. 5.2 I am in favour of the ordination of women as priests: estimated means

support among the Broad church, with least support among Anglo-catholics. The cohort analysis reveals interesting details on how opinion shifted between 2001 and 2013. For the Broad church the already strong support shifted in all cohorts, so it was above 90% across the board in 2013. Anglo-catholic opinion also moved towards full acceptance, and the shifts were greater in older cohorts, so by 2013 support was at 80–90% across the board. How far this was due to people leaving, and how far to change in those who stayed is hard to tell, through the latter is more likely because most had already left by 2001. Evangelicals showed a rather different pattern: for those born in the 1950s or earlier, opinion became more accepting, rising from 80 to 90%, whereas for cohorts born after the 1950s opinion was if anything hardening, with less than 50% agreement for those born in the 1970s or 1980s (Fig. 5.3).

I Am in Favour of the Ordination of Women as Bishops

The patterns of differences between groups for the ordination of women as bishops was very similar to those for women as priests, but overall acceptance was about 10% lower at 78% (Fig. 5.4). Here there was a shaper difference between age groups, but this was largely due to the 2001 survey, and by 2013 this age difference had virtually disappeared. The cohort analysis (Fig. 5.5) shows how opinion shifted dramatically among the older cohorts, suggesting the advent of change was not so much about the coming of liberal youngsters and the loss of traditional older generations, as about change in people as the decade progressed. Once again, the conservatism of young Evangelicals is apparent.

Who were the people who supported women as priests, but not as bishops? Analysis of this small group showed they made up 15% of the sample in 2001 but only 4% in 2013. It seemed that the alongside a generally increasing acceptance of women in ministry, they was an erosion of the position that could justify women priests, but deny them access to the episcopate. Evangelicals had a higher proportion (11%) in favour of priests but not bishops than either Broad church or Anglo-catholics (7% each). This makes sense given that Evangelical arguments against women in ministry have been centred on leadership, and more would be likely to oppose the leadership of women over fellow priests.

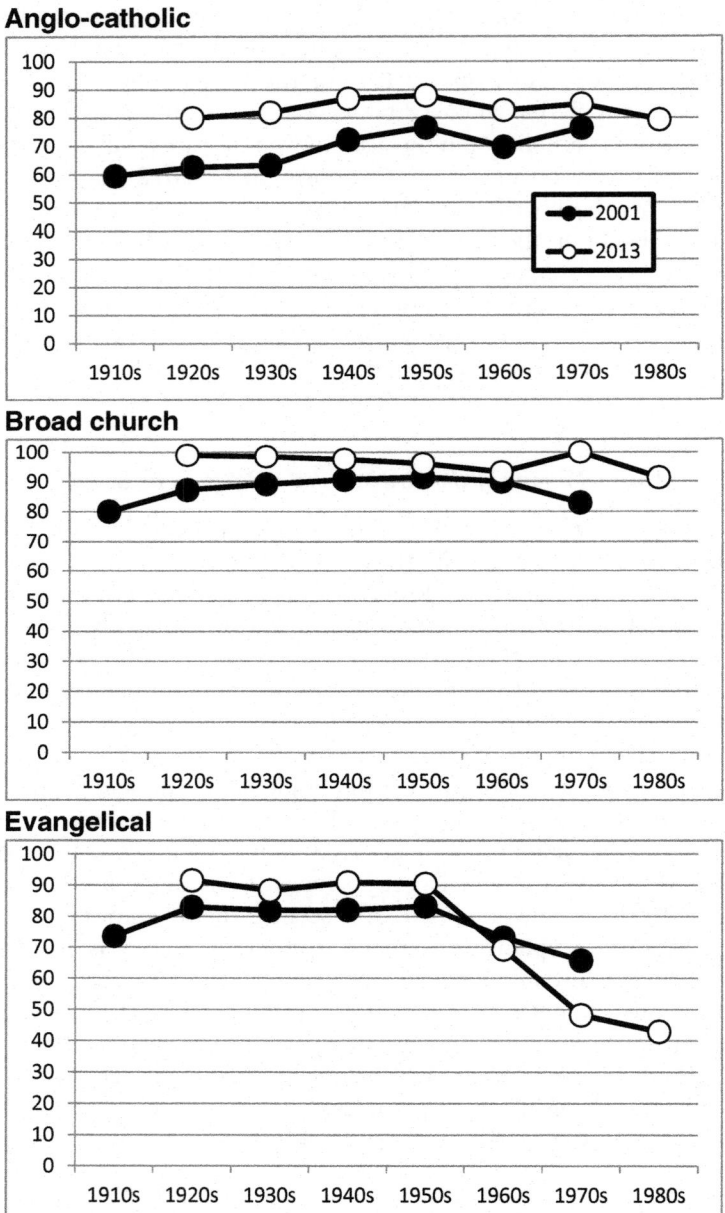

Fig. 5.3 I am in favour of the ordination of women as priests: cohort changes

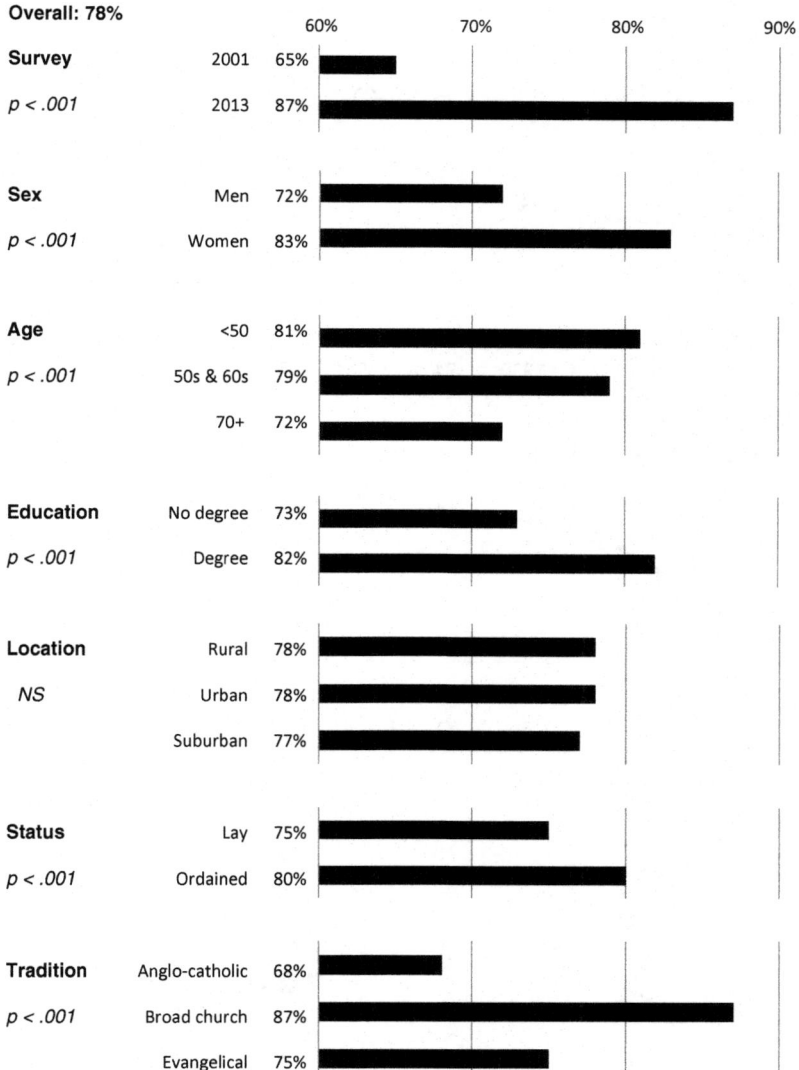

Fig. 5.4 I am in favour of the ordination of women as bishops: estimated means

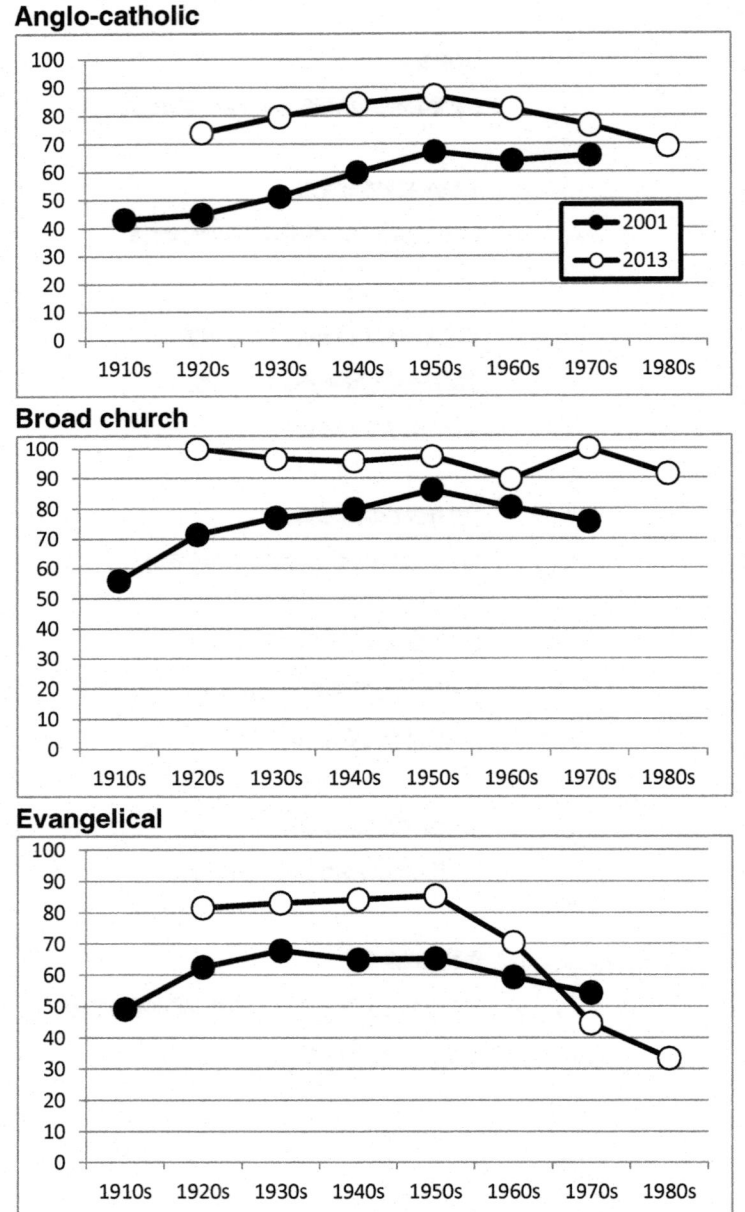

Fig. 5.5 I am in favour of the ordination of women as bishops: cohort changes

CONCLUSIONS

The data help to confirm the narratives that have been written about the way in which different parts of the Church of England responded to the notion of women having equality with men in the area of ministry. While it would have been ideal to have surveyed opinion every decade from the 1970s, the first *Church Times* survey was strategically located near the midpoint of women being allowed to priests and women being allowed to be bishops. The initial divisions following women's ordination had somewhat settled, and some of the clergy most strongly opposed had left the Church of England. Nonetheless, the issue remained divisive, especially with the moves to allow the consecration of women as bishops. In 2011, the Roman Catholic Church established the Personal Ordinariate of Our Lady of Walsingham as a structure that would allow Anglicans from the Church of England to have full communion with Catholic Church while at the same time retaining much of their Anglican traditions and practice (Hill, 2010). Even this long after the Church of England began ordaining women, there still seemed to be a need to create a space that would allow Anglicanism without the ministry of ordained women. The extent to which people left the Anglican Church as a result of the changing status of women is unclear and exact figures are hard to find. In 2018, the Anglican ordinariate listed some 50 groups in England (Ordinariate, 2018), but most of these were probably quite small. The advent of women bishops made the 1993 Act of Synod redundant, so Resolution AB parishes (those under alternative episcopal oversight) were asked to reapply for alternative arrangements (the previous measure having been replaced by a new one in 2014). By 2017, around 450 (3.7% of all parishes) had requested alternative arrangements (Williams, 2017), which shows that relatively few parishes seemed to be totally opposed to women's ministry by then. This is line with the *Church Times* data for 2013 where only 13% of the sample were opposed to women bishops in 2013. Given the sample is likely to over-represent Anglo-catholics and traditionalists, it seems there is a wide measure of support for women having leadership roles in the Church of England.

Although some of the changes between surveys could have been due to traditionalists leaving the Anglican Church, the scale of the changes suggests it was due at least in part to shifts in attitudes within birth cohorts. The shifts were most apparent in those who were born prior to the 1960s, and these people became more accepting across all traditions.

This may represent the shedding of stereotyped beliefs that reflected assumptions and norms that were acquired at a time when women generally had very different roles, both within and beyond the church. Psychologists have long argued that prejudice can be reduced by contact with 'outgroups' (Dovidio, Gaertner, & Kawakami, 2003) and this may well have been what happened to many in the Church of England. As women priests became more common, even parishioners who were opposed and pastored only by male clergy were likely to encounter clergywomen in deanery or diocesan meetings and to see them portrayed in the media. By 2001, women held many senior diocesan roles including being archdeacons and cathedral deans. The realization that women could do these roles as well as, or better than, the men who preceded them may have made many question the reasons for their objections.

The marked changes between surveys in cohorts born before the 1960s may be linked to the change in age profile of women clergy in the first decade of this century. Figures from the Church of England show that the number of stipendiary female clergy aged 50–65 almost doubled between 2001 and 2011, in marked contrast to the static picture for younger clergywomen and the decline in the number of clergymen in this age group over the same period (Research and Statistics, 2012, Figure 28). The data show the change in profile was not due to age cohorts of clergywomen getting older, but rather because recruitment in this age group over the decade increased faster than for younger women or men generally. These were women from the war and post-war cohorts, which is where those where opinions changed most markedly over the same period. The change was not simply because more clergywomen appeared in these survey cohorts: they formed a small proportion of the overall survey and the changes were apparent in laywomen as well as laymen and clergymen. There are two explanations for this association, which are not mutually exclusive. One explanation is that it was the vocation and example of these women that helped the continuing acceptance of women's ministry in this period. The other is that as opinions changed in these age cohorts women found that it was more acceptable to offer themselves for the priesthood. Either way, the change was marked and seemed to pave the way for the changes that enabled women to become bishops.

The consistent liberalization of opinion among the older cohorts in all traditions throws into contrast the very different pattern among younger cohorts of Evangelicals. Here there seems to have been a reduction in support for women's ministry, both as priests and as bishops. Examining these trends more closely showed that they held among Evangelical men (clergy and lay) but not women.[2] This pattern is present in some other areas of opinion reported in other chapters and will be discussed in more detail in Chapter 11. In this case, it suggests that there may be cohorts of Evangelical Anglicans born after the 1960s who are resisting the changing roles of men and women in the Church, and perhaps in society at large. They form a small proportion of *Church Times* readers, but a larger proportion of the Church generally, so may represent an important minority that could have a strong influence in the future. The validity of the claim that this resistance is based solely on trying to be faithful to scripture, and not unjustifiable patriarchy, would be given more weight if it was a view more strongly supported by Evangelical women, who are as likely as their male counterparts to take a conservative and literal approach when interpreting the Bible (Village, 2012).

If bishops are the equivalent (in terms of leadership) of executive directors in other institutions, then the progress of the Church of England has been remarkable: in 2017 there were 25 female executive directorships of FSTE 100 companies, representing 9.8% of the total; in 2018 there were 15 women bishops in office or about to be consecrated, representing some 13% of all bishops. This might be a short-term effect because the experience of many clergywomen is of an ongoing struggle to find full acceptance (Greene & Robbins, 2015; Percy, 2017; Peyton & Gatrell, 2013), a finding that was also apparent in data for the Episcopal Church in America in 1999, some 25 years after they were first ordained in that province (Sullins, 2000). Nonetheless, it shows that once the Church of England was able to enact the legislation regarding women bishops it moved quickly to redress the balance. If the Church does eventually come to fully reflect English society in terms of the gender balance in leadership, it may still find that women are over-represented among laity and under represented among clergy. Whatever the pressures or expectations of some sections of society that women should work outside the home, it seems likely that some will always choose to devote all or most of their time to bringing up children. The fact that

---

[2] For those born after the 1950s, 56% of Evangelical men supported women as bishops, compared with 75% of Evangelical women. The comparable figure for Anglo-catholics were 67% for men and 86% for women; for Broad church the figures were 80% for men and 93% for women.

there is widespread support for allowing women to be priests and bishops does not necessarily mean that women will be as likely as men to offer themselves for ordained ministry. Ordination figures show that by 2015 women comprised 41% of those going into stipendiary ministry and 59% of those going into self-supporting (i.e. mainly part-time) ministry (Research and Statistics, 2015). However, the figures on the ages of those ordained show that of 998 men of known age at ordination from 2012 to 2015, 49% were under 40, compared to just 17% of 870 women (Research and Statistics, 2015 from Tables 5 and 6). Unless those selecting for training are heavily biased against women of child-bearing age (which seems very unlikely) it appears that young women may be more reluctant than young men to put themselves forward for priesthood, and women seem to prefer the flexibility of being unpaid to the demands of stipendiary positions. Whether this is a short-term residual effect of previous patterns and expectations, or an ongoing reluctance of women to combine having children with the demands of ministry only time will tell. The proportion of women among ordinands is continuing to increase (Williams, 2017), but as women comprise some two-thirds of the laity the figures will have to rise considerably before it can be argued that both sexes in the Church of England are equally likely to become priests.

REFERENCES

Avis, P. D. L. (2003). *Seeking the truth of change in the church: Reception, communion and the ordination of women.* London: T&T Clark.

Dovidio, J. F., Gaertner, S. L., & Kawakami, K. (2003). Intergroup contact: The past, present, and the future. *Group Processes & Intergroup Relations, 6*(1), 5–21. https://doi.org/10.1177/1368430203006001009.

Francis, L. J., Robbins, M., & Astley, J. (2005). *Fragmented faith? Exposing the fault-lines in the Church of England.* Milton Keynes: Paternoster Press.

Furlong, M. (1998). *Act of Synod–Act of folly?* London: SCM Press.

Gill, S. (1994). *Women and the Church of England: From the eighteenth century to the present.* London: SPCK.

Glick, P., & Fiske, S. T. (1996). The ambivalent sexism inventory: Differentiating hostile and benevolent sexism. *Journal of Personality and Social Psychology, 70*(3), 491–512. https://doi.org/10.1037/0022-3514.70.3.491.

Glick, P., & Fiske, S. T. (1999). The ambivalence toward men inventory: Differentiating hostile and benevolent beliefs about men. *Psychology of Women*

Quarterly, 23(3), 519–536. https://doi.org/10.1111/j.1471-6402.1999. tb00379.x.

Glick, P., Fiske, S. T., Mladinic, A., Saiz, J. L., Abrams, D., Masser, B., … López, W. L. (2000). Beyond prejudice as simple antipathy: Hostile and benevolent sexism across cultures. *Journal of Personality and Social Psychology, 79*(5), 763–775. https://doi.org/10.1037/0022-3514.79.5.763.

Glick, P., Lameiras, M., & Rodriguez Castro, Y. (2002). Education and Catholic religiosity as predictors of hostile and benevolent sexism toward women and men. *Sex Roles, 47*(9–10), 433–441. https://doi.org/10.102 3/A:1021696209949.

Greene, A.-M., & Robbins, M. (2015). The cost of a calling? Clergywomen and work in the Church of England. *Gender, Work & Organization, 22*(4), 405–420. https://doi.org/10.1111/gwao.12101.

Hill, C. (2010). What is the personal ordinariate? Canonical and liturgical observations. *Ecclesiastical Law Journal, 12*(2), 202–208. https://doi.org/10.1017/S0956618X10000062.

House of Bishops. (1988). *The ordination of women to the priesthood.* London: General Synod of the Church of England.

Keen, R., & Cracknell, R. (2018). *Women in Parliament and Government.* London: House of Commons Library.

Kuhrt, G. W. (2001). Women and ordained ministry. In G. W. Kuhrt (Ed.), *Ministry issues for the Church of England: Mapping the trends* (pp. 234–239). London: Church House Publishing.

ONS. (2013). *Women in the labour market: 2013.* London: Office for National Statistics.

ONS. (2018). *Understanding the gender pay gap in the UK.* London: Office for National Statistics.

Ordinariate. (2018). Retrieved June 29, 2018, from http://www.ordinariate. org.uk.

Park, A., Bryson, C., Clery, E., Curtice, J., & Phillips, M. (2013). Gender roles: An incomplete revolution? In A. Park, C. Bryson, E. Clery, J. Curtice, & M. Phillips (Eds.), *British Social Attitudes: The 30th Report* (pp. 115–138). London: NatCen Social Research.

Percy, E. (2017). Women, ordination and the Church of England: An ambiguous welcome. *Feminist Theology, 26*(1), 90–101. https://doi.org/10.1177/0966735017714405.

Petre, J. (1994). *By sex divided: The Church of England and women priests.* London: Fount.

Peyton, N., & Gatrell, C. (2013). *Managing clergy lives: Obedience, sacrifice, intimacy.* London: Bloomsbury.

Research and Statistics. (2012). *Ministry statistics 2011.* London: Archbishops' Council.

Research and Statistics. (2015). *Ministry statistics 2012 to 2015*. London: Archbishops' Council.

Sealy, R., & Vinnicombe, S. (2013). *Female FSTE Board Report 2013*. Cranfield School of Management (Online).

Singh, V., & Vinnicombe, S. (2001). *Women directors: Swimming, sinking, or not even in the pool?* Report on female directors in the top 100 companies index, 2001. Bedford, UK: Cranfield University School of Management.

Sullins, P. (2000). The stained glass ceiling: Career attainment for women clergy. *Sociology of Religion, 61*(3), 243–266. https://doi.org/10.2307/3712578.

Village, A. (2012). Biblical literalism: A test of the compensatory schema hypothesis among Anglicans in England. *Review of Religious Research, 54*(2), 175–196. https://doi.org/10.1007/s13644-012-0055-4.

Williams, H. (2017, September 29). More women than men enter clergy training, latest figures show. *Church Times*, p. 5.

CHAPTER 6

Sexual Orientation

Introduction

The notion of 'sexuality' is relatively new, and it was not until the latter part of the nineteenth century that the word 'homosexual' entered the English language. A phenomenon that had previously been understood as sinful behaviour driven by lust gradually came to be seen as a characteristic of some people. In the last century, perceptions of homosexuality ranged from a form of illness akin to insanity, through a life style choice, to a basic orientation that sits alongside a range of others related to gender and identity. For the Church of England, the changes have meant that some of its members are no longer willing to hide their sexual orientation, nor accept the idea that it is wrong for it to be expressed in sexual activity. As with other areas such as divorce and remarriage, changing social values in Britain have led to pressure on the Church of England to change its beliefs and practices to reflect more closely the society in which it is set. As with those other areas, the issues have tended to be focused on the orientation and behaviour of clergy. This chapter reports on items in the *Church Times* surveys related attitudes to the idea of same-sex relationships generally, and to the idea of ordaining practicing homosexuals. This was a hotly debated issue in the Church of England through the first decade of the twenty-first century, and the results demonstrate the marked changes in attitudes in some quarters during

© The Author(s) 2018
A. Village, *The Church of England
in the First Decade of the 21st Century*,
https://doi.org/10.1007/978-3-030-04528-9_6

this time. Before looking at how this issue developed in the Church, it is worth looking at how attitudes have shifted in society at large.

Attitudes Towards Homosexuality in British Society

Attitudes towards same-sex relationships have been becoming more liberal in the UK for many decades and these changes have gradually led to revisions of the laws related to homosexual acts and same-sex partnerships. Prior to the 1960s, homosexual acts between men (but not women) were treated as a crime, and there were several high-profile court cases in the 1950s that resulted in convictions. Newspapers at the time reflected the growing unease with what was seen as unnecessary victimization, and the Wolfenden report of 1957 recommended that homosexuality should no longer be illegal. It took some time for this view to prevail, and homosexual acts between men were not decriminalized until 1967 in England and Wales and not until 1980 in Scotland. The homosexual age of consent was reduced from 21 to 18 years in 1994 but did not reach parity with heterosexual consent until 2001, when the age was reduced to 16. The latter change was not without considerable opposition from the House of Lords, where it was opposed by Church of England bishops, and only became law because the Parliament Act allows the House of Commons to overrule repeated rejections of bills by the upper chamber. So at the time of the first *Church Times* survey significant changes in the law were being made, but these changes were being strongly resisted in some Church quarters.

Legal changes to the status of same-sex partnerships followed on the heels of the change in the age of consent as the Blair Labour Government pursued its goal of ensuring sexual orientation did not affect a person's status before the law. For many, this was seen as a matter of equal rights, and the drive for change was underpinned by the UK adopting the European Convention of Human Rights into law in 2000. Gay couples were allowed to adopt from 2002, and the Civil Partnership Act of 2004 gave some legal status to same-sex partnerships without going as far as parity with married couples. This final step did not happen until the time of the second *Church Times* survey, with the passing of the Marriage (Same-Sex Couples) Act in 2013. In the decade before this landmark, there had been several laws that were aimed at removing discrimination on the grounds of sexual orientation. Changes in regulations in 2007 meant it became illegal to deny goods and services to gay people, and this was a direct confrontation to some Christian organizations. Most notable was the Catholic Church's adoption agency, Catholic Care, which hitherto had not been willing to place children with gay couples. The agency fought a legal battle to keep this stance, which it ultimately lost (BBC, 2012), resulting in the closure of its adoption service (Catholic Care, 2018). Similar cases of businesses refusing to offer services to gay couples on religious grounds were also lost after protracted appeals that led all the way to the European Court (Pigott, 2013). This starkly raised the issue of competing human rights: do religious people have the right to uphold their beliefs if those beliefs deny that homosexual and heterosexual partnerships are equally valid?

Changes in law are one way of documenting changes in social attitudes since the Second World War. A more direct way is to examine beliefs among the general population, and there have been several ongoing surveys of attitudes and practices related to sexuality over the last few decades. Some of the most comprehensive have been the National Surveys of Sexual Attitudes and Lifestyles (Natsal), which have studied the British population at the start of each of the last three decades (Mercer et al., 2013). Among younger people (aged 16–44), there has been a marked change in attitudes towards same-sex relationships. In 1990–1991, around 23% of men and 28% of women agreed that there was nothing wrong at all in same-sex partnerships. By 2000–2001, this had risen to around 39% of men and 52% of women, and by 2010–2012 the figures were around 50 and 66%, respectively. This level of change is reflected in other national surveys that have asked similar sorts of questions. Since 1983, the British Social Attitudes Surveys have asked about sexual relationships between two adults of the same sex. In the 1980s, somewhere between 11 and 17% of the population said this was 'not wrong at all', in the 1990s the figure ranged from 15 to 27%, in the 2000s the figure ranged from 34 to 39%, and by 2012 it was 47% (Park & Rhead, 2013).

The overall pattern of increasing acceptance of homosexuality belies variations between different sections of the population. Not surprisingly, older people have consistently shown more conservative views, though this may be partly a cohort effect rather than a change in attitude with age. So, for example, in the mid-1980s around 85% of people born in the 1930s felt homosexuality was wrong, compared with only 60% of those born in the 1950s. By 2012, the figure for the 1930s cohort had fallen to around 55% and that of the 1950s cohort to around 30%

(Park & Rhead, 2013, Figure 1.5). Both generations had become more liberal, but the difference between them remained. It seems that people have become more accepting of homosexuality during their lifetimes, but this is relative to the level of acceptance that was prevalent in society when they were young adults. The projections suggest that virtually none of those being born today will consider homosexuality is wrong by the time they reach adulthood.

Responses in the Church of England

The pace of change in attitudes to sexuality has been hard for churches, especially the Church of England. This is not because the Church is uniformly against homosexual practice, but rather because it has long been a Church which has been ambivalent on the matter. In the nineteenth century, when Victorian attitudes were hardening against homosexuals, the Church of England made little official comment. Timothy Jones (2011) points out that there was no pronouncement on the infamous trials of Oscar Wilde in 1895, and it was a Church of England clergyman, Stewart Headlam, who posted bail for the offender. The Anglo-catholic movement in particular seems to have been a place where homosexual men could find a niche, partly because of the growth of celibacy and celibate orders, and partly because of the style of worship and ritualism (Hilliard, 1982). Although acceptance of homosexual men was by no means widespread in Anglo-catholic circles, it was certainly more prevalent than among Evangelicals or society at large. The affinity between a minority religious movement in the Church of England and a sexual minority may have allowed homosexuals to find companionship and networks of like-minded people long before the overt changes in British society after the 1950s.

It was out of this stable of liberal Catholicism that the Church of England Moral Welfare Council commissioned a report, *The problem of homosexuality*, written by Derrick Bailey and published in 1954. It proposed decriminalization of homosexuality several years in advance of the Wolfenden Report, and indeed formed the basis of the Church of England's submission to the commission (Jones, 2011). Bailey (1955) also produced a major historical study that argued there was no biblical or theological warrant for treating homosexuality differently from heterosexuality in terms of moral prescriptions. It was work such as this that led to the Church Assembly (forerunner of the General Synod) to support, albeit by a narrow majority, the recommendation to decriminalize homosexuality. This does not mean that the Church of England has come to accept fully homosexuality, and the official position remains that expressed in the statement by the House of Bishops *Issues of human sexuality* (House of Bishops, 1991). This cautiously worded document referred to 'homophile orientation and practice' as something which could not be endorsed by the Church, but also said the Church must '... not reject those who sincerely believe it is God's call to them' (paragraph 5.6, p. 41). The tone is one of not condoning same-sex relationships, but not condemning those who hold to that orientation or practice. The report distinguishes between clergy and others because of their 'representative and pastoral responsibilities' (paragraph 5.12, p. 44). On these grounds, the bishops decided '...the clergy cannot claim the liberty to enter into sexually active homophile relationships' (paragraph 5.17, p. 45). This view allowed for the open acceptance of gay couples without conceding that their orientation or behaviour was entirely equivalent to heterosexual partnership. The caveat was that the acceptance was conditional on neither partner being ordained (unless they were also celibate).

This stance on homosexual clergy was to be severely tested by events within and beyond the Church of England in the period before and after the first *Church Times* survey. The 1998 Lambeth Conference gathered bishops from across the Anglican Communion and, despite the efforts of the then Archbishop of Canterbury, George Carey, public reporting was dominated by the issue of homosexuality (Bates, 2004, p. 125). The conference passed a resolution (I.10) that reaffirmed the acceptance of those with homosexual orientation, but could not 'advise the legitimising or blessing of same sex unions nor ordaining those involved in same gender unions' (Anglican Consultative Council, 2005, p. 9). This may have been an attempt to hold the line, but it was undermined in 2003 when Gene Robinson, an openly gay priest in a long-term same-sex partnership, was elected as a diocesan bishop in the Episcopal Church of the USA. In the same year, Jeffery John, an openly gay, but celibate, priest was nominated by the Bishop of Oxford to be Bishop of Reading. The nomination failed, but not before it had exposed the division of opinion among English Anglicans on this subject. Rowan Williams assumed office in February that year and immediately set up the Lambeth Commission on Communion, chaired by Archbishop Robin Eames. The aim of the Windsor Report (Eames, 2004) was ostensibly to deal with issues of unity and communion in general, but its recommendations included the suspension of any further consecration of gay bishops, a halt to blessings of same-sex unions, and an invitation for those involved in these causes to express public regret. In the decade that followed the Windsor Report the issue continued to cause tensions, though the sundering apart of the Anglican Communion that some predicted has not yet happened. The 2008 Lambeth Conference was boycotted by some primates and bishops opposed to same-sex unions, but on the whole it managed to avoid producing more resolutions that would further divide the Communion.

The advent of civil partnerships in the UK in 2005 raised issues for the Church in terms of whether such partnerships might be blessed in church services and whether they were an option for clergy. The House of Bishops released a pastoral statement prior to the legislation coming into force that allowed priests to register in civil partnerships, allowed priests to pray for same-sex couples in church and care for them pastorally, but prohibited the introduction of formal liturgy for the blessing of such partnerships (House of Bishops, 2005). There was inevitably a mixed reaction to the change in law and the stance that the bishops had taken, with feelings that the latter did not go far enough in either direction or was too ambiguous in its wording (Boulding, 2005; Harden, 2005a, 2005b). The question of whether priests in civil partnerships should be eligible for the episcopate was reviewed by a working party of bishops set up in 2011, which recommended in 2013 that this should be allowed to happen, provided candidates were celibate (Thornton, 2013).

The 1998 Lambeth Conference had urged Anglican Churches to set up listening processes as part of the way forward. In 2011, the Church of England House of Bishops set up a working group on human sexuality, chaired by Sir Joseph Pilling, to 'reflect upon biblical, historical and ecumenical explorations on human sexuality and material from the listening process undertaken in the light of the 1998 Lambeth Conference resolution' (House of Bishops, 2013, p. 1). The Pilling Report was published in 2013 just after the second *Church Times* survey was completed. It found that the listening process across the Church of England had been patchy rather than systematic and dependent on local initiatives. The group made a number of observations that summed up the state of the issue for the Church of England at the time. They noted among other things the marked difference between generations, with homosexuality not being an issue for young people. They believed teaching and practice were deeply off-putting to those outside the Church and therefore harmful to mission. They had also heard that the rules for ordinands and clergy were inconsistently applied, encouraging dishonesty and the avoidance of open or formal partnerships. Some gay and lesbian clergy reported difficulty in securing appointments due to the views of conservative groups and congregation members. At the same time, gay people who believed that scripture forbids same-sex attraction found that Church teaching helped them to resist temptation and would view relaxation of the rules as a betrayal.

The Pilling Report illustrates the way in which the Church of England seems to be gradually changing its beliefs and practices with regard to same-sex relationships. The majority report is affirming of gay people and recognizes the hurt caused by the Church in the past. It moves cautiously in the direction of affirming same-sex relationships, recommending at one point that 'there can be circumstances where a priest, with the agreement of the relevant PCC, should be free to mark the formation of a permanent same sex relationship in a public service but should be under no obligation to do so. Some of us do not believe that this can be extended to same sex marriage' (p. 118). At the same time, the report includes a 30-page 'Dissenting Statement' from the Bishop of Birkenhead, Keith Sinclair, which reflects that by no means all of the Church of England wishes to see a gradual accommodation.

At the time of the first *Church Times* survey, the Church of England was trying to respond to the 1998 Lambeth Conference by engaging in discussions and dialogue. The major changes in the legal rights of same-sex partners were a few years away, and the issue of consecrating openly homosexual bishops had not yet reached public attention. By and large most members of the Church of England would be aware of the arguments surrounding sexuality, but perhaps other issues would be seen as more pressing. By the time of the second *Church Times* survey things had moved on considerably, with civil partnerships being commonplace, and same-sex marriages about to become permitted by law. The Church of England was still officially maintaining the views of sexuality defined in 1991 by the House of Bishops, but the Pilling Report was about to be published and this showed the extent to which many in the Church were willing to see changes in practice that would de facto undermine some of the traditionally held theological beliefs about sexuality. Others were still unwilling to allow the Church to make this sort of accommodation to wider social change.

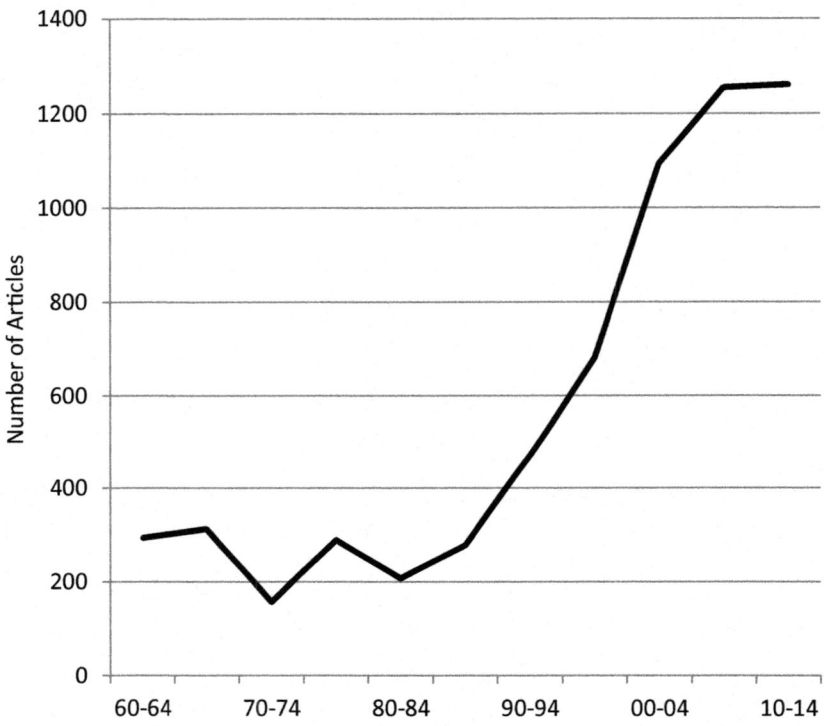

Fig. 6.1 Number of *Church Times* articles related to homosexuality in five-year periods

The level of interest in the issue in the Church of England is indicated by the number of *Church Times* articles on the subject since the 1960s (Fig. 6.1).[1] There was ongoing interest at a low level until the early 1990s, when the number of articles began to rise steeply, which they continued to do until the time of the second *Church Times* survey. The number of articles currently exceeds 1000 in any five-year period, making it one of the key topics referred by the paper.

[1] Searches of the *Church Times* archive used the following terms: 'homosexual*'; 'gay'; LGB*; 'same sex'.

EXPLORING THE DATA

It Is Wrong for People of the Same Gender to Have Sex

When exploring attitudes towards homosexuality among church people it is common to employ two slightly different types of question, one related to the issue of whether homosexuality is wrong generally, and the other related to whether homosexuality is compatible with being in ordained ministry. The Church of England has for some time tended to accept homosexual orientation but rejected homosexual sex, so it is important to specify the distinction in the items used to test opinion. Both *Church Times* surveys included the item 'It is wrong for people of the same gender to have sex'. Across both surveys, the adjusted average proportion of respondents who agreed or agreed strongly that gay sex was wrong was 46% (Fig. 6.2). In other words, over half (54%) were either neutral or did not think that gay sex is wrong.

Some of the differences between groups were much as we might expect to find in the population at large (Crockett & Voas, 2003; Mercer et al., 2013; Park & Rhead, 2013): men were more likely than women to agree same sex was wrong (50% versus 42%), older people more likely than younger people (59% of those 70 or older versus 34% of those under 50), and those without degrees more likely than those with degrees (52% versus 41%). The sex difference was in the same direction but slightly smaller (9%) than reported in some national surveys. There was no indication that attitudes varied systematically between rural and urban areas, so the idea of greater conservativism in these matters in the countryside may be a myth. Clergy were more accepting of same-sex relationships than were laity: overall, 42% of clergy agreed it is wrong for people of the same gender to have sex, compared with 50% of laity. This allows for the fact that clergy were predominantly male and laity predominately female, and for the fact the lay people in the surveys tended to be older and less well education, on average, than the clergy.

There was a marked difference between people who identified with different traditions with the Church of England. Rejection of same-sex relationships ran at 29% among Anglo-catholics and 34% among those from the Broad church, but 74% among Evangelicals. This was the biggest disparity among any of the groups tested and shows the marked difference between Evangelicals and the rest of the Church of England on this issue.

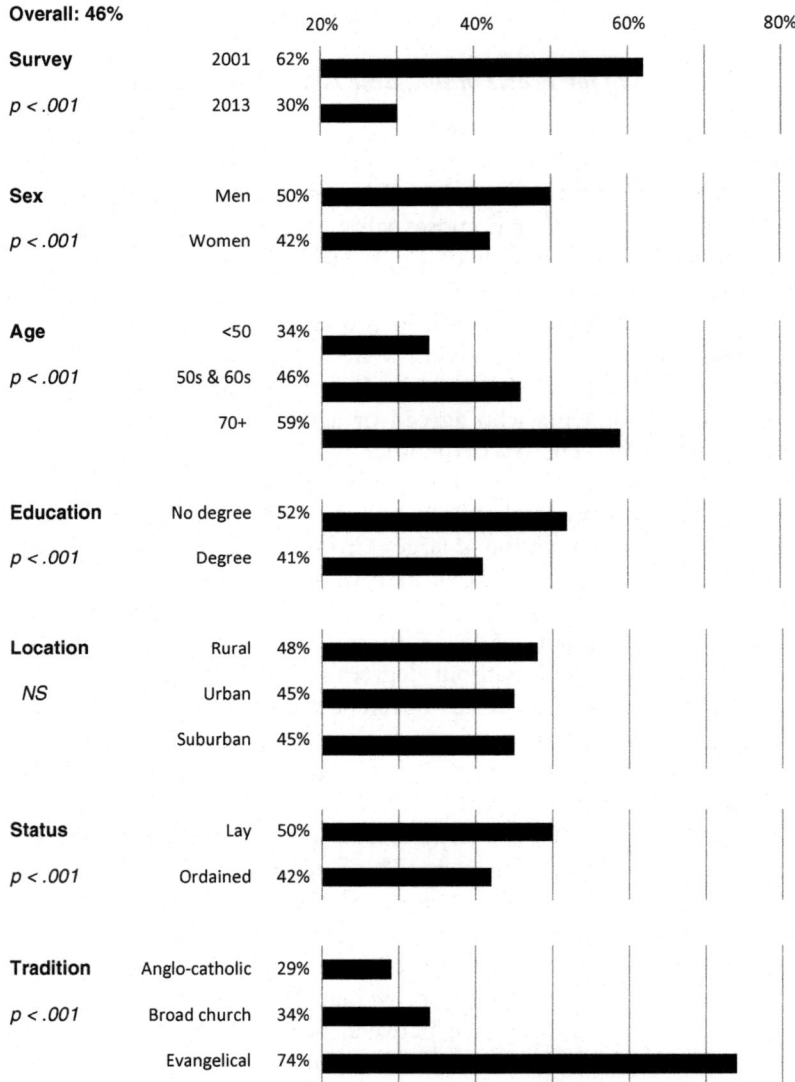

Fig. 6.2 It is wrong for people of the same gender to have sex: estimated means

Besides the difference between traditions, the most obvious change was between surveys, with rejection of same-sex relationships falling from 62% in 2001 to 30% in 2013. The nearest equivalent figures from national surveys would be 46% in 2000 to 28% in 2012,[2] suggesting people in the Church of England have moved further in their opinions of this period and are now almost similar in their views to the general population. Detailed cohort analysis showed that in virtually all birth-cohorts opinion had become more liberal over the decade (Fig. 6.3). The reduced opposition to same sex was most obvious among Anglo-catholics, averaging between 10 and 25%, with around 10% of those born after the 1940s agreeing with this item. Over half of Broad church respondents born after the 1930s were already accepting of gay sex in the 2001 survey. Opposition to same-sex relationships declined across the board, but at 10–30% in 2013 it remained slightly higher than among Anglo-catholics. The situation among Evangelicals, who tended to be much more likely to agree that same sex is wrong, was very different, with declining rejection among Evangelicals born in the 1960s and earlier, but similar or increased opposition among those born after the 1960s.

I Am in Favour of the Ordination of Practicing Homosexuals as Priests

Both surveys included two items related the ordination of practicing homosexuals: 'I am in favor of the ordination of practicing homosexuals as priests' and 'I am in favor of the ordination of practicing homosexuals as bishops'. These items are phrased in the opposite direction to the previous one, so here an increase in agreement meant a more positive attitude towards homosexuality. Responses to the two items were almost identical, but in each survey around 5% were in favour of allowing homosexuals to be ordained as priests but not as bishops. The results here are given for attitudes towards priesthood, where across both surveys the adjusted average support for ordaining homosexual priests was 30%.

---

[2] These figures are from the British Social Attitudes Surveys for 2000 and 2012, where 46 and 28% respectively said 'homosexuality is always/mostly wrong' (Park & Rhead, 2013, Table A.4).

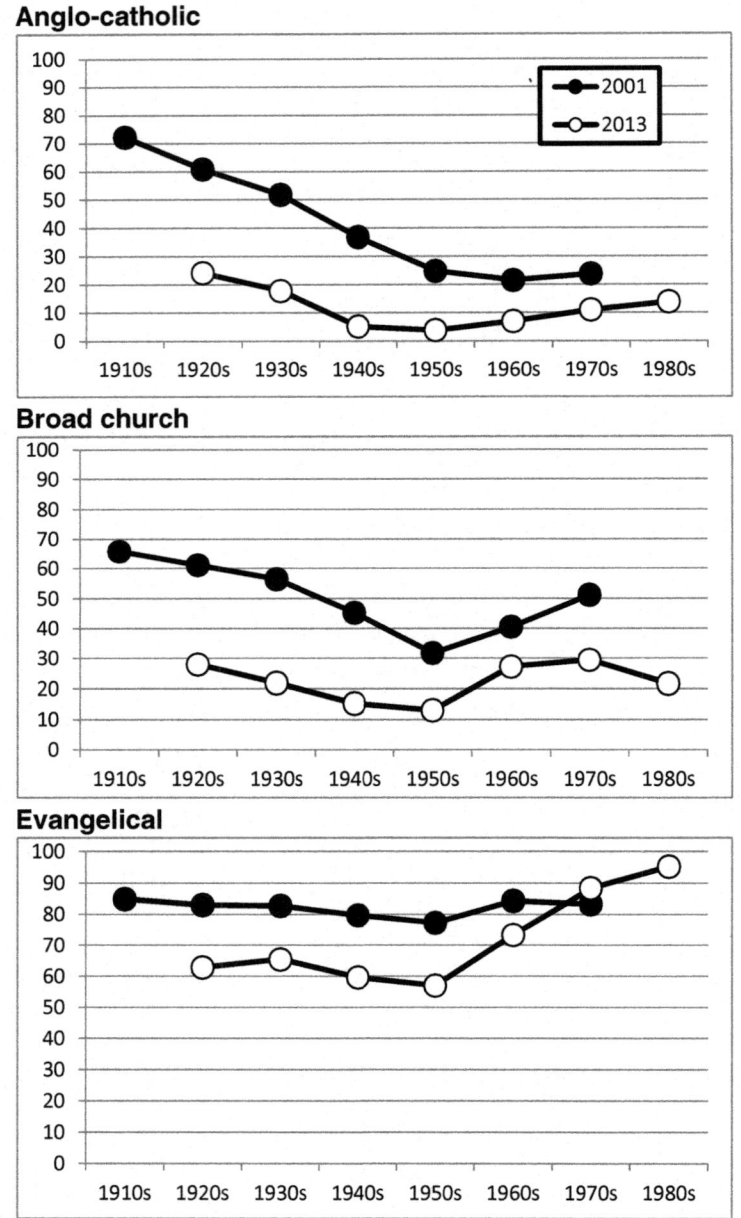

Fig. 6.3   It is wrong for people of the same gender to have sex: cohort changes

The differences between groups (Fig. 6.4) were as expected from the previous items, with greater acceptance among women (34%) than men (27%), among those under 50 (42%) compared with those 70 or older (21%), among graduates (36%) compared to those without degrees (25%), and among clergy (35%) compared to laity (26%). Unlike the previous item, there was a difference between locations in this item: in rural areas, 28% were in favour compared with 31% in urban areas and 33% in suburban areas. There was again a marked difference between people who identified with different traditions within the Church of England. Acceptance of ordaining practicing homosexuals ran at 49% among Anglo-catholics, 42% among the Broad church, but only 11% among Evangelicals. This is one issue where Evangelicals in particular seemed reluctant for any change in the official Church position.

The change in opinion between the surveys was again striking, with support for the ordination of homosexuals as priests more than doubling between the surveys, from 18% in 2001 to 47% in 2013. Detailed examination of the cohort breakdown shows that in all birth-cohorts opinion had become more liberal over the decade, though for Evangelicals born in the 1970s, the age-corrected 2013 figure was only 2% higher than the 3% recorded in 2001. The increased support was most obvious among Anglo-catholics, averaging around 30% after correcting for age, with some evidence of a 'ceiling' effect at around 80% support in 2013 among those born after the 1940s. For the Broad church, over half of those born in the 1950s and 1960s already supported the ordination of homosexual priests in the 2001 survey. The levels rose across the board, with a suggestion of a ceiling at around 85–90% support. The situation among Evangelicals was very different, with an adjusted average of only 11% across both surveys. Although starting from a low base in 2001, support among cohorts born before the 1970s more than doubled between the surveys. The situation was different for younger Evangelicals, who seem to remain almost unanimously opposed to the ordination of practicing homosexuals. The striking difference between Evangelicals and other traditions was nowhere more apparent than in the 1980s cohort, where there was no support for this issue (Fig. 6.5).

There were three items related to homosexuality included on the 2013 survey that were not present in 2001, two of which were related to the issue of liturgical provisions for same-sex couples. Of 3922 responses, 68% were in favour of homosexual couples being able to receive a blessing in church, but only 33% thought homosexual couples

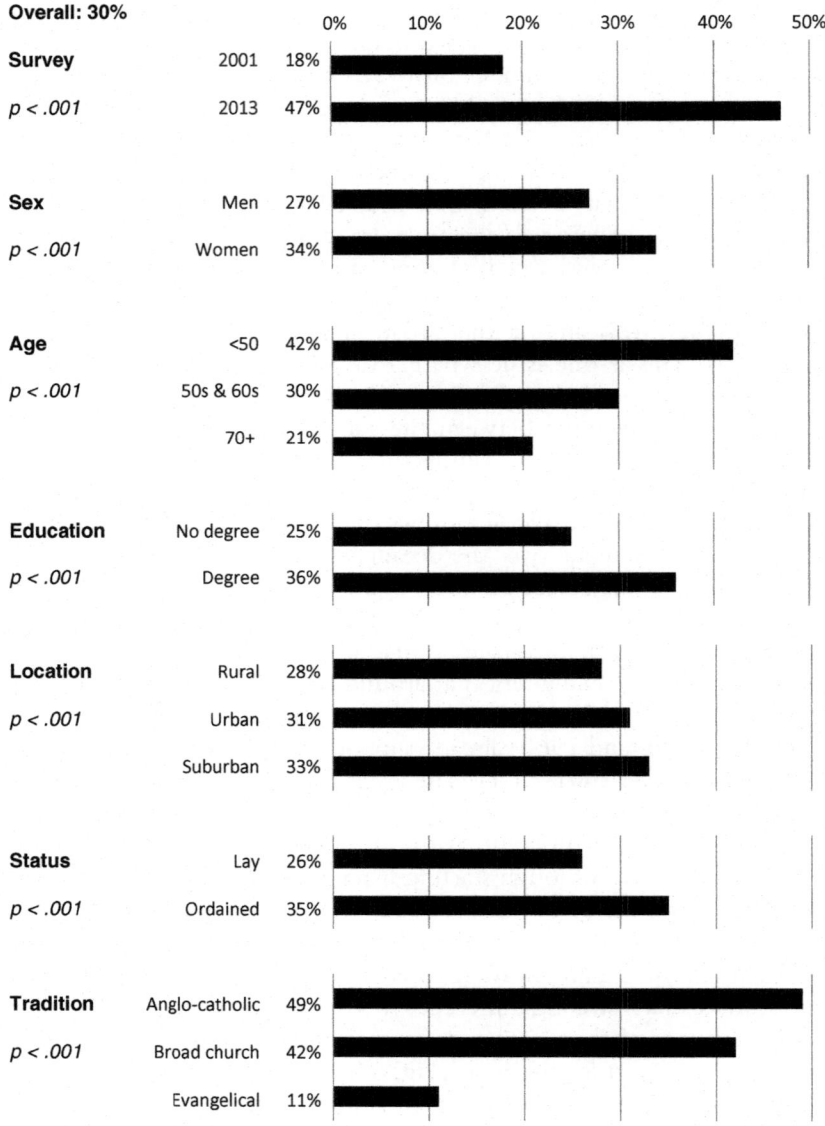

Fig. 6.4 I am in favour of the ordination of practicing homosexuals as priests: estimated means

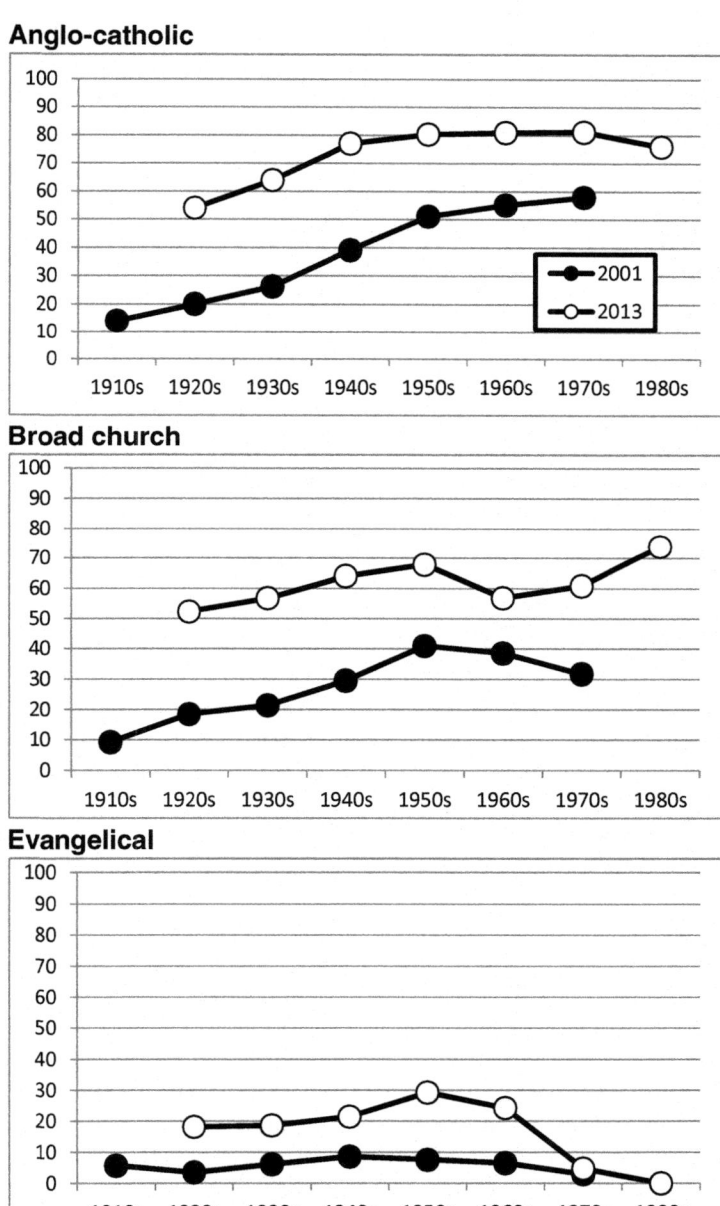

Fig. 6.5 I am in favour of the ordination of practicing homosexuals as priests: cohort changes

should be allowed to marry in church. This sort of distinction probably echoes opinions on the remarriage of divorcees in the period before the rules were changed. The third item 'Homosexual couples should not be allowed to adopt children' made it onto the online version of the 2013 questionnaire, and was answered by 1723 participants; only 27% agreed with this statement and 51% disagreed, suggesting substantial support for gay adoptions.

Conclusions

Both measures of attitudes towards homosexuality gave broadly the same results (though worded in opposite directions), but accepting that practicing homosexuals can be priests or bishops was less likely than accepting gay sex in general. As with some of the other issues that have faced the Church of England over the last few years, there is a deep-seated feeling that clergy should be exemplars of 'ideal' behaviour. This, as the Pilling Report pointed out, highlights an inconsistency in thought about this issue. If, as is increasingly the case, the Church argues that there is nothing wrong with homosexual love expressed physically, then why should this be denied for clergy? Looked at another way, is it not demeaning to the laity to assume that they need not strive for ideals that are required of those who are ordained? The history of practice in other areas suggests that the distinction between rules for clergy and laity will slowly decline as homosexuality continues to become more acceptable across the Church of England.

The differences between various groups mirrored those found in society at large. The more accepting attitude of women compared with men is a widespread finding in this country and elsewhere (Kite & Whitley, 1996; Mercer et al., 2013; Whitley 2001). The gender difference is complicated because detailed national studies have shown that men are more accepting of female same-sex partnerships than male same-sex partnerships, whereas women are equally accepting of both. Social psychologists have put forward a number of theories to explain this finding, often related to attitudes towards traditional gender roles: men tend to be less flexible about gender roles than women, and male homosexuality in particular is seen as a violation of those roles. The age difference is well-documented and almost certainly reflects the changing status of homosexuality in society during the last century or so. National data show a gradual increase in acceptance with successive cohorts, so even if people retain the attitudes they grew up with, as time goes by younger people will be more accepting and society will change. The data in the *Church Times* surveys showed that, for most of the Church of England, changes in attitude are happening for two reasons. First, successive cohorts are more and more accepting: those born in the early twentieth century were much less accepting in 2001 and in 2013 compared with those born in the latter part of the century. Second, people within those cohorts had become more accepting between the two surveys. This effect was smaller, but consistent more or less across the board and suggests that whatever their beliefs at the start of this century, people were likely to be more accepting a decade later. This combination of cohort difference and change over time means that attitudes in relation to homosexuality in large parts of the Church of England are changing very rapidly, and it will soon cease to be an issue for many people, reflecting the situation in society at large.

This average picture hides the very marked variation between the three main traditions in the Church. Older Anglo-catholics have shown the most marked changes in attitude. In 2001, between 40 and 70% of Anglo-catholics born before the War believed gay sex was wrong, but this had fallen to between 5 and 25% by 2013. The nearest equivalent figures in the population at large were between 30 and 40% in 2003 and about 20% in 2012 (Park & Rhead, 2013), suggesting that in this area Anglo-catholic opinion has been ahead of public opinion for some time. For the Broad church, equivalent figures for pre-war generations in 2001 were between 30 and 65% agreeing that same sex was wrong, a figure that fell to less than 30% by 2013, suggesting that by then they pretty much reflected public opinion at large. The marked exception has been Evangelicals, who have maintained attitudes in this area that are increasingly at odds with society as a whole and with their fellow Anglican churchgoers. This is not to say there has been no shift in opinion at all, and for older Evangelical birth-cohorts rejecting gay sex declined from 80% or more in 2001 to between 60 and 70% in 2013. The picture among younger Evangelical birth-cohorts was, however, very different. The lack of change suggests that younger Evangelicals have not responded to the liberalizing attitudes of their Church and non-church peers. The movement seen in some older Evangelicals is by no means evidence of any rapprochement with other traditions; the gap is still very large and, if trends among younger Evangelicals (which are admittedly based on rather low numbers in this sample) are maintained, it could be widening.

Of all the issues examined in the *Church Times* surveys, this was probably the one that had engendered the most interest and controversy in the period under study. To be sure, the area of biggest change in practice was the ordination of women bishops, where it was clear that objections were going to be overruled and a change in practice was going to happen. For the issue of homosexuality the matter is different, at least in terms of theology. The Anglican Church decades ago recognized no theological impediment to ordaining women, and the protracted period leading to women's ordination in the Church of England was about finding ways of accommodating those who disagreed with this widely held stance. There has been less movement in finding consensus in being able to remove theological objections to same-sex relationships. To date, statements from bishops and the official position of the Church of England have been about recognizing the harm done to gay people by the way they have been treated, and urging the whole Church to have more charity in accepting what gay people have to offer as examples of faith. But this still leaves the fundamental issue of whether being gay, or having same sex is wrong. Officially to date, the Church has accepted the orientation but not practice, but this may not be a position that it can maintain for much longer in the face of overwhelming changes in attitudes in society and in the Church.

Since the surveys were run, other related issues have come into focus in society and subsequently in the Church. Among these is the issue of transgender people, and whether to allow them to be ordained and married in church (Davies, 2015). Gender has moved rapidly from being a relatively minor issue in society to one that is becoming a major preoccupation, especially among younger generations. The Church is having to respond to another change in society that causes it to review its theology and practice with respect to minority groups (Dormor, 2015).

REFERENCES

Anglican Consultative Council. (2005). *The Lambeth conference resolutions archive from 1998*. London: Anglican Communion Office.

Bailey, D. S. (1955). *Homosexuality and the Western Christian tradition*. New York: Longmans, Green.

Bates, S. (2004). *A church at war: Anglicans and homosexuality*. London: I.B. Tauris.

BBC. (2012). *Catholic Care loses gay adoption fight*. Retrieved August 7, 2018, from https://www.bbc.co.uk/news/uk-england-leeds-20184133.

Boulding, R. (2005, August 19). Selby breaks bishops' ranks. *Church Times*, p. 3.

Catholic Care. (2018). *Our history*. Retrieved August 7, 2018, from http://www.catholic-care.org.uk/about-us/history/.

Crockett, A., & Voas, D. (2003). A divergence of views: Attitude change and the religious crisis over homosexuality. *Sociological Research Online, 8*(4). http://www.socresonline.org.uk/8/4/crockett.html.

Davies, M. (2015, December 4). *Support 'growing' for transgendered Christians. Church Times*, p. 8.

Dormor, D. (2015). Transgenderism and the Christian church: An overview. In J. M. Scherpe (Ed.), *The legal status of transsexual and transgender persons* (pp. 27–76). Cambridge: Intersentia.

Eames, R. (2004). *The Windsor report*. London: The Lambeth Commission on Communion.

Harden, R. (2005a, July 29). *Civil partnerships require sensitivity, say bishops. Church Times*, p. 3.

Harden, R. (2005b, September 30). Evangelicals criticise Bishops over Civil Partnership Act. *Church Times*, p. 7.

Hilliard, D. (1982). Unenglish and unmanly: Anglo-Catholicism and homosexuality. *Victorian Studies, 25*(2), 181–210.

House of Bishops. (1991). *Issues in human sexuality: A statement by the House of Bishops of the General Synod of the Church of England*. London: Church of England.

House of Bishops. (2005). *Civil Partnerships—A pastoral statement from the House of Bishops of the Church of England*. London: Church of England.

House of Bishops. (2013). *Working group on human sexuality: Final report*. London: Church House Publishing.

Jones, T. (2011). The stained glass closet: Celibacy and homosexuality in the Church of England to 1955. *Journal of the History of Sexuality, 20*(1), 132–152.

Kite, M. E., & Whitley, B. E. (1996). Sex differences in attitudes toward homosexual persons, behaviors, and civil rights: A meta-analysis. *Personality and Social Psychology Bulletin, 22*(4), 336–353. https://doi.org/10.1177/0146167296224002.

Mercer, C. H., Tanton, C., Prah, P., Erens, B., Sonnenberg, P., Clifton, S., … Johnson, A. M. (2013). Changes in sexual attitudes and lifestyles in Britain through the life course and over time: Findings from the National Surveys of Sexual Attitudes and Lifestyles (Natsal). *The Lancet, 382*(9907), 1781–1794. http://dx.doi.org/10.1016/S0140-6736(13)62035-8.

Park, A., & Rhead, R. (2013). Personal relationships: Changing attitudes towards sex, marriage and parenthood. In A. Park, C. Bryson, E. Clery, J. Curtice, & M. Phillips (Eds.), *British Social Attitudes* (Vol. 30, pp. 1–32). London: NatCen Social Research.

Pigott, R. (2013). British Airways Christian employee Nadia Eweida wins case. Retrieved July 25, 2018, from https://www.bbc.co.uk/news/uk-21025332.

Thornton, E. (2013, September 30). Civil partnerships: 'We should have shown workings'. *Church Times*, p. 5.

Whitley, B. E., Jr. (2001). Gender-role variables and attitudes toward homosexuality. *Sex Roles, 45*(11/12), 691–721. https://doi.org/10.1023/A:1015640318045.

CHAPTER 7

Confidence in Leadership

INTRODUCTION

The period spanning the two *Church Times* surveys (2001–2013) enclosed the tenure of Rowan Williams as Archbishop of Canterbury (2002–2012). As we have seen in earlier chapters, this was a time of some turbulence both in the Church of England and in the Anglican Communion, with issues such as sexuality and the ordination of women as bishops leading to heated debates and evident divisions. In such circumstances, it is worth asking how members viewed those individuals and institutions that had the unenviable tasking of guiding the Church through the stormy seas of deciding how to respond internally to the external changes in society. The *Church Times* questionnaires contained several different items headed by the phrase 'I have confidence in the leadership given by:', which was followed by 'the Archbishops' Council', 'the Archbishop of Canterbury', 'the General Synod', 'my diocesan bishop' and 'my local clergy'. Between them, these represent some of the offices and institutions that shape the Church of England and the extent to which it evolves and changes over time. This chapter first outlines the way in which direction and leadership are manifest in the Church of England before asking if confidence in the different parts of the hierarchy varied within or between the surveys.

Governance in the Church of England is a complicated business. This is partly a matter of history and partly a matter of the desire to balance

© The Author(s) 2018
A. Village, *The Church of England
in the First Decade of the 21st Century*,
https://doi.org/10.1007/978-3-030-04528-9_7

episcopal authority with democracy. The diocese is the fundamental unit of the Church of England (Podmore, 2009), which means diocesan bishops carry a key responsibility for pastoring clergy and laity, safeguarding doctrine, teaching the faith, the ordering of worship and overseeing the conduct of the Church. Bishops work locally with councils and diocesan synods, but it is bishops who tend to be the visible figureheads of the diocese. For most parishioners (including many clergy), the bishop may be someone encountered at occasional visitations or meetings, or someone they see in the media, but who is otherwise a rather distant figure. For most lay people, the key figures who represent the presence of the Church are the local clergy: incumbents or priests-in-charge plus curates, deacons and other ordained people who might lead worship. Parochial clergy usually belong to their local chapter, which may or may not be a place to find encouragement and support from those who share similar experiences of ministry. In local terms, the diocesan bishop and parish clergy are key leaders who need the confidence and support of those they work with and serve.

The Archbishop of Canterbury is the senior bishop of the Church of England and traditionally also the diocesan bishop of Canterbury. The office holder is also the symbolic head of the Anglican Communion; Rowan Williams wrote of the Archbishop being '...the focus and spokesman of its [the Anglican Communion] unity today' (Williams, n.d.). The role tends to have influence rather than direct power, and part of the art of office lies in managing media scrutiny on the one hand and expectations of the Church on the other. Williams' predecessor was George Carey, an Evangelical who took office in 1991 and retired in 2002, so he was Archbishop at the time of the first *Church Times* survey. In office, Carey was a firm supporter of the ordination of women, tolerant of divorce and the remarriage of divorcees, but firmly resisted moves to change the Church's traditional teaching on sexuality. He was succeeded by Rowan Williams who was Archbishop of Wales and a leading academic theologian with a more Anglo-catholic background than his predecessor. He worked hard to try and hold together the liberal and conservative wings of the Church and wider Anglican Communion, while at the same time recognizing the need for the Church to be more mission-focused than it had been (Goddard, 2013; Shortt, 2014). Williams resigned at the end of 2012, and his successor, Justin Welby, had been in office less than six months at the time of the second *Church Times* survey. Welby, the current incumbent, came to faith through the

Evangelical tradition (Atherstone, 2013, 2014) but admits to being something of a 'spiritual magpie' (Moore, 2013). He strongly supported the move to allow the ordination of women as bishops and saw the Measure through Synod in 2014. He has trodden a careful line on the issue of same-sex marriages, outspokenly rejecting homophobia and affirming the quality of such relationships, but showing little support for changing the current prohibition on same-sex marriage in the Church. His tenure has included an emphasis on social issues related to poverty, austerity and justice for refugees.

It is at national institutional level that the process of managing change becomes particularly difficult to decipher unless you are familiar with history and ecclesiastical processes. The origin of the Church of England means that the English monarch is its 'Supreme Governor' and the Church is 'established' insofar as its laws are subject to the same authority as those of the state. The Sovereign-in-Parliament demonstrates that authority by giving Royal Assent to laws and measures affecting the Church. Although Parliament was for centuries the body which managed all the minutiae of the Church's legislation, this changed in the early twentieth century as powers were passed to the General Assembly and then to its replacement, the General Synod, in 1970. The Enabling Act of 1919 allowed the Church to produce 'measures' which are the equivalent of acts of Parliament, but which relate to the way that the Church operates internally and in its relationships to society. For example, changing who can marry in parish churches has implications for many people within and beyond church congregations, so this was a measure that required the approval of Parliament. Measures have the full force of law and can only be submitted for Royal Assent if Parliament agrees, which it usually does without debate or disagreement. Nonetheless, Parliament has the right to amend or reject measures, as happened on the revision of the Prayer Book in the 1920s. The laws relating to the Church also include canons, a complex body of rules inherited from the Roman Catholic Church, altered and formally established in 1603, substantially revised in the 1960s, and modified from time to time as the Church sees fit (Briden, 2013). Canons tend to relate to detailed matters of church order and are therefore more limited in scope than measures, but they must still obtain Royal Assent in a similar procedure to measures. A third category of secondary or subordinate legislation may involve guidelines issued by General Synod or the House of Bishops, which usually do not need to go before Parliament.

Towards the end of the nineteenth century, there was pressure to widen representation on national church bodies by electing lay people (at that time laymen), and this happened in the Convocation of Canterbury in 1886 and York in 1892 (Buchanan, 2015). Lay representation was retained in the Church Assembly and in the General Synod, which has three houses representing bishops, clergy and laity. Each house has a veto on crucial legislation, which must pass in each to go forward. When the bar is set at a two-thirds majority in each house, as it was for measures associated with the ordination of women, it can be all but impossible to make changes unless there is widespread agreement across different sections of the Church. The House of Bishops, which consists of all diocesan bishops plus some elected suffragan or assistant bishops, also meets separately to discuss various matters that are particular episcopal responsibilities, such as doctrine, worship and pastoral matters. Over the years, the House of Bishops has produced key reports and guidance which has shaped the way in which legislation is framed and put forward to Synod.

General Synod has featured prominently in the debates over the ordination of women, where measures were introduced that required a two-thirds majority in each house. The way in which debates are organized tends to follow a parliamentary model, though usually with a sense that Christian charity should be more in evidence than it is in Westminster. Public attention is aroused when one or other house fails to approve a change, as happen with the women bishops (Davies, 2012) and the blessing of same-sex relationships in church (Sherwood, 2017). When change is blocked or change comes about in areas that are contentious, it can be Synod that takes the blame. Some see it as a body that has legislated on matters that should lie well outside its jurisdiction, while others become frustrated at its inability to keep in touch with the rank and file of the Church, let alone wider society. After the House of Laity narrowly defeated the measure to allow the ordination of women bishops in 2012, Mark Chapman, the Vice Principal of Ripon College, wrote an article in which he expressed something of the frustration felt by some at this form of government:

> ...even when synods are discussing such worldly matters as parochial fees, it remains important to think through the theology of the synodical system. The problem, however – and this is something that has been blindingly obvious in recent years – is that they do not seem very theological. Instead they are messy, full of conflict and very political. Often they do not

appear to be possessed of the great Christian virtues of faith, hope and love at all. And furthermore they seldom embody anything more than a modicum of unity or consensus. (Chapman, 2013, p. 18)

Much of the work of the Synod is through committees and commissions, which deal with various matters such as liturgy, business and appointments. In 1998, some of the responsibility of Synod was moved to the Archbishops' Council, a body that consists of the Archbishops of Canterbury and York, various ex officio members of the Convocations, representatives of the three houses of Synod and members appointed by the Archbishops. It acts as a corporate executive for the Church and as such tends to be an enabling and supportive body rather than a representative or legislative body, as is General Synod. Since its formation, it has taken an increasing leadership role through shaping legislation, supporting and directing ministry, managing funds and promoting particular goals (Church of England, 2018).

In the years leading up to 2001, the Church of England had been embroiled in a number of issues that might have affected confidence in the leadership offered by these various bodies (see Chapter 1). The ongoing debate about women's ordination continued, and the issue of women being allowed to be bishops was gaining momentum. The introduction of Common Worship in 2000 marked a milestone in liturgical reform that was welcomed by many, but not by everyone. Between 2001 and 2013, there was growing controversy over the matters related to sexuality, fuelled partly by the fallout from the 1998 Lambeth Conference and the subsequent actions of the Episcopal Church in the USA, who appointed an openly gay bishop in 2003. Synod continued to push forward the ordination of women bishops, and this led to several contentious debates and votes. In addition, there were changes that affected clergy, such as the Clergy Discipline Measure (2003) and the Ecclesiastical Offices (Terms of Service) Measure (2009). The latter removed some of the safeguards associated with incumbency, introducing appointments of limited duration and removing the freehold of property, while at the same time introducing protection against unfair dismissal. While some saw this as necessary progress towards aligning the working life of clergy with the rest of society, others saw it as a threat their independence and security (Editorial, 2007). How then, did the rank and file of the Church of England view the leadership of the Church over this period?

EXPLORING THE DATA

I Have Confidence in the Leadership Given by My Diocesan Bishop/Local Clergy

The overall figure for confidence in diocesan bishops was high (70%, Fig. 7.1) and on a par with that for the Archbishop of Canterbury (73%). Confidence was higher among women than men (72% versus 68%), higher among those 70 or older (72%) than in the other age groups (70 and 68%). There was no difference by education in this case, but those in rural areas had higher confidence (72%) than elsewhere. Clergy were more likely than laity to express confidence in their diocesan bishop (73% versus 67%). There was rather little difference between traditions, though Anglo-catholics showed the lowest levels of confidence. Overall, there was a slight fall in confidence between surveys (73% in 2001 versus 66% in 2013), which seemed to occur in all three traditions and nearly all age cohorts (Fig. 7.2).

Similar trends applied at parish level, and local clergy enjoyed the highest overall level of confidence in their leadership (74%). It probably makes sense to look at just lay people for this item, though the trends were mostly similar in each group when clergy were included. Among lay people, 77% had confidence in their local clergy, though this declined slightly between surveys from 79 to 75%. Unlike diocesan bishops, confidence in local clergy was lowest in rural areas (75%) and highest in urban areas (79%). Among lay people, confidence declined once their congregation size fell below about 100 people, and this may be linked to the smaller congregations in rural areas.

I Have Confidence in the Leadership Given by the Archbishop of Canterbury

This item could partly reflect views about the office in general, but probably more directly relates to the people occupying the office at that time. Overall, there was much higher confidence in the Archbishop's leadership (73%) than for either the General Synod (34%) or the Archbishops' Council (41%). Given that much of the change that archbishops achieve comes through those institutions, this may indicate that, when it comes to being led, people generally prefer a human face over a faceless institution. Across the two surveys, there were some consistent differences between groups (Fig. 7.3). As with diocesan bishops, women had more

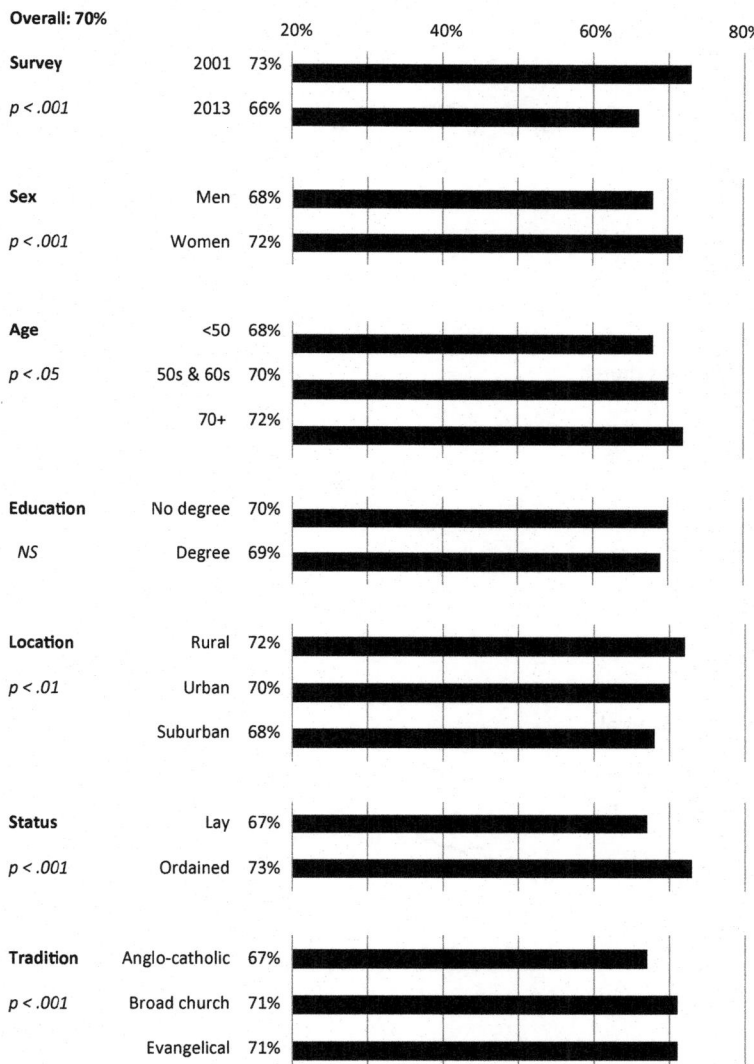

Fig. 7.1 I have confidence in the leadership given by my diocesan bishop: estimated means

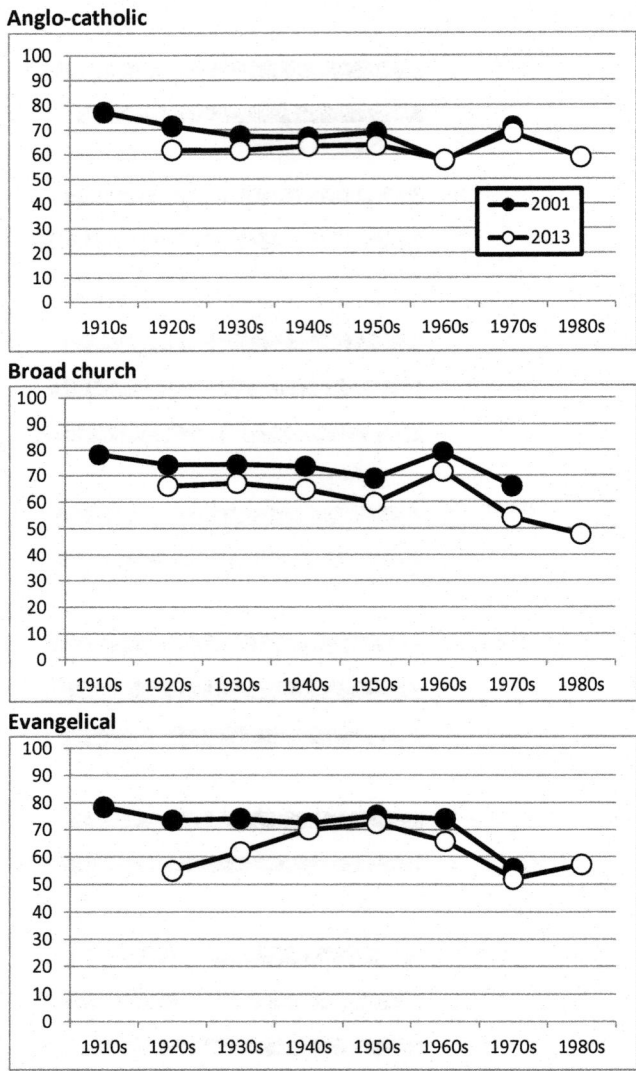

Fig. 7.2 I have confidence in the leadership given by my diocesan bishop: cohort changes

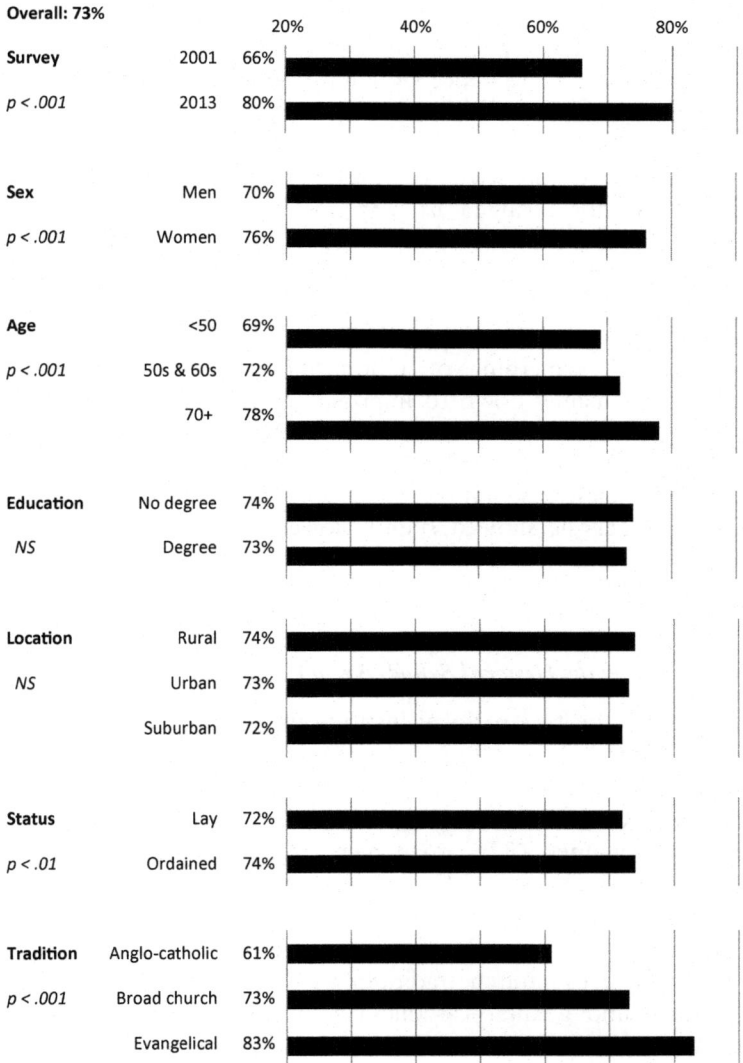

Fig. 7.3 I have confidence in the leadership given by the Archbishop of Canterbury: estimated means

confidence than did men (76% versus 70%), and confidence was higher among those 70 or older (78%) than in the other age groups (72 and 69%). There was no difference by education in this case, or by location. Clergy were more likely than laity to express confidence, but the difference was small (74% versus 72%). Evangelicals were much more confident the leadership of the Archbishop than those in the other two traditions (83% for Evangelicals, 73% for Broad church and 61% for Anglo-catholics). Confidence in the Archbishop's leadership increased considerably between the surveys from 66% in 2001 to 80% in 2013. This may have been due to the characters of the two men involved, though it is also true that Justin Welby was new in the post and was probably still in something of a honeymoon period. The improved confidence was mainly down to improving confidence among all birth cohorts in the Broad church and Anglo-catholic traditions (Fig. 7.4). Evangelicals had generally high confidence, even in 2001, and there was just a slight increase among those born from the 1930s to 1950s. Younger Evangelicals showed slightly lower values compared to their older ones.

I Have Confidence in the Leadership Given by the General Synod/Archbishops' Council

The results for the two national institutions of leadership will be considered together because the pattern of responses between groups was almost identical. Across both surveys, only 34% indicated that they had confidence in General Synod (Fig. 7.5). There was slightly great confidence among women (37%) than men (31%), among those aged 70 or older (38%) compared with younger age groups (33 and 31%) and among those without degrees (36%) compared with graduates (32%). There was no significant difference by location, nor between clergy and laity. Confidence by church tradition was highest among Evangelicals (38%), lowest among Anglo-catholics (29%) and intermediate among the Broad church (35%). There was a marked decline in confidence between 2001 (44%) and 2013 (25%), which the cohort analysis showed was present across all cohorts in all three traditions (Fig. 7.6). In most cases, in 2013 less than 20% of those born after the 1950s agreed that they had confidence in the leadership of the General Synod.

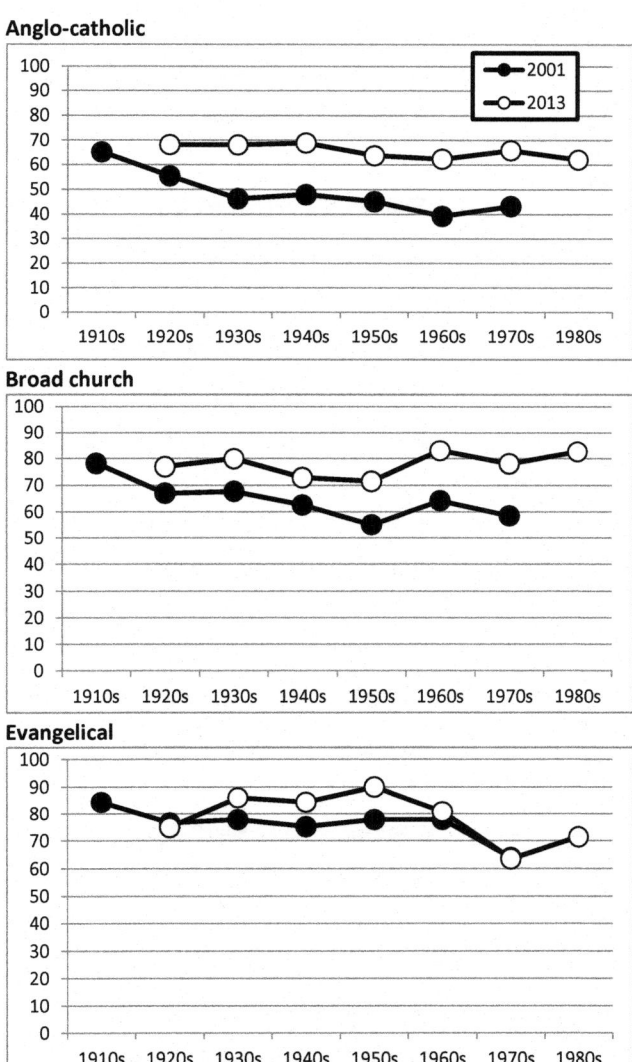

Fig. 7.4 I have confidence in the leadership given by the Archbishop of Canterbury: cohort changes

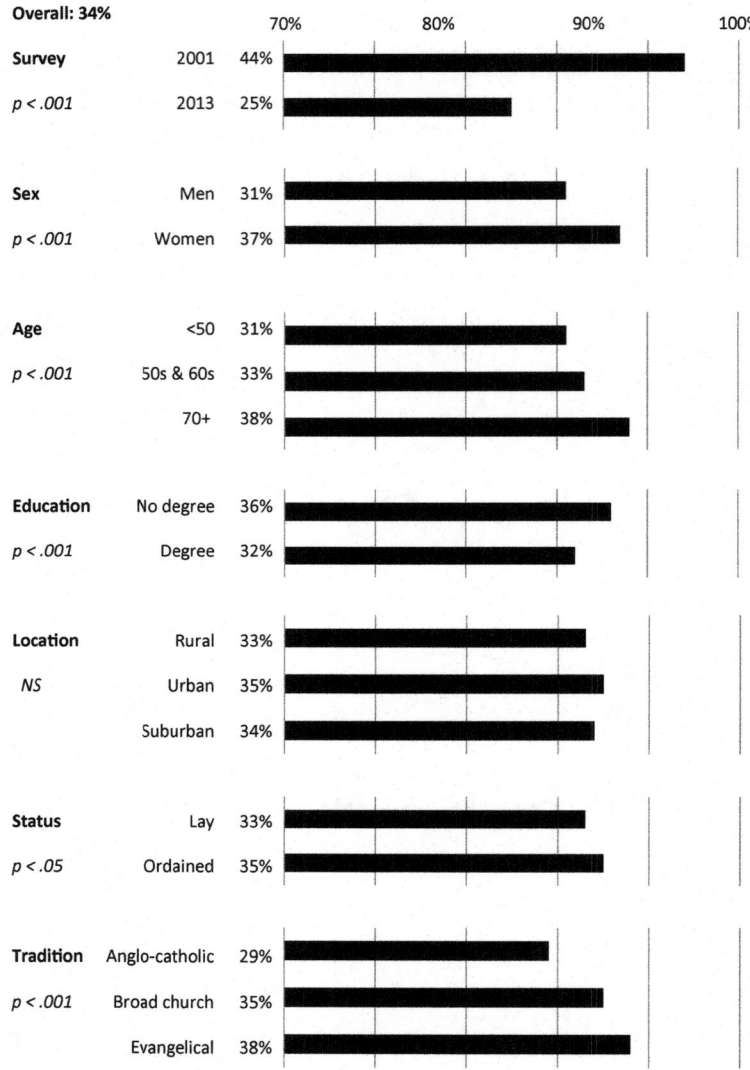

Fig. 7.5 I have confidence in the leadership given by the General Synod: estimated means

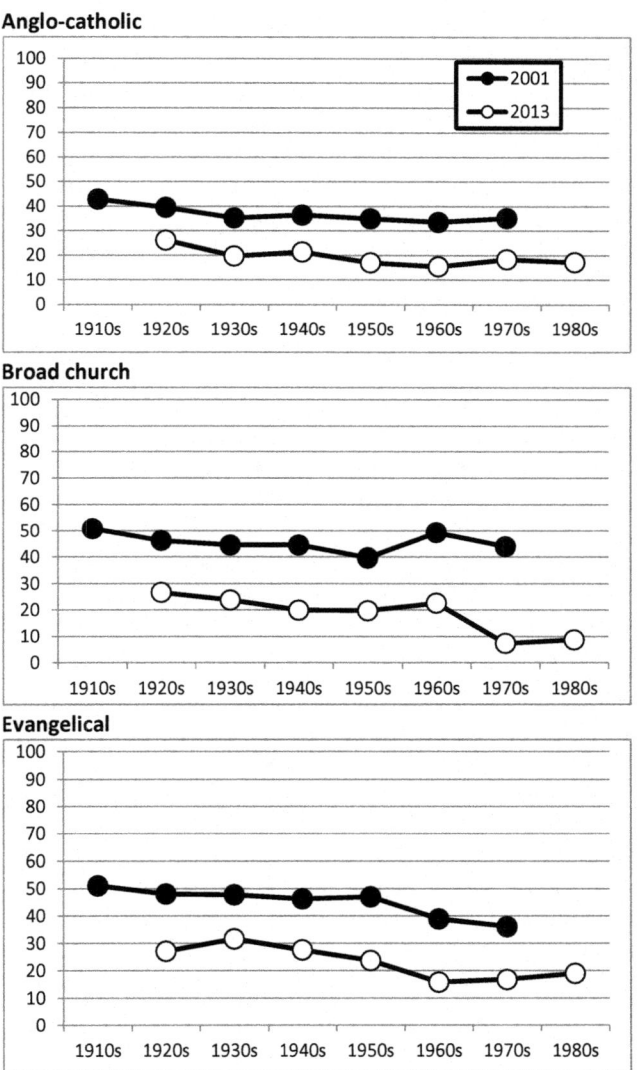

Fig. 7.6 I have confidence in the leadership given by the General Synod: cohort changes

The Archbishops' Council was relatively new in 2001, but well established by 2013. Its overall rating was slightly higher than for General Synod (41% versus 34%), but still low in absolute terms. The same patterns of differences between groups held as for the General Synod, but there was no change between the surveys, and the cohort analysis (not shown) indicated virtually identical values in each survey in most cohorts. The only exception was a marked decline among Evangelicals born after the 1950s, where confidence declined from 40–50% to 10–30% from 2001 to 2013.

Stance on Issues and Confidence in General Synod

The generally low confidence in General Synod is worth examining is a little more detail. In particular, it is worth asking whether or not someone's level of confidence was related to their stance on particular issues that were being debated in Synod around that time. The two issues that perhaps encapsulate the debates of the first decade of the century are the ordination of women as bishops and the ordination of practicing homosexuals as bishops. How did these relate to confidence in the leadership given by General Synod? For this analysis, I have used the original five-point scales for each variable and separated the results by church tradition. The results show the way that stances varied in relation to confidence in Synod, but this depended on tradition and the issue in question. For women bishops (Fig. 7.7), those in the Broad church were strongly supportive, and their stance (shown here as the average score on this item) was not related to their response to the confidence in Synod question. Among both Anglo-catholics and Evangelicals, where opinion on this issue was more divided, those that were most opposed to ordaining women priests tended to be those who had least confidence in Synod. In this case, the Church was moving forward change and confidence in Synod depended partly on how far someone wanted things to remain the same. For practicing homosexuals being allowed to be bishops (Fig. 7.8), Evangelicals were strongly opposed, and their stance was not related to their response to the confidence in Synod question. In the other two traditions, where there was more variation in opinion, those who were most strongly in favour tended to be those who had least confidence in Synod. In this case, the Church was resisting any change and confidence in Synod depended partly on how far someone wanted the prohibitions to be removed. In some ways, these results are hardly surprising, but they give some clue about the reasons why people might lack

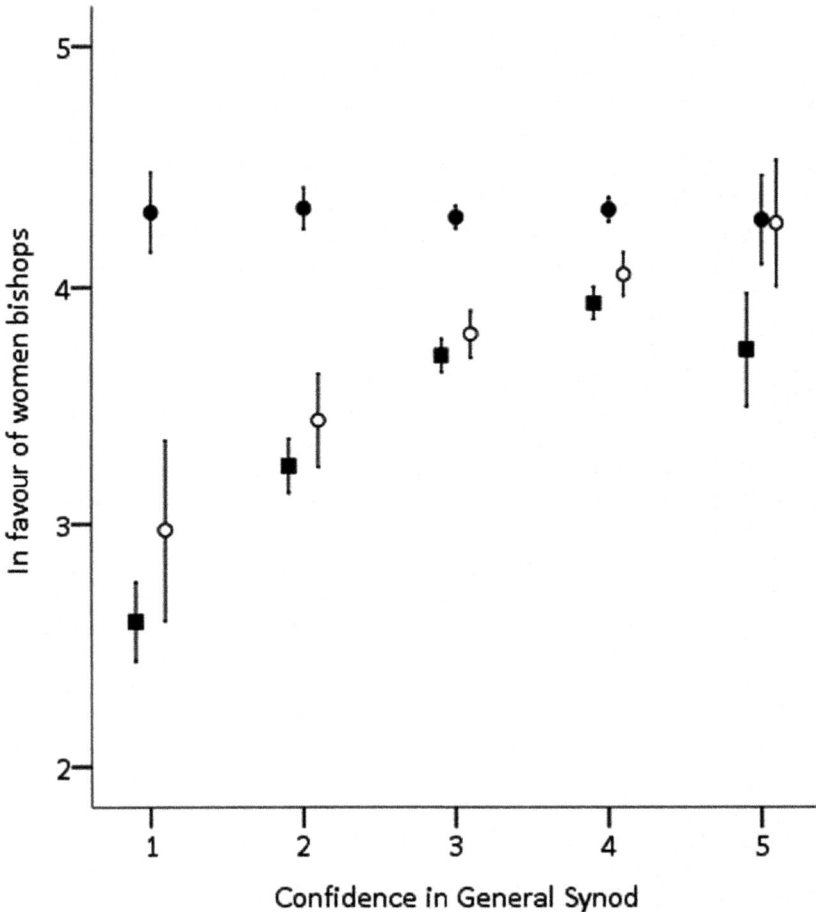

Fig. 7.7 Support for the ordination of women bishops in relation to confidence in General Synod (*Note* Anglo-catholic, solid squares; Broad church, solid circles; Evangelical, open circles. Error bars are 95% confidence limits)

confidence in the Church's main legislative body. It becomes the focus for grievances related to specific issues, and its leadership can be rejected by some whether it resists or promotes change. As those who serve on Synod probably already realize, when it comes to key issues of the day and the need to hold to tradition or to change with the times, you can be damned if you do and damned if you don't.

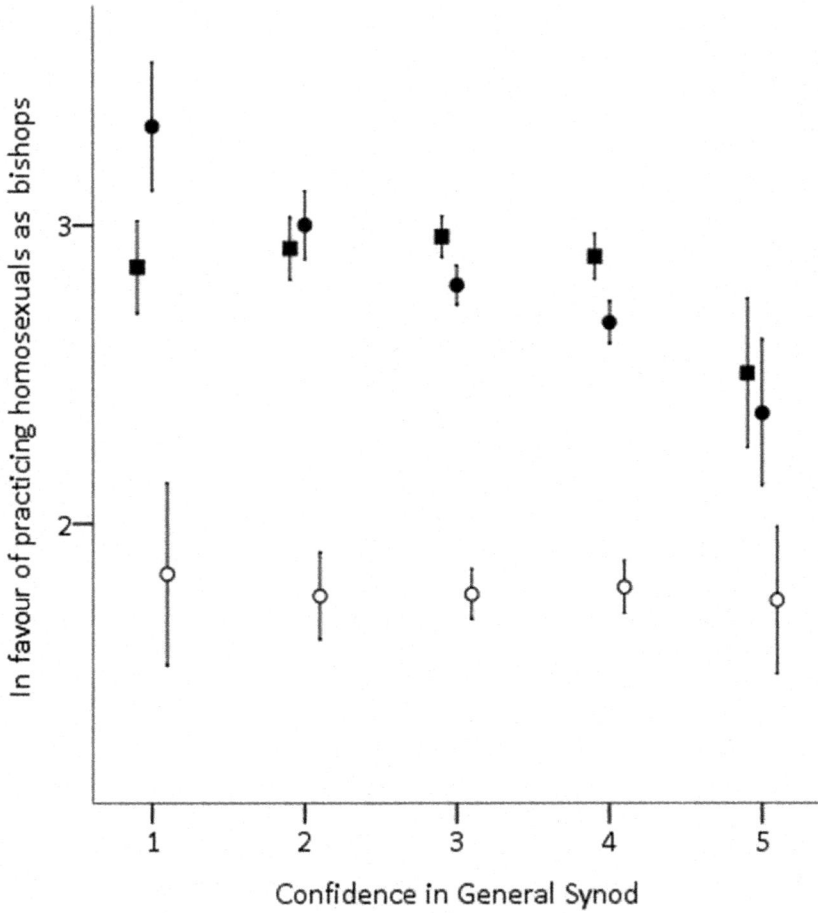

Fig. 7.8 Support for the ordination of practicing homosexual bishops in relation to confidence in General Synod (*Note* Anglo-catholic, solid squares; Broad church, solid circles; Evangelical, open circles. Error bars are 95% confidence limits)

CONCLUSIONS

This analysis of attitudes towards the leadership of the Church of England suggests that there is generally more confidence in local leaders, such as diocesan bishops, than for national synods or councils. Clergy are likely to know their diocesan bishop better than do most laity, and they also tended to have greater confidence in their leadership than did laity. When it came to General Synod and Archbishops' Council, there was no clergy–laity difference, perhaps because both groups were equally distant from these institutions. Much of the literature that has emerged from business or church circles stresses the importance of the human side of leadership, with terms such as 'relational leadership' (Wright, 2000). Some of the models proposed specifically for episcopal ministry imply an oversight that is built on close relationships between those leading and those being led (Grundy, 2011). The Church has known for some time that diocesan bishops, even more than parish clergy, can be caught up in managing an institution rather than pastoring a people and that carving time to create personal relationships with followers is not an optional extra (Archbishop of Canterbury and Archbishop of York, 2001). A recent study of a ministry development programme in the Diocese of Truro showed the benefits of close involvement of the two bishops with clergy and lay people in parishes when managing change, but also the costs in time of getting to know scattered and isolated rural churches (Village & Muskett, 2018).

In the two surveys, local leadership was one of relatively few cases where there was a slight but statistically significant difference between those living in rural or urban areas. Confidence in bishops was highest in rural areas, perhaps because bishops have a higher profile and more influence in such communities than they do in more multi-ethnic urban areas, where bishops are but one voice among many. Among lay people, confidence in local clergy was slightly lower in rural areas than elsewhere, perhaps reflecting the fact that many rural parishes have been combined into larger benefices, and share stipendiary priests who work alongside self-supporting clergy and lay ministers. Another factor may be the small size of rural congregations as this was generally associated with lower confidence. Small congregations that perhaps see their incumbent only a few times a month can feel burdened by responsibilities that they might feel properly lie with the local clergy.

The Archbishop of Canterbury is a key figure in both the Church of England and more widely in the Anglican Communion. A typical pattern in recent decades is for them to receive as great deal of media attention beyond church circles when they are first appointed, which declines somewhat as their tenure in office lengthens. This is partly fuelled by the eagerness with which the press pounces on anything slightly controversial, so that incumbents of the post soon learn to temper their comments to avoid unhelpful attention. It is also partly because most Archbishops of Canterbury want to visit the provinces of the Anglican Communion, a time-consuming activity that tends to lower their profile at home. Furthermore, leaders are often most popular when they first begin their terms in office, and this might partly explain the higher confidence in Justin Welby in 2013 than in George Carey in 2001. The fact that both were Evangelicals may explain the higher support among this constituency that among Anglo-catholics: it would have been interesting to see the results of the survey if Rowan Williams had been in office in 2013, but surveyors cannot always manage the timing of episcopal resignations.

The generally high levels of confidence in the senior leader of the Church are in contrast to the generally low levels of confidence or trust expressed in national political leaders in most surveys. Ipsos MORI have run a UK poll on public trust in professions since 1983 (Ipsos MORI, 2017).[1] Politicians and government ministers have consistently polled below 20%, the lowest of a long list of professions, whereas clergy average about 65%, on par with television newsreaders and 'the ordinary man/woman in the street'. The figures for clergy have shown a long-term decline since the 1980s, when they were around 85%, putting them in the same league as teachers and nurses. The reasons for this loss in trust may be related to sex-abuse scandals in some churches, and perhaps because more and more people have less connection with their local priest. The lack of trust in politicians is often focused on key figures; in the USA, a great deal of attention has been given to presidential leadership, which many have recognized is one that may have great influence, but which usually lacks the power to make significant changes (Genovese, 2017). Political scientists have returned to the study of leadership with renewed vigour over the last decade or so, trying to understand the factors that make leaders effective or ineffective. The notion of 'leadership capital' seems to offer a way of integrating the influence of personal, institutional and contextual factors in shaping leadership (Bennister, 't Hart, & Worthy, 2017). Such capital is a composite of matters such as vision, communicative performance, longevity in office and levels of public trust.

The *Church Times* surveys suggest that within Church of England circles the Archbishop of Canterbury may hold a high level of this sort of capital, though they were not surveys that could examine this in detail.

---

[1] Participants are given a list of professions and asked in each case 'do you generally trust them to tell the truth or not?'

The ability of archbishops to shape the future direction of the Church may depend on their ability to create and maintain leadership capital among the constituencies they are seeking to influence. The wisdom of archbishops leading through the strength of their charisma and personal relationships was questioned when Justin Welby (a former business executive) took over from Rowan Williams, a man from a more scholarly background. Martyn Percy (2015), addressing the change in archiepiscopal leadership style, warned that when it comes to shaping ecclesial polity the charismatic manager and hero figure may be no substitute for the spiritual theologian deeply embedded in the institution. What is needed, he argued, is less emphasis on creating personal relationships and more emphasis on linking at the institutional level. In response, Richard Harries (2016) stressed that while it is clearly important that leaders understand the intricacies of the institutions they lead, breaking deadlocks and reconciling parties often relies on the type of personal gifts that Welby demonstrated in helping to reach the goal of allowing women to be consecrated as bishops.

Judged by the survey results on the General Synod, the Church would do well to try and maintain the personal face of leadership as a counterbalance to the under-whelming confidence in the institutional instruments of governance. Almost by definition, leadership in the Christian faith is based strongly on the messianic and prophetic model, and perhaps the similarity of synodical and parliamentary functioning means the former suffers by association with the latter. Although corporate decision-making is nothing new in the Church, the tension between governing an institution and leading a people of faith is present at all levels. Parochial Church Councils can be discussing church drains one minute and spiritual renewal the next. Synods in deaneries and dioceses can similarly be caught between the profound and the mundane. Chapman (2013) makes the same point about synods, which have always tended towards being politicized and therefore must inherently deal with divisions within the Church. His suggestion for a 'theology of General Synod' eschews the obvious choice of Trinitarian theology on the grounds that such relationship modelling is simply out of touch with the reality of what a synod is. Augustine's understanding of the church seems better fitted for the role, Chapman argues, because it allows synods to be fallible human institutions that carry sufficient authority to at least allow people to live decently with divisions. The data from the *Church Times* surveys presented in earlier chapters have shown that the divisions remain and in some instances may be growing. The one group that seems to stand out are younger Evangelicals, who seem to have views that are at odds with much of the rest of the Church. In this chapter, we have seen that they have less confidence in the General Synod and Archbishops' Council than any other segment of the Church, but this disparity disappears when it comes to confidence in the leadership of diocesan bishops and the Archbishop of Canterbury. The latter might be a temporary matter, linked to the background of the particular archbishops in question, but it nonetheless suggests that those who hold that office can find themselves in a good position to be the sign and creator of unity, as Rowan Williams suggested they should be. If General Synod is to be the means of containing division in the Church, then it may need particular encouragement and support from those in key offices who do enjoy the confidence of the Church generally.

The analysis of confidence in General Synod in relation to specific issues shows that it is not necessarily the institution per se that is at fault, but perhaps simply the fact that people have less confidence in leadership that does not lead them where they want to go. The two issues used as examples were ones where one tradition or another had strong views for or against the change. Someone who believes something must be so (e.g. practicing homosexuals must never be made bishops) will see this as something that lies beyond the jurisdiction of a body such as the Synod. It is among those groups where some conceive that change could or could not happen that the competence of Synod becomes an issue, whether this is about coming to the right decision or how the final decision is reached. The Council of Jerusalem recorded in Acts 15 has been used as something of a paradigm of how churches might come to decide on crucial matters (Fowl, 1998; Harries, 2016; Johnson, 1996). The issue at stake, whether Gentiles could be followers of Jesus without first becoming Jews, implied a radical departure of theology and practice and would have profound consequences for the future of the fledgling faith. A number of writers have noted Peter's crucial intervention, which shows both the importance of personal witness, and the power of individuals to persuade and (patently in this case) to guide people in the right direction. It was Peter's personal encounter with Gentiles that enabled him to speak with authority on the matter and that encounter occurred because his reputation went before him. Councils and synods cannot have such personal experiences, and they rely on the witness and testimony of those who do. Individuals cannot make changes without taking followers with them, and synods and councils ensure followers have choice and control. The synergy between individual leaders such as archbishops and governing institutions such as synods is probably the best way of achieving divine purposes. The *Church Times* surveys suggest the Church of England has some work to do to help its members to appreciate and respect some of its institutions of governance.

References

Archbishop of Canterbury and Archbishop of York. (2001). *Resourcing bishops: The first report of the Archbishops' Review Group on bishops' needs and resources.* London: Church House Publishing.

Atherstone, A. (2013). *Archbishop Justin Welby: The road to Canterbury.* London: Darton, Longman and Todd.

Atherstone, A. (2014). *Archbishop Justin Welby: Risk-taker and reconciler.* London: Darton Longman & Todd.

Bennister, M., 't Hart, P., & Worthy, B. (2017). Understanding political leadership: The leadership capital approach. In M. Bennister, P. 't Hart, & B. Worthy (Eds.), *The leadership capital index* (pp. 1–26). Oxford: Oxford University Press. https://doi.org/10.1093/oso/9780198783848.003.0001.

Briden, T. (2013). *Moore's introduction to English Canon Law* (4th ed.). London: Bloomsbury.

Buchanan, C. (2015). Church Assembly. In C. Buchanan (Ed.), *Historical dictionary of Anglicanism* (p. 151). Lanham, MD: Rowan & Littlefield.

Chapman, M. D. (2013). Does the Church of England have a theology of general synod? *Journal of Anglican Studies, 11*(1), 15–31. https://doi.org/10.1017/s1740355312000368.

Church of England. (2018). *Archbishops' Council.* Retrieved July 3, 2018, from https://www.churchofengland.org/about/leadership-and-governance/archbishops-council#na.

Davies, L. (2012, November 21). Church in crisis as it turns its back on women bishops. *The Guardian,* p. 1.

Editorial. (2007, March 2). Synod airs hope and fear on clergy terms. *Church Times,* p. 28.

Fowl, S. E. (1998). *Engaging scripture.* Oxford: Blackwell.

Genovese, M. (2017). *The presidential dilemma: Revisiting democratic leadership in the American system* (3rd ed.). New York: Routledge.

Goddard, A. (2013). *Rowan Williams: His legacy.* Oxford: Lion.

Grundy, M. (2011). *Leadership and oversight: New models of episcopal leadership.* London and New York: Mowbray.

Harries, R. (2016). Justin Welby's leadership. *Journal of Anglican Studies, 14*(2), 131–133. https://doi.org/10.1017/s174035531600019x.

Ipsos MORI. (2017). Trust in professions: Long-term trends. Retrieved July 5, 2018, from https://www.ipsos.com/ipsos-mori/en-uk/trust-professions-long-term-trends.

Johnson, L. T. (1996). *Scripture and discernment*. Nashville, TN: Abingdon Press.

Moore, C. (2013, July 12). Archbishop Justin Welby: 'I was embarrassed—It was like getting measles'. *The Telegraph*. Retrieved from https://www.telegraph.co.uk/news/religion/10176190/Archbishop-Justin-Welby-I-was-embarrassed.-It-was-like-getting-measles.html.

Percy, M. (2015). Emergent archiepiscopal leadership within the Anglican Communion. *Journal of Anglican Studies, 14*(1), 46–70. https://doi.org/10.1017/s1740355315000029.

Podmore, C. (2009). *The governance of the Church of England and the Anglican Communion*. London: General Synod.

Sherwood, H. (2017, February 15). Church of England in turmoil as synod rejects report on same-sex relationships. *The Guardian*. Retrieved from https://www.theguardian.com/world/2017/feb/15/church-of-england-in-turmoil-as-synod-rejects-report-on-same-sex-relationships.

Shortt, R. (2014). *Rowan's rule: The biography of the Archbishop*. London: Hodder & Stoughton.

Village, A., & Muskett, J. A. (2018). Knowing their people and being known by them: A changing episcopal role within Accompanied Ministry Development in the Diocese of Truro. *Ecclesial Practices* (in press).

Williams, R. (n.d.). *Roles and priorities*. Retrieved July 4, 2018, from http://aoc2013.brix.fatbeehive.com/pages/roles-and-priorities.html.

Wright, W. C. (2000). *Relational leadership*. Milton Keynes: Paternoster.

CHAPTER 8

Discipleship

INTRODUCTION

From its earliest days, the Christian church has understood that belief and faith are not 'all or nothing' categories. Jesus was sometimes frustrated by the lack of faith of those around him (Mark 9:19) and saw that even a little faith can go a long way (Matthew 17:20). He also experienced the frustration of the teacher who has taught so much yet does not seem to be getting the message across (John 14:9), and he clearly knew that his disciples would need to keep learning after he had gone (John 16:12–13). St. Paul felt a similar frustration in having to give his charges 'milk, not solid food' (1 Cor. 3:2), a sentiment echoed elsewhere in the epistles (Hebrews 5:12). Although conversions and baptisms could be sudden, as in the Ethiopian with Philip (Acts 8:26–40) or the jailer with Paul and Silas (Acts 16:25–34), many would have been a gradual change during a period of preparation leading to baptism. The tradition of preparing people for baptism in the weeks before Easter seems to have been a practice that developed early on in the life of the church (Kavanagh, 1991). Initiation into the faith was a process of learning about faith and learning to live it. For baptized believers, there has always been the expectation that following the way of Jesus, Christian discipleship, is a continuing journey of learning and growing in faith.

The purpose of this development and growth is expressed in the New Testament in different ways. Paul in writing to the Ephesians (4:13)

© The Author(s) 2018
A. Village, *The Church of England
in the First Decade of the 21st Century*,
https://doi.org/10.1007/978-3-030-04528-9_8

looks forward to a time when '...all of us come to the unity of faith and the knowledge of the Son of God, to maturity, to the measure of the full stature of Christ'. One benefit of this is that mature Christians are not '...children, tossed to and fro and blown about by every wind of doctrine, by people's trickery, by their craftiness in deceitful scheming'. Clearly, learning and growth are about intellectual integrity, resilience and spiritual formation that equips individuals in their own understanding and faith journey, with the ultimate prize being personal salvation (Phil. 3:10–11). Yet alongside this personal end is the ever-present command to share faith with others, be that through proclamation (Matt. 28:19) or the witness of holy lives (Matt. 5:16). Paul's eloquent personal testimony in 2 Corinthians 4–5 speaks of ambassadors carrying the sacred Gospel message in earthen vessels, striving and suffering in order to bring that message to others. Sharing faith can mean many different things, but in some sense it must be one of the purposes and ends of the Church.

This chapter looks at three individual items from the *Church Times* surveys that relate broadly to Christian discipleship: learning about faith, growing in faith, and sharing faith. These are each big and complicated areas of church life, and the survey was never going to be able to examine them in any detail. It was not intended, for example, to assess the level of individual knowledge about faith, nor the extent to which participants shared faith with others. I suspect *Church Times* readers might have distained a biblical literacy test or a question asking about how many times they had spoken to others about Jesus in the last week. Instead, the items were designed to probe their self-perceptions in these areas. For learning, the items asked if they would 'welcome more opportunities to learn about Christianity'. If many people agree with this statement, it might indicate a deficit in learning opportunities and/or an unfulfilled desire to learn more. Measuring someone's growth in faith is always likely to be a subjective exercise because there are so many different ways that this might be understood. The item used here was a simple statement 'I am growing in my Christian faith', which measures a subjective perception based on individual interpretations of what growth in faith might be. Despite the obvious ambiguities that attend such a statement it does, nonetheless, directly address a question that many church-goers might ask of themselves from time to time. The item related to sharing faith takes one aspect which is that of explaining faith to others. This narrows the scope because it rules out faith sharing that might be implicit through acts of service or kindness. Instead, the word 'explaining' links to the idea of knowing about faith and being able to articulate it. Rather than ask people how often they do this, or if they are good at it, the item was phrased as 'I feel confident at explaining my faith to other people'. The reason for this was to link sharing more closely to learning and growth: being confident in explaining implies someone who has a certain level of knowledge and clarity of understanding. If few people agree with this statement, it might suggest that even if they are growing in faith and feel they know enough about faith, they are unlikely to want to explain it to others outside the church.

These items together relate to the area of discipleship: the practice of following Jesus by living your life in a particular way. How that is done varies enormously and depends on the characteristics of individual believers, how they understand the Christian faith and the sorts of traditions to which they belong. Before exploring the data related to the items in the *Church Times* surveys it is worth exploring how the Church of England has understood and engaged with the area of discipleship in recent years.

Learning and Growing in Faith

Jeff Astley (2002) makes the helpful distinction between Christian education that is education *about* Christianity, education *into* Christianity, and education that is done in a Christian manner. These may be linked but they are distinctly different sorts of processes. The first implies the possibility of a rather detached information gathering exercise that may promote understanding without necessarily making much difference to someone's life. Learning about Christianity could be little different from learning about any religion, or learning about English literature or quantum mechanics. This is the sort of learning we associate with schools and universities: it can be exciting and life-changing, but not in quite the same way as being educated *into* Christianity. This sort of learning is often linked to the notion of 'formation', a process of acquiring the habits and characteristics that are the hallmarks of those who follow the Christian way. If learning about Christianity is a matter of the intellect (the head), then formation into Christianity is a matter of the heart and soul. Jeff Astley also points out that the term 'formation' is often ill-defined and sometimes used as a catch-all phrase (Astley, 2015b). It is, nonetheless, a word that has been widely used in Church of England circles over the last few decades. It may involve personal reflection, developing patterns of prayer, and the conscious or unconscious application of particular beliefs and values in everyday life.

The tension between these two different sorts of learning is clearly seen in the Church of England debates about how to train people for ordained ministry. The Church of England has for some time acknowledged the need for ministers to have credibility in a society of increasingly educated lay people (Wilton, 2007a). The New Labour government's aspiration of having half of school leavers attend university has not quite been achieved, but by 2016 just under a third of school leavers went to university (Universities UK, 2017) and in September 2017, 42% of adults aged between 21 and 64 were graduates (ONS, 2017). A succession of Church reports about ministerial training have wrestled with the issue of what that training should look like in terms of the balance between critical academic education and spiritual formation (Archbishops' Council, 2003; Groom, 2017). Linking church-based training with universities gives ministerial qualifications the assurance of external academic validity and exposes candidates to at least some of the critical insights into Christianity that are needed in order to understand those in society who are increasingly sceptical of the Christian religion. Candidates, it is argued, should be expected to critically engage with biblical studies, theology, church history and so on. This sort of education might not look all that different from what we would expect of a university course, and validating training for ordained and lay ministries by partnering with universities has been a long-standing practice for Church of England theological colleges and regional training courses (Archbishops' Council, 2003; Higton, 2013; Wilton, 2007b).

Alongside issues of what make for good learning about Christianity, the question of formation as education *into* Christianity has continued to occupy the attention of those who are responsible for training clergy (Bunting, 2009; Williams, 2013; Wilton, 2007a). A number of writers have suggested various characteristics that should typify someone in ordained ministry and suggested ways that these might be developed during and after training. Mike Harrison (2014) suggests nine outcomes of theological education that might not be easily incorporated into the typical learning outcomes of a university theology course: gratitude, joy, attention to beauty, responsiveness, humility, vulnerability in learning, listening, awareness of the presence of God and leisured diligence. Marrying these sorts of objectives with what is learnt through university-type courses is difficult but not impossible. David Heywood (2013) emphasizes the importance of 'tacit' knowledge that enables ministers to 'interpret the world through the lens of Christian faith and respond habitually in a way that expressed Christian character' (p. 17). Key in the process of integrating learning into life, he argues, is reflective practice, an idea that has been widely discussed in the context of adults learning about faith (Le Cornu, 2005; Heywood, 2009; Nichols & Dewerse, 2010). Paul Overend (2007) contrasts the individualistic and competitive model of learning typical of a university with the distinctive approach of developing practitioners that stresses the importance of personhood in community. The debate between the conflicting paradigms involved in 'learning about' and 'formation into' Christianity have continued as the Church developed its Common Awards framework in partnership with the University of Durham (Groom, 2017; Higton, 2013; Williams, 2013).

In the meantime, the Church of England had been somewhat slow to recognize the impact of rising education levels on the faith and discipleship of lay people. Until comparatively recently the focus of 'religious education' has been in schools, while the focus of 'theological education' has been on those preparing for ministry. Education for the 'whole people of God' has been a relatively new catch phrase. Parish churches have traditionally taught children through Sunday school and confirmation classes, but once they graduate from these there may be little expectation, and few opportunities, for adults to learn about their faith or to be educated into faith. The drift away from churches by teenagers and young adults means that even if they do return later in life, they probably have ideas and knowledge more suited to their childhood than their adulthood (Village, 2016). Unless there are opportunities for adults to develop their understanding there is a risk that belief becomes detached from reality and faith does not link to everyday life. Many parishes do offer courses of study (often around Lent) and many will also have some home groups where people meet regularly to study the Bible, pray together, and support one another in their faith, and these can be important places for learning (Walton, 2011). Overall, across the two *Church Times* surveys, 62% of lay people indicated that they had attended at least one church or diocesan course in the previous five years, but for most it was just one course and over a third had not done even that. In the same sample just under a third of participants were part of a home group, though the figure varied from just over half of Evangelicals to about a fifth of Anglo-catholics. The quality of teaching and learning in a home group may be very variable and those that rely solely on members sharing their ideas about a Bible passage may be less likely to draw on external ideas that contradict the group norms.

The importance of adult Christian education and discipleship formation for all Christians has been emphasized from time to time over the last half century, both in the USA (McKenzie & Harton, 2002; Roehlkepartain, 1993) and in the UK (Astley, 2000, 2015a). The Church of England termed this 'Education for Discipleship' in a report that set this sort of education alongside training for particular lay or ordained ministries (Archbishops' Council, 2006). Towards the end of the period between the *Church Times* surveys, the General Synod began to give the issue of developing discipleship some more attention (Jordan, 2015). This arose partly out of the Church's quinquennial goals for 2010–2015, which identified three main tasks for the church, one of which was related to spiritual and numerical growth (House of Bishops and Archbishops' Council, 2011). It was this goal that drew attention to the need to review the way the Church developed and sustained disciples. In 2013, around the time of the second survey, the Church launched the Pilgrim course, aimed at teaching about Christianity and (as the name implies) helping people on their journey of faith (Church of England, 2018b). This programme consists of a mix of education *about* and education *into* that is the hallmark of many such courses. One of the originators of Pilgrim was Stephen Croft, Bishop of Sheffield at the time, who also drew up a discussion document for General Synod in 2015 which highlighted some of the issues related to learning and growing in faith (Church of England, 2015). The document notes that the failure of the Church to form and sustain disciples is partly due to clericalism, which creates a context that tends to give low priority to the life and work of lay people, especially those who are not involved in recognized ministries.

Sharing Faith

The need for the Church to pass on the faith that it has received is becoming ever more critical and ever more difficult. Several surveys in the UK have shown the importance of parents in socializing their children into faith, the difficulties in doing this, and the decline in knowledge about Christianity among younger generations (Bible Society, 2014; Care for the Family, 2017). There is a growing recognition that adult members of the Church of England will have to share their faith beyond their immediate family, and with adults as well as children, if the long-term decline in numbers is to be reversed. Just what it means to 'share faith' is a crucial question because the answer will shape the kind of witness that is given to the increasingly large majority of the country who have little or no contact with Christianity.

So what does the Church of England mean by 'sharing faith'? The Church of England website has threads headed 'Our Faith' and 'Faith in Action' (Church of England, 2018a). The former has a page 'Living out our faith', which includes a short video depicting people answering the question 'How do you express your love of God?' A variety of people give different answers that include personal spirituality (prayer, worship, daily offices), living daily life with family and at work, serving and caring for others, and (in a few cases) speaking about their faith with others. There is a similar mix under the thread 'Faith in Action', and the resources offered under 'Social engagement and evangelism' (Richards, 2017) include themes of trust, sharing, confidence and hope. The emphasis is on building relationships that become the place where faith can be shared and explained. The Fresh Expressions movement has wrestled with what it means to share faith in our current culture (Croft, 2005; Hollinghurst, 2010), and this mixture of living lives that are shaped by faith and being willing to articulate to others the core motivation of that life is summed up in the idea of being a 'witness'.

In a society where faith has been largely privatized, it is becoming increasingly quirky to talk about it openly in public. A key issue may be the how much confidence people have in their faith. Using the 2013 *Church Times* survey data for lay people, I developed a five-item 'Confidence in Faith' scale that included two of the items reported here (Village, 2015).[1] The aim was to see how far confidence might be something that depends on someone's personality ('nature') as opposed to the educational experiences they have had ('nurture'). The results showed that these things independently predicted levels of confidence: certain personality types tended to have higher scores on the confidence scale, as did those who had attended diocesan courses or Higher Education courses in theology. Tradition also had a part to play, with Charismatics and Evangelicals having more confidence that other groups.

---

[1] The five items were: 'I am growing in my Christian faith'; 'I feel confident in explaining my faith to others'; 'My Christian faith influences my important decisions in life'; 'My Christian faith influences my attitude toward other people'; 'Nowadays I feel closer to God than I used to'.

There is no doubt that the Church is beginning to focus attention on discipleship as a key issue for its future strategy. It can no longer sustain a model of operating that gives so much attention to educating ministers and so little to educating lay people. Although this may be changing grass-roots attitudes within the Church, this may take some time to show any effect in terms of changing the culture and stemming the decline in membership. It is worth remembering in the context of this study that much of the growth in interest in this area has happened after the second *Church Times* survey was completed.

Exploring the Data

We might expect major differences between clergy and laity in this area, given their probably very different experiences of learning about faith and how it is manifest in daily life. There were instances where the two groups had different levels of response to the items, but the patterns across groups and cohort analyses were surprisingly similar, so I have retained the full sample for this analysis.

I Would Welcome Opportunities to Learn About the Christian Faith

Across the two surveys, two thirds indicated that they would welcome opportunities to learn more about the Christian faith (Fig. 8.1). This suggests that there is a sizeable constituency across the Church of England that feels a need to learn more and who might be willing to engage in some sort of educational programme or course. Whether they would or not is, of course, another question that may depend on the Church being able to provide the right sort of opportunities. Targeting may be important here, and so it is useful to look at which groups were the most and least open to learning. There was no difference by location and (perhaps surprisingly) very little between laity and clergy, but there was some significant variation in other categories. Women were more likely to endorse this item than were men, though the absolute difference was relatively small (68% versus 64%). The disparity across the age groups was the most marked for this item, with three-quarters of the under 50s endorsing it compared to only around a half of those over 70. This might simply reflect the possibility that younger people have more to learn and older people have nothing to learn, though neither of these possibilities may actually be the case. Seventy would seem to be

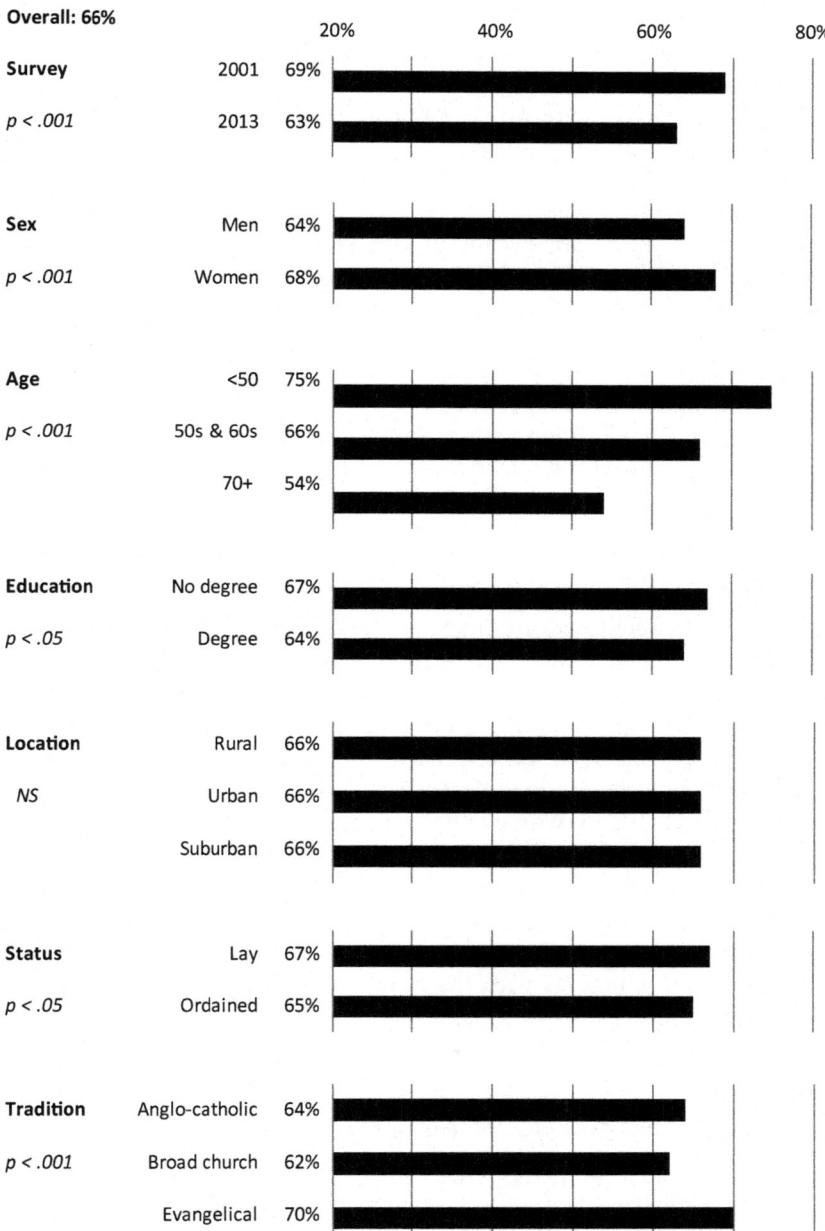

Fig. 8.1 I would welcome opportunities to learn about the Christian faith: estimated means

a rather young age at which to stop learning these days, and perhaps the low score for the oldest age group points to the need to shift attitudes in relation to life-long learning. Those without degrees were slightly more likely to welcome learning opportunities than those with degrees, though the difference was again small (67% versus 64%) and barely statistically significant. Evangelicals were most likely, and the Broad church least likely, to endorse this item.

There was a significant decline in openness to learning opportunities from 2001 (69%) to 2013 (63%). Cohort analysis suggested there was small but consistent decline across all traditions and nearly all cohorts (Fig. 8.2), so the change was not simply the result of an ageing population among churchgoers. Although this was a small change it suggests there is a need to find out if this is because of a general decline in interest to learn about the Christian faith, a sense of not having time to spend on learning, or a result of the quality of learning that is on offer.

I Am Growing in My Christian Faith

Very few people in this sample did *not* feel they were growing in their faith, and the overall endorsement was 84% (Fig. 8.3). Growth in faith is difficult to define, however, and there may also have been a strong pressure to give a positive answer here. Nonetheless, the perception of growing was widespread and that has to be a good thing for the Church. The differences between groups partly mirrored those for the learning item, with little or no differences by education level or location, higher endorsement by women (86%) than men (82%), by Evangelicals (89%) than others (82 and 80%) and lower endorsement by those over 70 (79%) compared with younger age groups (86%). The clergy were generally much more likely than laity to indicate that they were growing in faith (88% versus 78%), though they were less likely to welcome learning opportunities. As with the results for learning, there was also a slight decline between surveys (86–82%), which in this case seemed to be mainly among those born prior to the 1960s (Fig. 8.4).

I Feel Confident at Explaining My Faith to Other People

Confidence in explaining faith to others was surprisingly high across the board, with 91% of the sample endorsing this item (Fig. 8.5). This does not mean that people were actually doing it, and again this may be an item where there was a lot of positive pressure to agree. Trends in

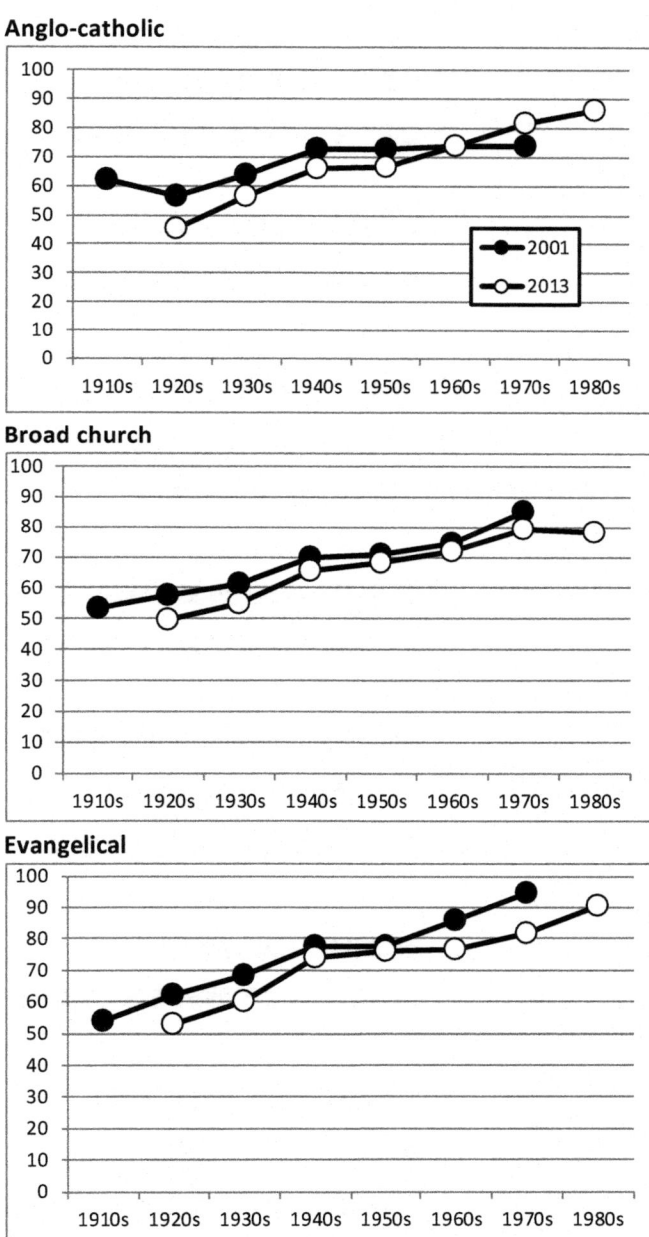

Fig. 8.2 I would welcome opportunities to learn about the Christian faith: cohort changes

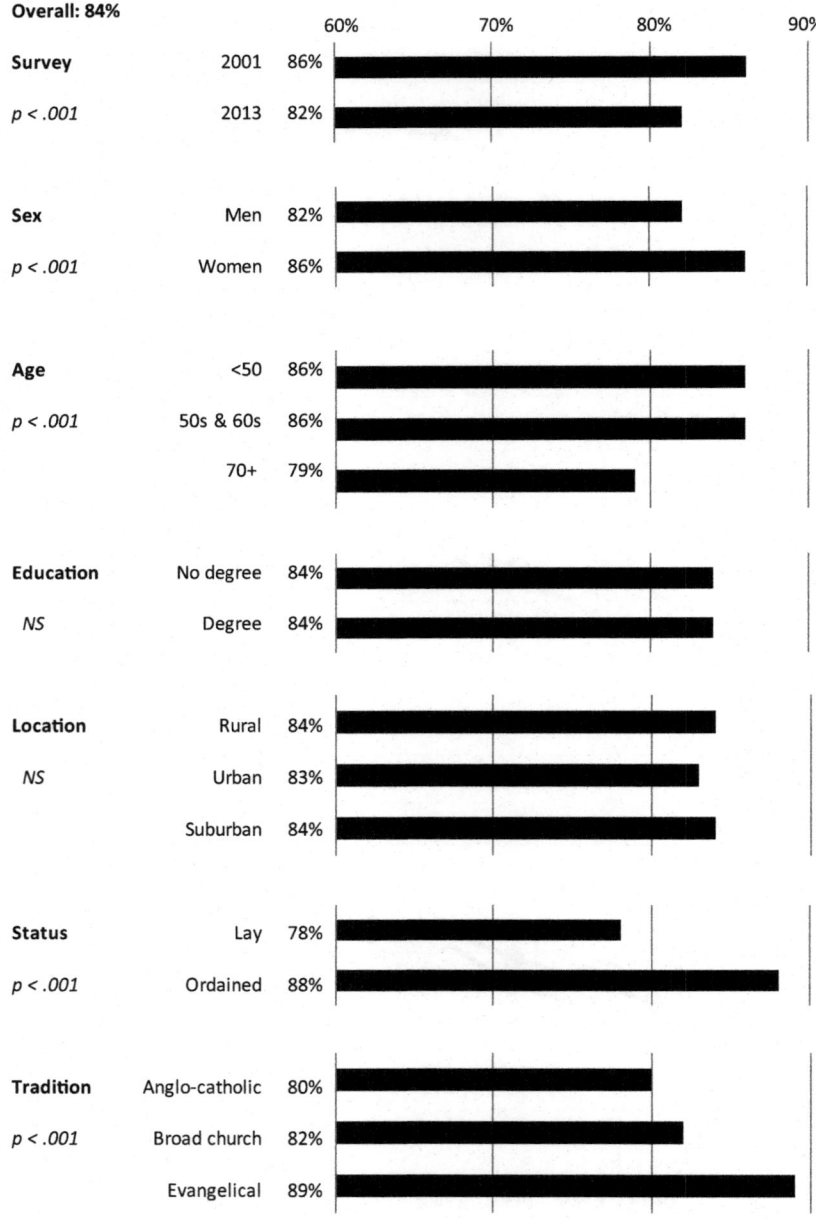

Fig. 8.3 I am growing in my Christian faith: estimated means

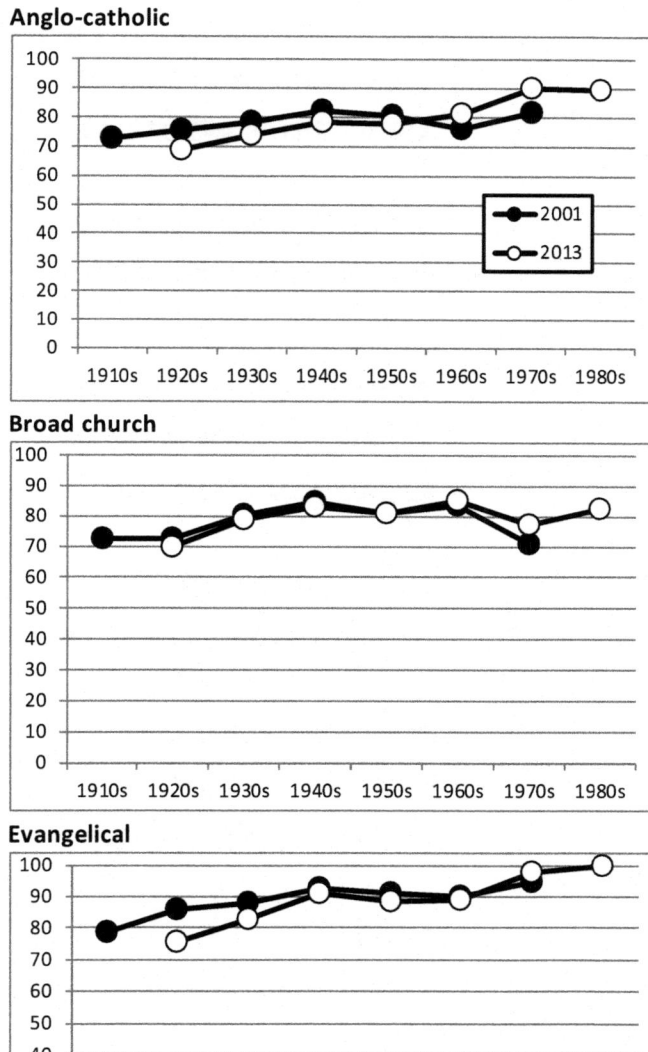

Fig. 8.4 I am growing in my Christian faith: cohort changes

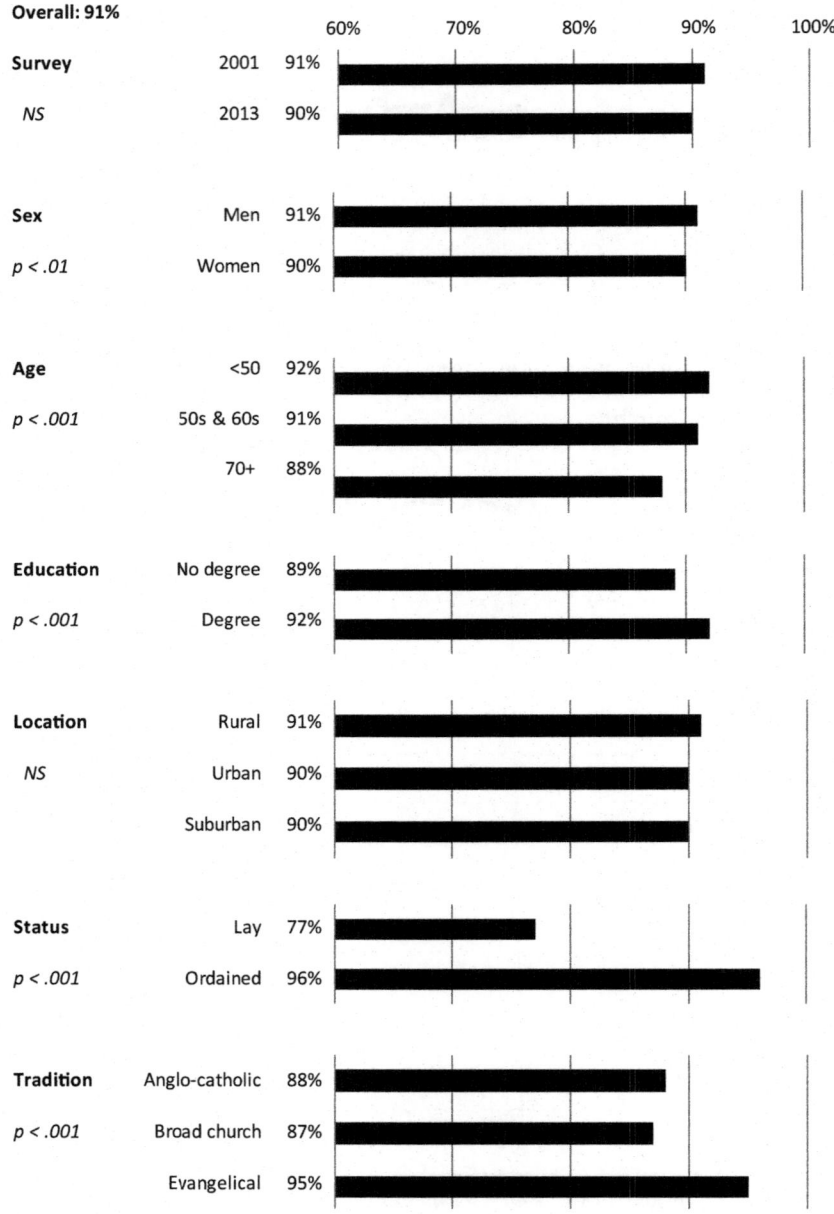

Fig. 8.5 I feel confident at explaining my faith to other people: estimated means

confidence in explaining faith did not necessarily reflect responses to the previous two items. In this case, men were slightly more confident than women, though women more likely to indicate they were growing in faith. Older people were less confident in sharing faith, and this was in line with their lower sense of growing in faith. The greater confidence of graduates (92% versus 89%) perhaps reflects a greater comfort in explaining and articulating things generally, rather than necessarily more knowledge. Once again there was no difference by location, but clergy were (as one would hope and expect) the most confident group in explaining faith (96% versus 77% for laity). Evangelicals (95%) also emerged as more confident than those from other traditions. Unlike the previous two items, there was no overall decline between surveys, and cohort analysis (not shown) suggested little or no change with cohorts over time.

CONCLUSIONS

The readership of the *Church Times* probably represents people who are more mature and confident in their faith than the Church of England at large. Whatever their understanding of faith may be, they seemed overwhelmingly to feel confident that they could share that faith. Admittedly this was to some extent because clergy were included in the analysis and this must surely be a group who are selected and trained precisely to explain their faith to others. Yet over three-quarters of lay people also expressed confidence in sharing their faith. Evangelicalism has traditionally stressed the need for Christians to share faith by being willing to speak about it with others and many in this tradition will have been helped and encouraged to do so. Evangelicals in this survey were slightly more likely than those in other traditions to agree that they felt confident in explaining their faith, but even among non-Evangelicals the overwhelming majority said they were confident they could do so. The Church's task in this area might be as much about helping people to find more opportunities and to share faith more effectively as about 'empowering' people. Just what it is that might be explained by those who participated is an interesting question and one that lies at the heart of the subject of this book. Is there 'a' faith that is common across the Church of England and which can be explained to those outside? Or are their different faiths that reflect the diversity of a national church serving a multitude of different people?

Confidence in explaining faith did not change between the surveys, despite what might have been an increasingly hostile environment for religion generally in England over the course of the decade. Younger people seemed to be more confident than those over 70, and perhaps one advantage of losing a national religion is that Christianity can gain a rightful place alongside any other creed or lifestyle. Offered as one choice among many it needs to explain why it claims to be the best way to live and what the evidence is to support those claims. This is where the mixed approach of caring and serving alongside proclaiming and explaining may be the best option for most churchgoers. To date the efforts of Fresh Expressions and other initiatives have not stemmed the numerical decline in churchgoing, so finding more effective ways of mobilizing the confidence expressed by the rank and file may be a key starting point.

As with explaining faith to others, there was also a high proportion of people who felt they were growing in their faith, with similar patterns of variations between groups. Sense of growth was related to confidence in sharing, and also to welcoming learning opportunities, and this was true for clergy and laity. Those who were most likely to welcome more opportunities to learn about faith were also those who were more likely to say they were growing in faith and confident in explaining it. This might be because some people are just more positive generally or feel pressure to be positive when they complete questionnaires; the inadequacies of the instruments have to be recognized. It might also be that there is a virtuous cycle here, with those who have attended some courses being those who are also open to more learning opportunities, who feel they are growing in faith, and who are more confident in sharing it. There was some evidence that this maybe the case: among laity in the 2013 survey, there was a positive correlation between agreeing with the three items reported here and the number of different types of lay training courses attended.[2] It may be that what is most crucial is to induct those who are willing to learn more about their faith into the virtuous circle by supporting them into their first experience of adult education in a church context. For some this may be the start of a process that will build confidence and lead to a desire for more learning.

The nature of 'education for discipleship' courses has been debated, especially how they might combine education about Christianity with

---

[2]For a sample of 2272 lay people, correlations with the number of different types of lay courses attended were as follows. 'I would welcome opportunities to learn about the Christian faith': $r = .16$, $p < .001$; 'I am growing in my Christian faith': $r = .23$, $p < .001$; 'I feel confident at explaining my faith to other people': $r = .19$, $p < .001$.

education into Christianity (John, Nixon, & Shepherd, 2018). Some programmes have been validated by universities, and participants are offered the chance to gain degree or sub-degree level awards (Francis, 2015; Neil, 2015). This can be helpful for different reasons. First, it may be for some an unexpected chance to find out that they are better at critical learning than they imagined, especially older people who were denied educational opportunities when they were young. New ways of understanding can be opened up, and this might lead to a thirst for learning in areas beyond just Christianity. Second, a more academically rigorous course could be helpful to what is rapidly becoming an increasing majority of churchgoers who already have experience of Higher Education. People training in critical thinking may need to be able to assimilate their faith into other areas of life and validated course may make this more likely. They are not a substitute for education into faith, but when delivered in church contexts there is the possibility of showing how critical knowledge of faith can lead to growth in discipleship.

References

Archbishops' Council. (2003). *Formation for ministry within a learning church.* London: Church of England.

Archbishops' Council. (2006). *Shaping the future: New patterns of training for lay and ordained.* London: Church House Publishing.

Astley, J. (Ed.). (2000). *Learning in the way.* Leominster: Gracewing Publishing.

Astley, J. (2002). Church schools and the theology of Christian education. *Journal of the Association of Anglican Secondary School Heads, 10,* 6–15.

Astley, J. (2015a). Discipleship learning. *Rural Theology, 13*(1), 1–3. https://doi.org/10.1179/1470499415Z.00000000035.

Astley, J. (2015b). Forming disciples: Some educational and biblical reflections. *Rural Theology, 13*(1), 4–17. https://doi.org/10.1179/1470499415Z.00000000037.

Bible Society. (2014). *Pass it on.* Retrieved October 28, 2015, from http://www.biblesociety.org.uk/press/uploads/final-copy-of-Pass-it-On-research-report_02070706.pdf.

Bunting, I. (2009). Formation and validity. *Journal of Adult Theological Education, 6*(1), 8–30. https://doi.org/10.1558/jate.v6i1.8.

Care for the Family. (2017). *Faith in our families.* Cardiff: Care for the Family.

Church of England. (2015). *Developing discipleship.* London: Church of England.

Church of England. (2018a, July 26). *The Church of England.* Retrieved from https://www.churchofengland.org/.

Church of England (Producer). (2018b, July 27). *Pilgrim: A course for the Christian journey.* Retrieved from http://www.pilgrimcourse.org/the-course.

Croft, S. (2005). *Evangelism in a spiritual age: Communicating faith in a changing culture.* London: Church House.

Francis, L. J. (2015). Taking discipleship learning seriously: Setting priorities for the rural church. *Rural Theology, 13*(1), 18–30. https://doi.org/10.1179/1470499415Z.00000000038.

Groom, S. (2017). The language of formation in official Church of England documents. *Anglican Theological Review, 99*(2), 233–255.

Harrison, M. (2014). What do the theologically educated look like? *Dialog, 53*(4), 345–355. https://doi.org/10.1111/dial.12138.

Heywood, D. (2009). Learning how to learn: Theological reflection at Cuddesdon. *Journal of Adult Theological Education, 6*(2), 164–175. https://doi.org/10.1558/jate.v6i2.164.

Heywood, D. (2013). Educating ministers of character. *Journal of Adult Theological Education, 10*(1), 4–24. https://doi.org/10.1179/1740714113Z.0000000001.

Higton, M. (2013). Theological education between the university and the church. *Journal of Adult Theological Education, 10*(1), 25–37. https://doi.org/10.1179/1740714113Z.0000000002.

Hollinghurst, S. (2010). *Mission-shaped evangelism.* Norwich: Canterbury Press.

House of Bishops and Archbishops' Council. (2011). *Challenges for the new quinquennium (GS1815).* London: Church of England.

John, E., Nixon, N., & Shepherd, N. (2018). Life-changing learning for Christian discipleship and ministry: A practical exploration. *Practical Theology,* 1–15. https://doi.org/10.1080/1756073x.2018.1458178.

Jordan, E. (2015). All God's people facing the same way: A theology of discipleship shaped by disciples—An Anglican perspective. *Journal of Adult Theological Education, 12*(2), 153–158. https://doi.org/10.1179/1740714115Z.00000000043.

Kavanagh, A. (1991). *The shape of baptism: The rite of Christian initiation.* Collegeville, MN: Liturgical Press.

Le Cornu, A. (2005). People's ways of believing: Learning processes and faith outcomes. *Religious Education, 100*(4), 425–446. https://doi.org/10.1080/00344080500308637.

McKenzie, L., & Harton, R. M. (2002). *The religious education of adults.* Macon, GA: Smyth & Helwys Publishing.

Neil, P. (2015). Exploring a formal model of discipleship in higher education: Case studies. *Rural Theology, 13*(1), 42–53. https://doi.org/10.1179/1470499415Z.00000000040.

Nichols, M., & Dewerse, R. (2010). Evaluating transformative learning in theological education: A multi-faceted approach. *Journal of Adult Theological Education, 7*(1), 44. https://doi.org/10.1558/jate.v7i1.44.

ONS. (2017). *Graduates in the UK labour market: 2017.* London: Office for National Statistics.

Overend, P. (2007). Education or formation? The issue of personhood in learning for ministry. *Journal of Adult Theological Education,* 4(2), 133–148. https://doi.org/10.1558/jate2007v4i2.133.

Richards, A. (2017). *Social engagement and evangelism resources.* Retrieved August 8, 2018, from https://www.churchofengland.org.

Roehlkepartain, E. (1993). *The teaching church: Moving Christian education to center stage.* Nashville, TN: Abingdon Press.

Universities UK. (2017). *Patterns and trends in UK higher education 2017.* London: Universities UK.

Village, A. (2015). Nature or nurture? What makes people feel confident in faith? *Rural Theology,* 13(1), 82–93. https://doi.org/10.1179/1470499415Z.00000000043.

Village, A. (2016). *Encountering the Bible.* London: SCM Press.

Walton, R. (2011). Disciples together: The small group as a vehicle for discipleship formation. *Journal of Adult Theological Education,* 8(2), 99–114. https://doi.org/10.1558/JATE.v8i2.99.

Williams, J. (2013). Conflicting paradigms in theological education for public ministry in the Church of England: Issues for church and academy. *International Journal of Public Theology,* 7(3), 275–296. https://doi.org/10.1163/15697320-12341295.

Wilton, G. (2007a). From ACCM22 to Hind via Athens and Berlin: A critical analysis of key documents shaping contemporary Church of England theological education with reference to the work of David Kelsey. *Journal of Adult Theological Education,* 4(1), 31–47. https://doi.org/10.1558/jate.v4i1.31.

Wilton, G. (2007b). The Hind Report: Theological education and cross sector partnerships. *Discourse,* 7(1), 153–178. https://doi.org/10.5840/discourse20077114.

CHAPTER 9

Belonging and Serving

INTRODUCTION

We can demonstrate belonging to a church in a variety of ways. Saying you belong (affiliating) and turning up for worship (attending) are obvious indicators, and they have been widely used to explore patterns of religion in society at large. They are not relevant here because the *Church Times* sample was entirely made up of frequently attending affiliates of the Church of England. An alternative approach is to measure congregants' sense of belonging, how important the congregation is for their social life, and how caring they think it is. We might also be able to judge the extent of a person's belonging by how many church groups they belong to. Lay people who are most closely involved in congregational life are likely to lead some aspect of ministry and be part of the decision-making process. Clergy in active ministry will have a different sense of what it means to belong to or lead a church, but they too will have perceptions of their congregation(s) in terms of belonging, social life and caring.

Christianity is not simply about belonging to a church; indeed, some might argue that it is not really about belonging to a church at all. Christians are called to love and serve others, not just other Christians but also those who never, or hardly ever, come to church. For some Christian traditions, meeting and serving unbelievers is a way of showing the love of Christ as a step towards bringing such people to faith

© The Author(s) 2018
A. Village, *The Church of England
in the First Decade of the 21st Century*,
https://doi.org/10.1007/978-3-030-04528-9_9

and encouraging them to join the church. From this perspective, sharing faith is, ultimately, helping others to own the same faith as you. Other traditions are more inclined to view service to others as an inevitable consequence of faith, and a duty for those who follow Christ. The love of Christ compels service to others irrespective of how they respond in religious terms. From this perspective, sharing faith is acting faithfully to help others in their need. Whatever the motivations and theologies that drive the outward impulse from church to wider society, there is plenty of scriptural warrant for such action: Jesus' parable of the sheep and goats (Matthew 25:31–46), Paul's call to care for strangers and enemies (Romans 12:9–21) and Peter's admonitions about 'living honorably among the Gentiles' (1 Peter 2:11–17), to name but a few. Serving society beyond the church is something that both clergy and laity may be involved with.

This chapter looks at three sorts of measures from the *Church Times* survey. The first are related to a sense of belonging to a congregation and measure respondents' attitudes towards their congregation as a place of socializing or mutual support and the extent of their involvement in church groups. The second are measures of how much responsibility someone has in terms of leadership roles and decision-making. The third look at involvement in society at large in terms of voluntary work. These measures allow us to explore which groups of people are most likely to be closely 'bonded' to their congregation and which are most likely to serve either within or beyond the Church. The two surveys allow us to see if there is any evidence that the extent or nature of belonging or serving in the Church of England changed in the first decade of this century. These issues have a wider relevance because sociologists have been debating whether or not people in Western societies are generally less likely to volunteer or to join associations than they used to a generation ago. Before dealing specifically with belonging or serving in the Church, it is worth looking briefly at the debate about what is happening in society at large.

Belonging and Serving in Society

One of the ongoing debates among sociologists is whether or not people in more recent generational cohorts are less inclined to join social groups or civic associations than were their parents or grandparents. This debate impinges on the Church of England because of the well-documented declines in attendance over the last fifty years. Are these about the general decline in religious belief, or might they also reflect a widespread tendency for people to be less inclined to join in with organized activities than they used to? In religious terms, sociologists have talked about 'believing without belonging'[1] as a way of expressing the move away from 'organized' religion to more individual and private manifestations of spirituality.

The question of the decline in formal social associations was raised by Robert Putnam in his widely read study of social life in the USA, which suggested that there had been a sharp decline in 'social capital' since the Second World War (Putnam, 2000). Putnam's definition of social capital stressed the personal relationships that develop in formal and informal networks, which he argued are important for developing trust between people. For Putnam, decline in social capital was apparent in the demise of voluntary and sporting associations (including the tenpin bowling groups that gave rise to the title of the book, *Bowling alone*), which he traced to a change between the pre- and post-war generations. Putnam suggested that the rise of television was largely to blame for the reluctance of post-war Americans to socialize in ways that their parents did. Since his study, there has been a massive growth in the Internet, which has even reached to the readers of the *Church Times*.[2] For good or for ill, social media may be replacing face-to-face contact as a key locus of social engagement.

The evidence for a general decline in cultural engagement or associational membership in Western societies has been hotly disputed (Stolle & Hooghe, 2004), and a number of studies using general social surveys have shown surprising stability between generations or over time (Clark, 2015; Dekker & Van Den Broek, 2005; Paxton, 1999). In the UK, changes in social capital seem to be mainly associated with the decline in working men's clubs and trade union affiliation among the working class (Li, Savage, & Pickles, 2003). Traditionally, it has been the middle class that have fostered and maintained voluntary groups and there is little to suggest this sort of behaviour has changed (Mohan & Bulloch, 2012). There are certainly cases where organizations dedicated to worthy causes

---

[1] This phrase was coined by Grace Davie (1994) and has sparked lively debate about what exactly it means for someone to affiliate to Christianity but not attend or belong to a church.

[2] In 2001, 42% of respondents reported they had no access to the Internet, but this had fallen to 11% by 2013.

have seen big increases in membership: the growth in the Royal Society for the Protection of Birds from 0.5 million in 1989 to 1.1 million in 2016 is a good example. Whether 'joining' always means forming close social ties is another matter, and 'belonging' can sometimes mean little more than paying dues and receiving newsletters.

The extent to which someone actively engages with voluntary groups is likely to depend on a number of factors such as their sex, age and educational experience. Men and women can differ in the type and levels of social engagement, but the direction of difference varies with particular circumstances and social contexts, and it is hard to generalize. Levels of social activity vary with age in a more predictable fashion, peaking in middle age and declining later in life as mobility and health become limiting factors (Smith, 1994). Some studies of the general population have shown a strong relationship between levels of civic engagement and education, with graduates being more active than those without degrees. This may partly be not only because of the social background of graduates, but also because graduates have more confidence and may know more people who are likely to encourage them to join voluntary associations (Egerton, 2002).

Changes in the Church of England

The Church of England has been measuring numbers over many years, but it is only comparatively recently that it has begun to collect and report attendance figures more systematically, and as a consequence begun to ask what factors might influence the growth and health of congregations. The number of people attending the Church of England has declined steadily over the last few decades as is evident in the official Church of England statistics for the period between the two *Church Times* surveys. Between 2001 and 2012, there was a fall of 191,500 in average Sunday attendance, representing an 18% decline over a period of about a decade.[3] Such figures have led to dire warnings about the likely demise of traditional churches, which have given urgency to the quest to understand the causes of declines and, conversely, what makes for healthy, growing churches.[4] To answer these sorts of questions, you

---

[3] Figures are from *Church Statistics 2001* and *Statistics for Mission 2013*, available on the Church of England website.

[4] See, for example, the Church of England growth project, http://www.churchgrowthresearch.org.uk/.

obviously need not only information on numbers (to give some sort of measure of growth and decline), but also some measure of the health of congregations. After all, the Christian faith is about transforming lives, not filling pews, and it is important to know if the people who do come have a sense that they belong to a worthwhile community that supports and promotes their journey of faith.

Robert Warren, former Rector of St. Thomas Crookes in Sheffield who was the Church of England's National Officer for Evangelism in the 1990s, has had an important influence through his work on developing the 'Healthy Churches' programme, which encourages churches to develop particular practices that are likely to create transformative congregations (Warren, 2004, 2012). Among the seven marks of a healthy church that he identified were those with an outward focus and those that operate as a community. Marks of an outward focus include working in partnership with other churches and secular groups in the local community, being passionate about justice and peace, making connections between faith and daily living, and responding to need by loving service. Marks of being a community are the quality of relationships, shared leadership between clergy and laity, and the development of lay ministry by valuing the gifts and experiences of everyone.

Underlying this need for quality of relationships was the understanding that it was part of making congregations attractive to outsiders. It became clear that the decline in membership could not be addressed by maintaining existing congregations and hoping they would self-perpetuate through the traditional processes by which parents pass faith to their children. New ways were needed for the church to become outward facing in order to reach adult unbelievers. An important response to this need is the Alpha Course (Gumbel, 1994), which has had a major impact within and beyond the Church of England (Heard, 2012; Hunt, 2005). The report *Mission-shaped Church* (Archbishops' Council, 2004) also propelled the Church to find new ways of reaching those who never attended traditional worship services. The growth of the Fresh Expressions movement was a key feature of the period between the two *Church Times* surveys (see Chapter 1) that led to local churches finding ways of meeting and worshipping that might be more likely to attract outsiders (Church Army's Research Unit, 2013).

One of the features of the changes over the last few decades has been the growth in the role of lay people in maintaining the ministry of the Church. This has partly been in response to declines in clergy, but has also reflected a growing sense that the quality of congregational life is improved if lay people are actively involved in running the church and decision-making (Kuhrt, 2001; Lay Ministries Working Group, 2017). The move towards lay ministry has been going on for many decades, with various initiatives at national and diocesan level. Whereas readers were the only licensed lay ministers in most dioceses in the middle of the last century, many dioceses now recognize a range of authorized roles that include pastoral assistants, parish evangelists and various kinds of worship leaders. Although the number of clergy relative to laity may have risen over the last decade or so, the trend to involve more lay people in leadership roles seems set to continue.

The need to be more outward facing in order to halt the decline in numbers may also have revitalized the notion of the Church having an active role in society. This has always been a significant feature of the Church of England: for example, Christian Socialism (Wilkinson, 1999) and particularly the work of William Temple (Kent, 1992) have long rooted the Church of England in social reform, even when this has meant challenging society at large or particular government policy. It is widely recognized, for example, that the Church's focus on the plight of the poor in urban areas in the 1980s brought it into direct conflict with the Thatcher government (Howes, 1998). In more recent years, the Church has responded to the notion of 'Big Society' promoted by David Cameron in 2009 (Kettell, 2012). In his presidential address to General Synod in November 2010, Rowan Williams urged the Church to '...take forward the spiritual and numerical growth of the Church of England –including the growth of its capacity to serve the whole community of this country'. This was expressed in terms of contributing to the 'common good' in the report that followed from the House of Bishops and Archbishop's Council:

> The increasingly secular assumptions within society make it all the more important that the Church takes seriously the need to celebrate, profile and support the work of active Anglicans making important contributions at all levels in the public and private sector. The huge contribution made by Anglicans, and other Christians, to voluntary and charitable activity outside the churches also needs celebrating and encouraging. (House of Bishops and Archbishops' Council, 2011)

The separation of congregational growth from serving the whole community in the report (unlike Rowan William's speech) has been noted by one observer who felt the move signalled an important and detrimental shift in thinking (Spencer, 2015). Whether this was intentional is unclear, but it highlights that church growth and church service are currently two important and related aspects of Church of England policy.

Changes in the size, social context and policy of the Church of England might influence the survey results on belonging, leadership and service in several ways. First, the stress on fostering healthy communities has meant a stress on developing relationships within a congregation, which might increase sense of belonging and involvement in church groups. Second, the stress on sharing ministry has meant more demands and more opportunities for lay people to be involved in decision-making and leadership responsibilities. Third, the stress on being outward facing and working for the common good might encourage more involvement in voluntary activities outside the church. The remainder of this chapter examines the data in terms of these three areas of faith practice.

Measuring Belonging, Leadership and Service

A worshipper's sense of belonging is related to the wider concept of the 'quality' of a congregation. High quality is associated with churches where there is a strong sense of engagement, mutual support and fellowship so that members benefit from being part of the congregation. Assessing numerically the quality of congregations is not easy, but a number of organizations have been attempting to do this for some years. Most notable are the National Church Life Surveys (NCLSs) that were started in Australia in 1991 and have been repeated elsewhere. These are large-scale surveys that collect information about churches alongside information from churchgoers, who complete a questionnaire during a worship service. This information allows researchers to identify a range of characteristics that are associated with congregations that are either growing numerically or where congregation members feel they are growing in their faith. The Australian NCLS has been repeated every five years, and a number of factors have been shown to be related to church vitality (Powell, 2013). The nine core qualities that emerged from this research can be categorized into three groups of three: internal core qualities (alive and growing faith, vital and nurturing worship, and strong and growing belonging), inspirational core qualities (clear and owned vision, inspiring and empowering leadership, and imaginative and flexible innovation) and outward core qualities (practical and diverse service, willing and effective faith sharing, and intentional and welcoming inclusion).

Notice that belonging features in the internal qualities and service in the outward qualities, so these are important measures for congregations as well as individuals.

Variations on this sort of list have been suggested by researchers and those promoting church growth in other countries such as the USA (Schwarz, 1996; Woolever & Bruce, 2004). This sort of approach has also been applied nationally in the Church of England, though without using such thorough congregational surveys. The 2013 study of church growth in the Church of England found that, while there was no single recipe for growth, there were a number of ingredients that tended to be associated with growing or healthy churches. Some of these were connected with the ability and vision of leadership, but others related to the culture of congregations, such as welcoming and relationship building, the nurturing of disciples, and the active involvement of lay people (Church Growth Research Programme, 2013).

The *Church Times* surveys were of individuals, not congregations, so there is no direct comparison with the studies such as the NCLS in Australia or the *Signs of Growth* survey in Southwark Diocese (Francis & Lankshear, 2015), which could rate congregations as a whole by summing the responses of individual members. However, the two *Church Times* surveys shared a number of questionnaire items with the *Signs of Growth* survey, so there is some comparison possible in this case. The three items reported here measured belonging directly ('I feel a strong sense of belonging to my church'), through social engagement ('My church is important for my social life'), and through a sense of mutual care ('Members of my church care deeply for one another'). A different measure of belonging was the number of groups someone belonged to, which was not asked in the *Signs of Growth* survey. This question had seventeen named responses that included membership of synods, the Parochial Church Council (PCC), children or youth groups, and groups such as Mother's Union or house groups.

Measuring leadership was through a measure of influence ('I can influence my church's decisions') and through asking about church leadership roles. This latter question had ten named responses that included licensed reader, churchwarden, organist/music director and youth leader. Service was measured by a single question that asked about volunteering outside the church and had 13 named areas of service ranging from education or children's work to human rights or political groups. For questions that asked about group memberships or roles, the analysis was slightly different because the outcome variable was a number between zero and up to 17, depending on the question.[5]

These sorts of questions are usually asked only of lay people, but the data used here included clergy, who might give very different answers, especially in terms of church roles. Clergy responses were included in the Likert (agree or disagree) responses, but only laity were used for church roles. Lay responses for Likert items were tested independently, but showed similar patterns to the overall data, so clergy and laity could both be included in the analyses of these items.

Exploring the Data

I Feel a Strong Sense of Belonging to My Church

Across both surveys, the sense of belonging was very high, with 91% agreeing or strongly agreeing that they felt a strong sense of belonging to their church (Fig. 9.1). This sort of positive response was also apparent in congregations that took part in the Southwark Diocese *Signs of Growth* survey, where the figure was 88% (Francis & Lankshear, 2015). The *Church Times* results are from a self-selecting group of committed churchgoers, so it is hardly surprising that they felt such a strong bond. This does not mean that virtually everyone who attends Church of England services feels they belong, and it is likely that those who do not soon go elsewhere or stop going to church altogether. What is of interest here is whether there are differences between groups that might suggest some feel more marginalized than others. The differences are likely to be small, but they may be an indication of which sorts of people are most strongly bonded to their congregations.

There were no significant differences by sex, education, location or ordination status, but there were some differences by age and between the different traditions. The most marked difference across all the groups was the lower sense of belonging to their church among the under 50s (87%) and the higher sense of belonging among those aged 70 or older (94%) compared with those in their 50s or 60s (91%). This is not a huge difference in absolute terms, but it does suggest that the Church of

---

[5] Analyses of questions using number of items mirrored those for the Likert items, but due to the nature of the distribution of responses, a negative binomial model was used to estimate means and statistical significance.

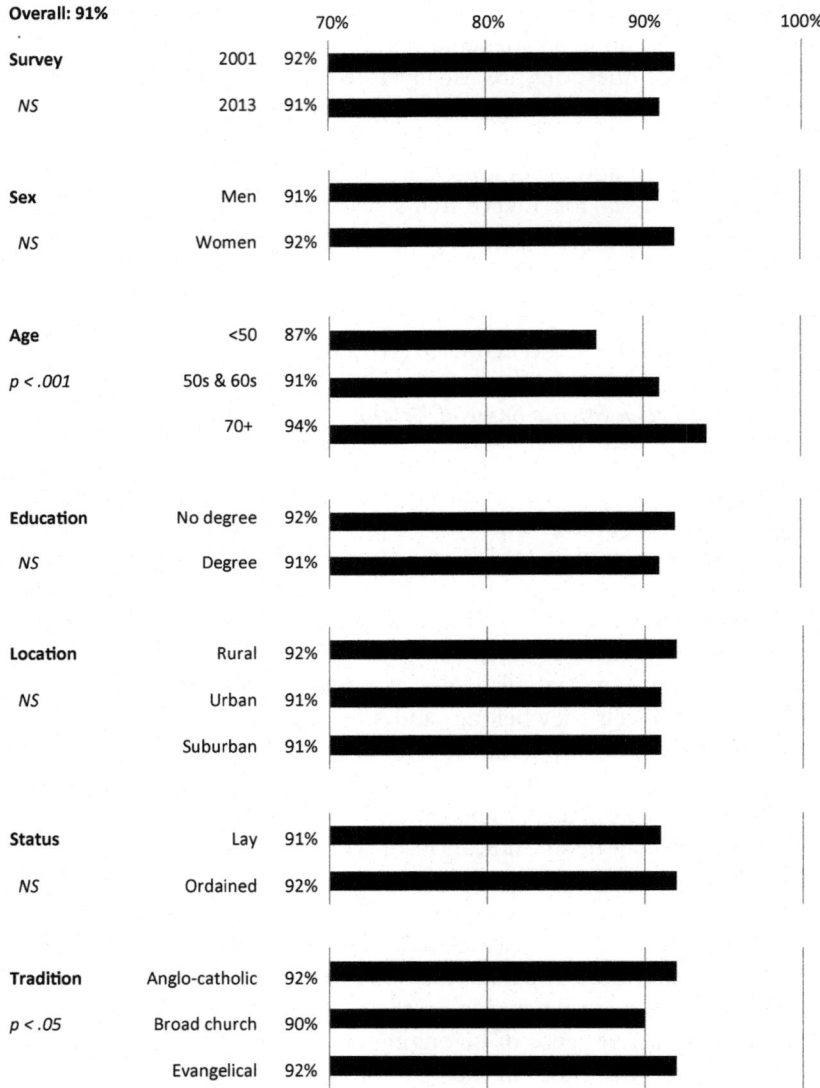

Fig. 9.1   I feel a strong sense of belonging to my church: estimated means

England has become a place most comfortable for the elderly. Examining the under 50s group in more detail suggested that this level of response (around 87% endorsement) was similar among those in their 20s, 30s and 40s. You would expect young people who read the *Church Times* to be among the most hefted of their generation to the Church, so it is likely that most young adults who attend the Church of England have an even lower sense of belonging than the young adults recorded here.

Evangelicals tended to be younger, so you might expect a generally lower sense of belonging. However, the statistical analysis allows for this age difference, and the figures suggest little difference in sense of belonging between Evangelicals and Anglo-catholics. The Broad-church respondents did show slightly lower levels of belonging, but this was barely statistically significant. It might be that being part of a specific tradition within the Church of England imparts a stronger sense of identity, but the evidence is that tradition per se is not that important.

Sense of belonging was maintained over the decade between the surveys, even though the overall numbers attending the Church declined during this period. For those that remain, bonding is still important. Cohort analysis (not shown) indicated no systematic changes across birth cohorts.

My Church Is Important to My Social Life

Responses to this item were mostly positive, but less so than for belonging, with an overall response of 73% (Fig. 9.2). People attend church for many reasons: for some, it is primarily a place to worship, and they do not want to foster friendships that extend beyond the courtesies of Sunday morning; for others, fellow worshippers are people they want to get to know well and who they would number among their most significant friends and neighbours. You might think that the level of socializing would vary between men and women and between the countryside and towns, but the survey data suggested no statistically significant difference when other factors are taken into account. There were, however, significant differences between other groups.

The age effect was similar to that for belonging, but differences were even more pronounced, with a 13% difference between the under 50s and the 70+ groups. This might reflect the fact that younger people are more mobile and have social networks that are related to work or having children at home, so church is a place that is one of many places to

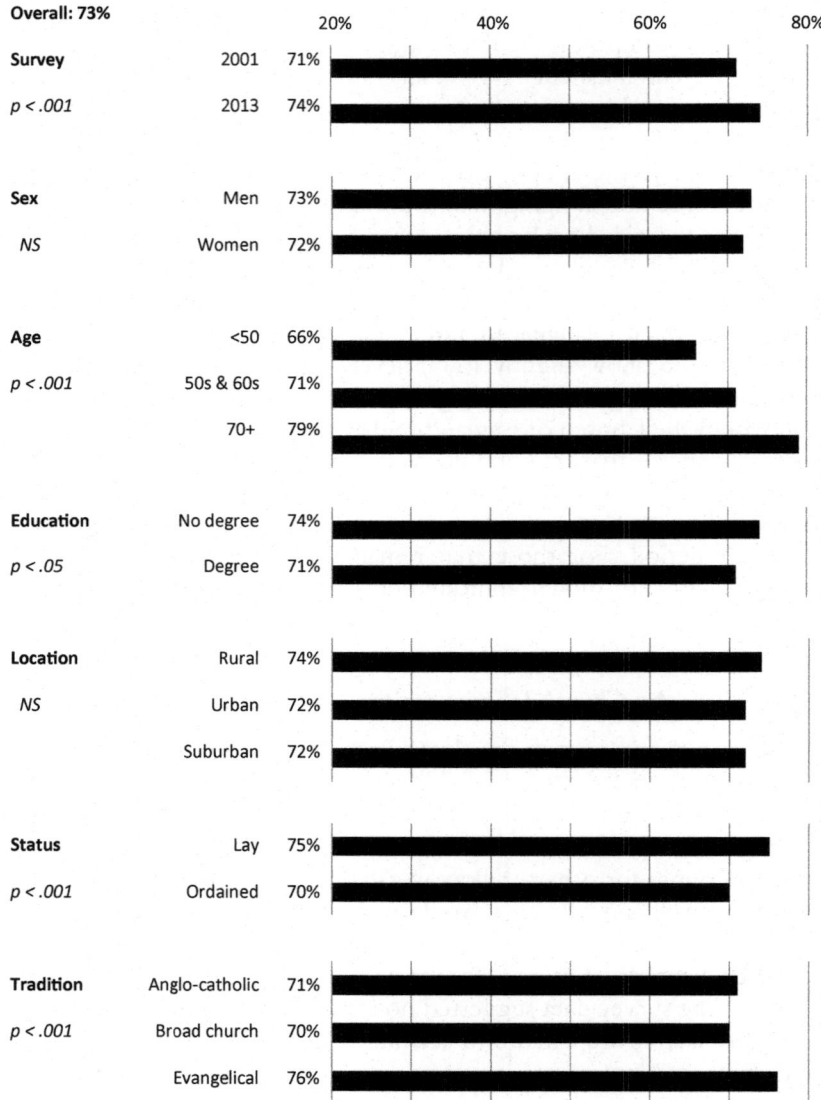

Fig. 9.2 My church is important for my social life: estimated means

socialize, whereas for older people other networks become less important relative to church. At a time when the trend has been to make services 'family friendly' and draw younger people into church through social activities, it is worth noting that it is the elderly retired for whom church may be a crucial social lifeline. Those with degrees were slightly less likely to endorse this item than those without degrees (71% versus 74%). This might reflect the different social networking patterns of graduates, who may have had more opportunities to form links with people beyond the church.

The difference between clergy and laity suggests that clergy may rely less on church for their social life than do their parishioners. Some clergy make a point of not making close friendships with their parishioners, perhaps for fear of what might happen if they are perceived as having 'favourites'. Others will believe that forming close bonds of friendship with their congregation that extend to a wider social life beyond Sundays is a crucial part of what it means to be a priest. There were interesting differences in the level of endorsement between the different sorts of ordained ministries: ordained local ministers 83%, retired clergy 72%, stipendiary clergy 70%, non-stipendiary clergy 64% and extra-parochial clergy only 46%. This shows the more socially 'embedded' nature of local ministry compared with stipendiary or non-stipendiary ministry. It also suggests that ordained clergy such as diocesan officers or bishops may lack the social ties with any particular church that perhaps should be integral to Christian life.

Evangelicals had a significantly higher level of endorsement (76%) than the other two traditions (70–71%), suggesting churches in this tradition might offer more opportunities for social engagement.

Unlike belonging, for socializing there was a significant change between the surveys, with higher endorsement in 2013 (74%) than in 2001 (71%). Again, the difference is small, but it seems to reflect some underlying trends. The cohort analysis showed some marked differences between cohorts and between traditions (Fig. 9.3). For all traditions, the cohorts born in the mid-century showed little change between surveys. There was some suggestion that church may have become more important for the social life of pre-war generations than you would predict solely from them becoming older between the surveys. This was even more so for those born in the 60s and 70s who attended Anglo-catholic or Broad-church congregations. In the 2001 survey, younger Evangelicals stood out in seeing church as more important to their

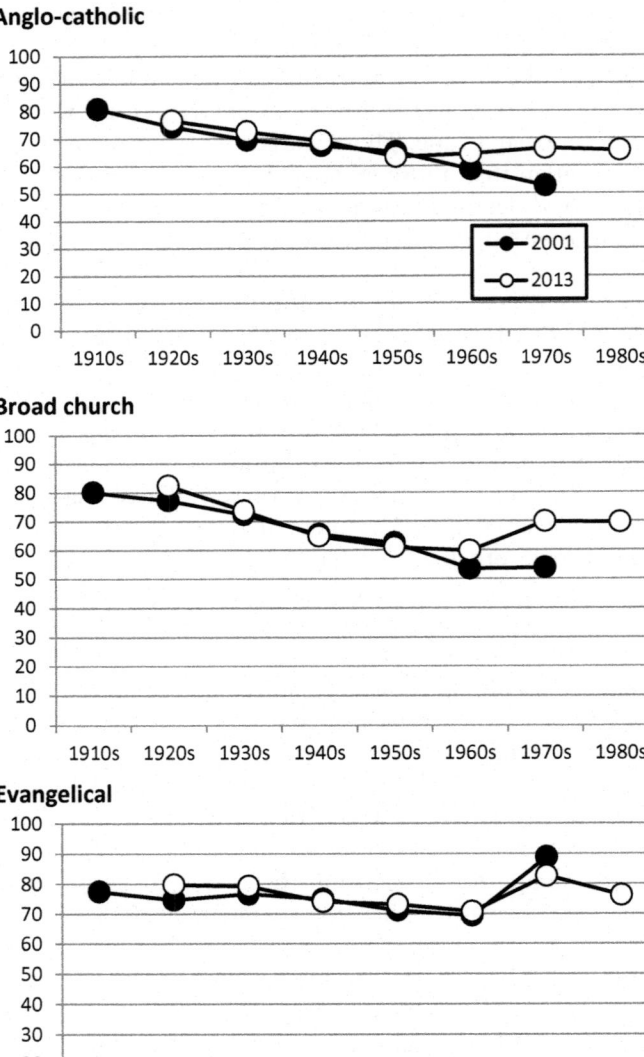

Fig. 9.3 My church is important for my social life: cohort changes

social life than equivalent age groups in other traditions. In the 2013 survey, there was much more parity between traditions, and the cohort graphs show this was mainly because younger adults in Anglo-catholic and Broad churches had similarly high scores to younger adults in Evangelical churches.

Members of My Church Care Deeply for One Another

Alongside the item of socializing was one on caring: 'members of my church care deeply for one another'. This is linked to socializing, but suggests relationships that go a little deeper and may involve more than social mixing. 'Caring' may be related to the pastoral support and encouragement that require more than superficial contact through Sunday worship. Unlike the previous item, this response is not about what individuals do, but about how they perceive the level of caring in their congregation generally. It may be driven not only by the actual level of caring that exists, but also by how much someone is aware of it happening and how important they think it should be. The pattern of responses was similar to socializing (77% endorsement), but there were some differences that might point to important underlying trends (Fig. 9.4). As with socializing, there was no difference between urban and rural locations, so the idea that rural churches can more easily foster close-knit, pastoral communities is not supported by this study. Unlike socializing, there was no significant effect of education on this variable. Women more often endorsed this item than did men (79% versus 75%). The difference was not because men were less certain about this (implying they may be less actively involved in caring) but because they seemed to be slightly less positive about the level of caring they perceived to be happening. Once again it was older people who were the most likely to endorse this item, with a 13% difference between the over 70s and the under 50s.

The difference with ordination was in the opposite direction to socializing, with clergy being more likely to endorse (79%) than laity (75%). This might represent a difference between clergy aspirations and the reality of congregational life as seen by laity, or it could reflect the possibility that clergy have greater inside knowledge about the caring that goes on quietly behind the scenes. Once again it was Evangelicals who were most likely to endorse this item. Perhaps caring and social interactions are seen

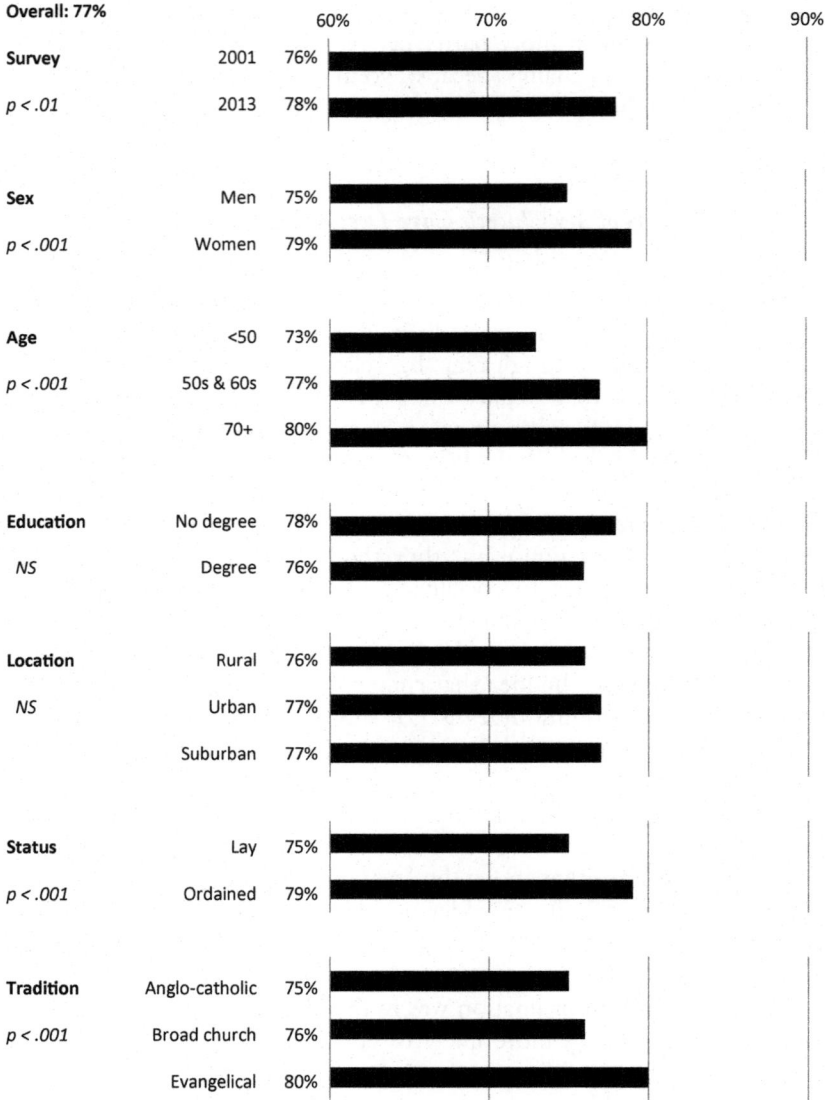

Overall: 77%

| | | 60% | 70% | 80% | 90% |

Survey — 2001 — 76%
p < .01 — 2013 — 78%

Sex — Men — 75%
p < .001 — Women — 79%

Age — <50 — 73%
p < .001 — 50s & 60s — 77%
— 70+ — 80%

Education — No degree — 78%
NS — Degree — 76%

Location — Rural — 76%
NS — Urban — 77%
— Suburban — 77%

Status — Lay — 75%
p < .001 — Ordained — 79%

Tradition — Anglo-catholic — 75%
p < .001 — Broad church — 76%
— Evangelical — 80%

Fig. 9.4 Members of my church care deeply for one another: estimated means

as intimately mixed within a theology that stresses the importance of living out salvation within the context of the Body of Christ.

There was, as with socializing, a slight increase in the level of endorsement between 2013 and 2011 (78% versus 76%), but this masked some much greater changes within some cohorts (Fig. 9.5). There was a consistent trend across all three traditions for positive change between surveys among the more recent cohorts. So whereas in 2001 there was a consistent change with age, with older people having a stronger sense of caring than younger people, in 2013 there was no difference between age groups. Cohorts born since the 1940s seem to have become more positive about the care that happens in their congregations, and this was not simply because they aged between surveys.

Membership of Church Groups

This analysis was restricted to lay people because clergy are likely to have profiles that are driven by the specific demands of their job. Church groups ranged from those where membership might involve some specific duties (such as being on the PCC or helping with children's groups) to those that were mainly related to fellowship (such as house groups). As with all the measures recording number of roles, there is a strong skew in the data, with large numbers reporting zero, and progressively fewer reporting one, two, three or more groups. This means the average number of groups was 2.1, with 24% belonging to no groups and 14% belonging to more than five. There was no overall change between surveys, so cohort graphs are not given for this variable. There were no significant differences between those with or without degrees, but there were some differences between other categories (Fig. 9.6).

Women belonged to slightly more groups, on average than men. This reflected a difference across most groups, including PCCs and synods, so it was not simply because women were more likely to be involved in children's work. The Church of England laity is predominantly female, and women seem, on this measure at least, to be more likely to get involved in activities outside worship. People in their 50s or 60s were most likely to belong to groups, with those 70 or over being least likely. This makes sense in terms of age distribution of congregations, with the majority age group also being the most active. Declines in the activity of older people are a common feature in general social surveys that measure voluntary association and group memberships. Rural churchgoers were slightly

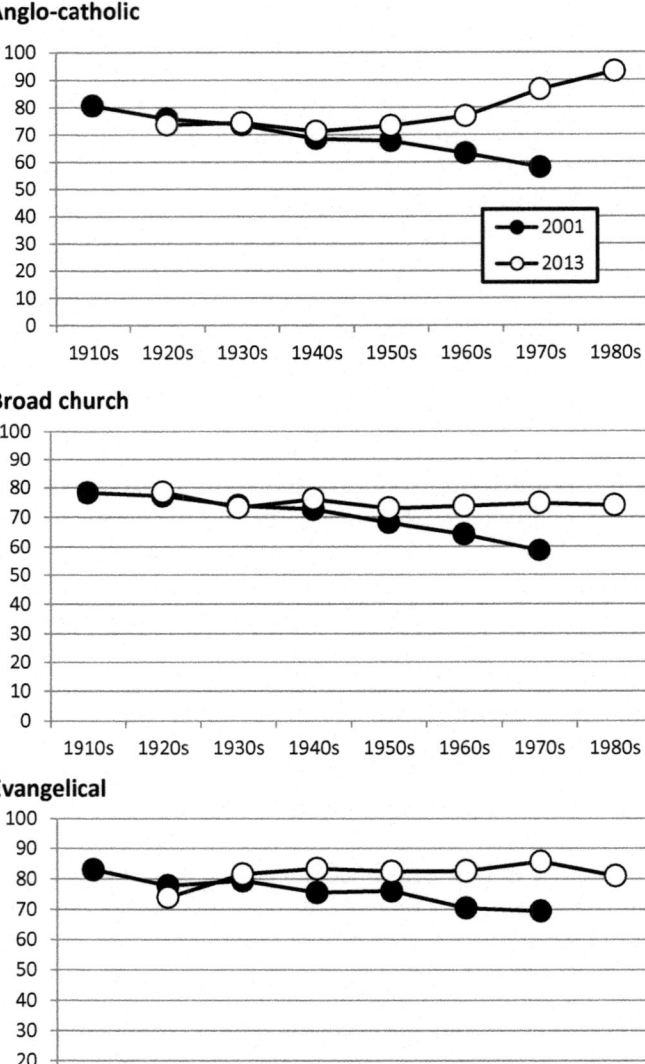

Fig. 9.5 Members of my church care deeply for one another: cohort changes

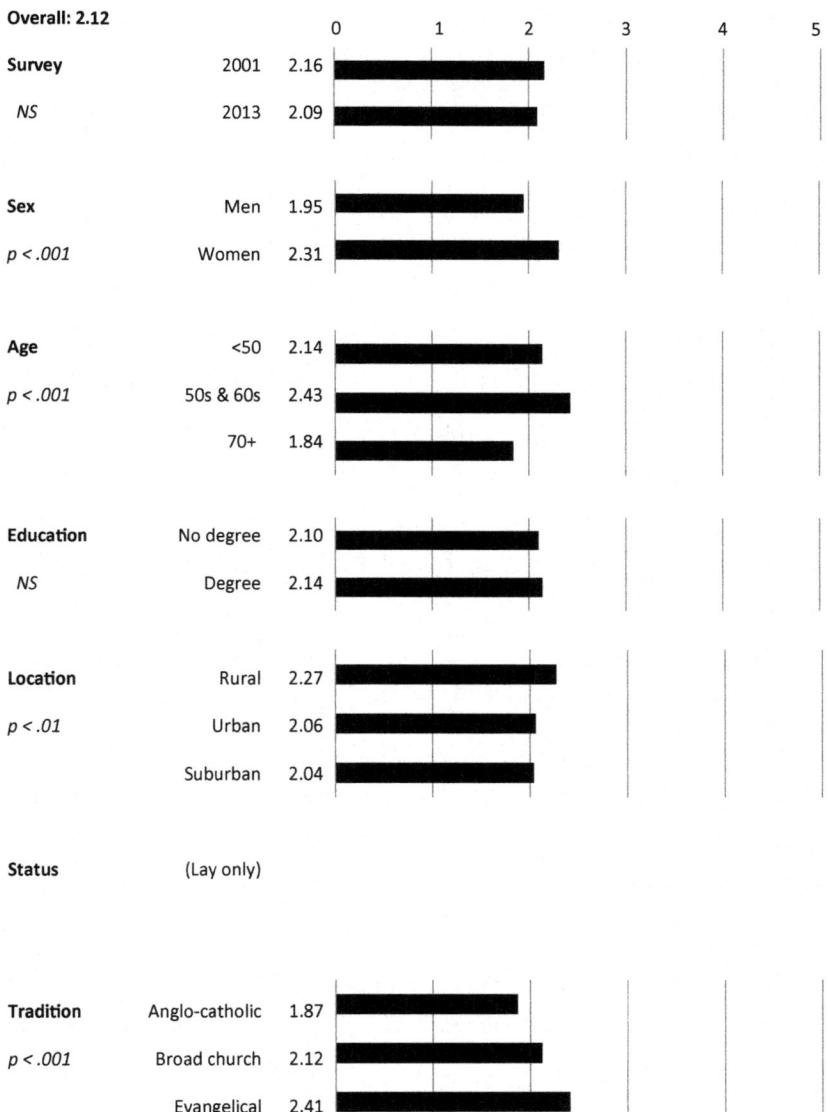

Fig. 9.6 Membership of church groups, laity: estimated means

more likely to belong to groups than those from towns or cities, though the difference was not great and this was one of the few measures where such a difference existed. Evangelical laity belonged to more groups, and Anglo-catholic laity belonged fewer groups, compared to people from Broad-church congregations. As with the sex difference, this was apparent across a range of different church groups, but here there was also a marked contrast in terms of house groups, where 40% of Evangelicals belonged to one, compared to only 20% of Anglo-catholics.

I Can Influence My Church's Decisions

Being bonded to your congregation and involved in its social and pastoral life is likely to give you more say in what goes on, but not necessarily so. The overall endorsement for this item was 66% (Fig. 9.7), which compares with 91% for a strong sense of belonging and 73% for the importance of church for the respondent's social life. Influence on decision-making is more likely if you belong to the formal decision-making bodies such as the PCC. Excluding clergy, those on the PCC were much more likely to endorse this item (81%) than those who were not (43%). Influence may also come through other means, and endorsement of this item was higher among those lay people who were *not* on their PCC but who were involved in groups such as choirs, youth and children's work, and house groups.[6] To some extent, the more people are involved with lay leadership or church groups the more they feel they have some influence on decision-making. This helps to explain some of the trends observed across both surveys.

Men generally felt they had more influence than women (68% versus 65%). This was after allowing for the fact that more clergy were men, and the trend held within laity alone. Women form the majority of congregations, but they may not have as much influence as men. The age difference was very marked and evident among those in the 70+ group, who were much less likely to endorse this item than younger people (56% versus 70 and 71%). Older people comprise the bulk of congregations and in this survey

[6]For lay people not on the PCC, membership of the following groups was associated with significantly higher endorsement of this item: choir, music/drama, youth group, Sunday school, uniform groups, house groups and other men's groups. There was no effect for those who were bell-ringers, in a mother-toddler group, in the Mother's Union or in other women's groups. This gives an interesting picture of where influence may reside among laity in the Church of England.

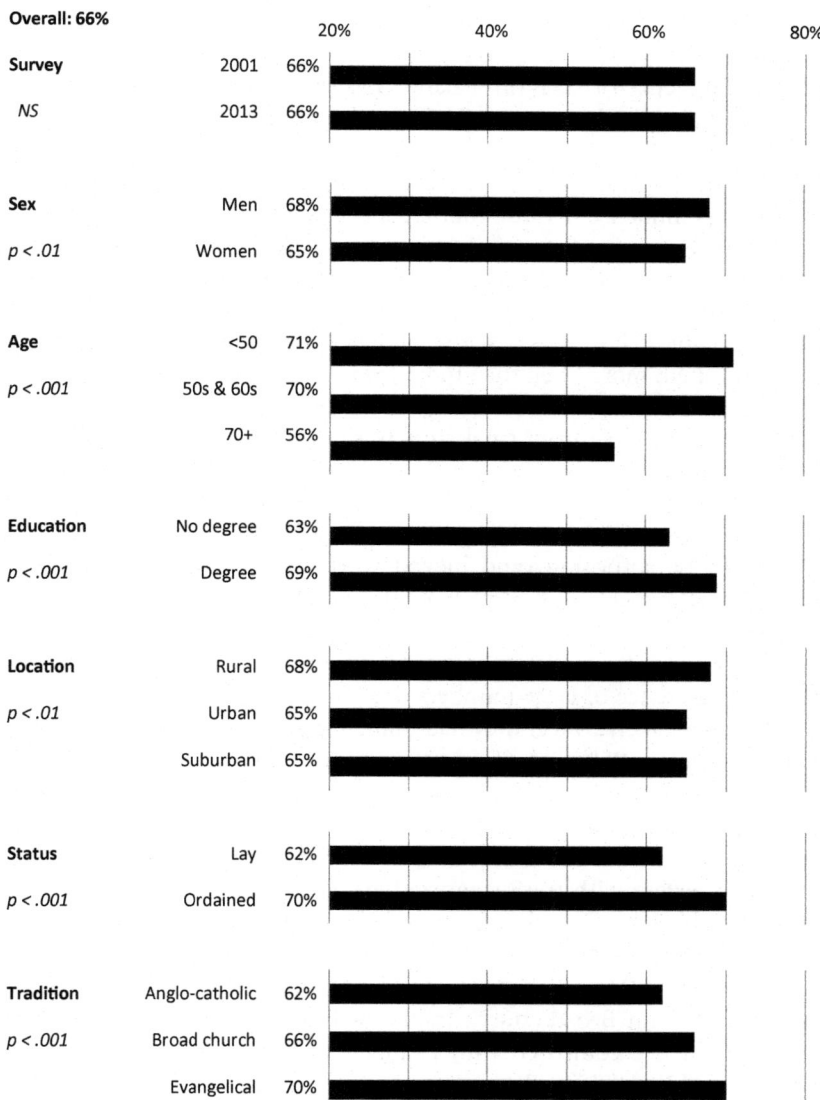

Fig. 9.7 I can influence my church's decisions: estimated means

were more likely to feel they belonged to their church and socialized in their congregation than did young people. Yet they also felt they had much less influence of decision-making. That may be as it should be since they are less likely to be in the centre of active ministry. Controlling statistically for the number of groups or leadership roles removed the age effect among lay people (but not among clergy), suggesting that older lay people may have less influence because they are less involved in church groups.

Those with degrees felt they had more influence than did those without degrees (69% versus 63%). This was not related to the number of roles they had and may reflect the skills that graduates have in negotiating and decision-making. There was a slight tendency for people in rural areas to endorse this item more often than those from urban or suburban areas (68% versus 65%). This was only so among lay people and could be explained by the fact that people from rural areas were more likely to be involved in groups or lay leadership roles. The shortage of people to lead ministries is most acute in rural areas, and it seems that the upside of this is that lay people get more involved and feel they have more influence on decisions.

It would be surprising (and indeed worrying) if clergy did not feel they could influence decision-making their churches, and it is comforting to see a marked difference between clergy and laity (70% versus 62%). Nonetheless, the overall clergy figure is lower than might be expected and reflects the presence of large numbers of retired clergy in the sample, who were much less likely to feel they had influence compared with stipendiary clergy (47% versus 95%). The figure for retired clergy is lower than for lay people, even allowing for differences in activity related to age. This may reflect a deliberate intent by the Church, or by retired clergy themselves, to exclude them from too much involvement in decision-making for fear they may interfere with the recognized leadership in a parish. While this may be sensible, the Church is also very happy to draw on the services of retired clergy when it needs them, which it increasingly does.

There was a difference between the three traditions, with those from Anglo-catholic and Broad-church traditions being much less likely to feel they had influence compared with Evangelicals. This was again linked to the number of leadership roles or group membership, with lay Evangelicals being more likely to have a leadership role than their Anglo-catholic or Broad-church counterparts.[7] This difference may be related to the greater clericalism in Broad or Anglo-catholic traditions within the Church.

[7]For Evangelicals, 68% had at least one leadership role, compared with 64% for those in Broad churches, and 58% for Anglo-catholics.

There was no overall difference between the surveys, with just under two-thirds of the sample in each case agreeing that they could influence decision-making in their church. There were differences between birth cohorts however (Fig. 9.8), and among Anglo-catholics and Evangelicals, the post-war cohorts in particular seemed to feel they had more influence in their churches in 2013 than 2001, even after allowing for changes expected with age. So although Anglo-catholics were generally less likely to feel they had influence over their church decisions, the situation seemed to improve between the surveys. In Broad churches, there was less change between surveys, and Evangelicals born in the pre-war decades seemed to feel they had much less influence in 2013 than in 2001.

Leadership Roles

The number of opportunities for lay people to lead ministry is likely to be less than the number of groups to which they can belong, and this is reflected in the fact that the average number of leadership roles was 1.1, around half the average number of group memberships (Fig. 9.9). Around 86% of laity reported no leadership roles, and only 6% had more than one role. In general, lay *Church Times* readers who completed the surveys seemed not to have leadership responsibilities in their church. There were no differences between men and women, or with education. The same pattern emerges as for lay membership of groups, with middle-aged churchgoers having the highest average number of roles and the elderly the least. Lay people in rural areas were more likely than those from urban or suburban areas to have leadership roles, which was in line with the greater sense of influencing decisions among this group. Rural churches may be better at giving laity responsibilities than churches where perhaps there are more people to take roles and clergy are more hands-on decision-makers. In line with influencing decisions, Evangelicals also scored higher than the other two traditions in terms of their leadership roles.

Voluntary Service Beyond the Church

The measure of service used here is the number of unpaid roles individuals had that were outside the church. The overall average was 1.0, with 41% having no such roles, and less than one per cent having more

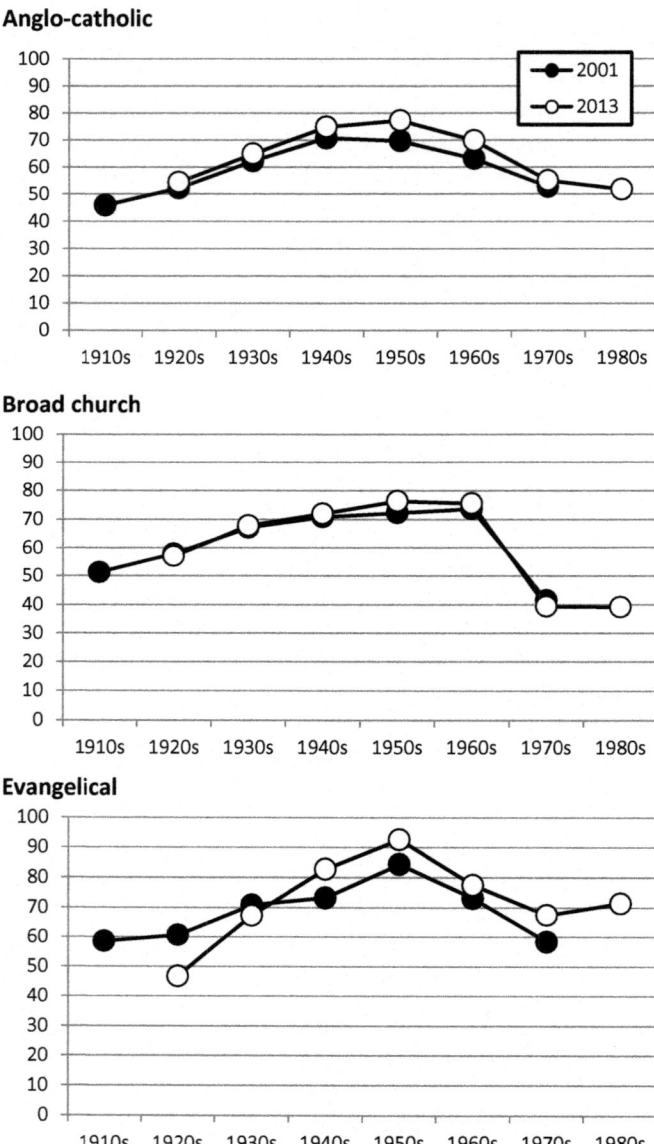

Fig. 9.8 I can influence my church's decisions: cohort changes

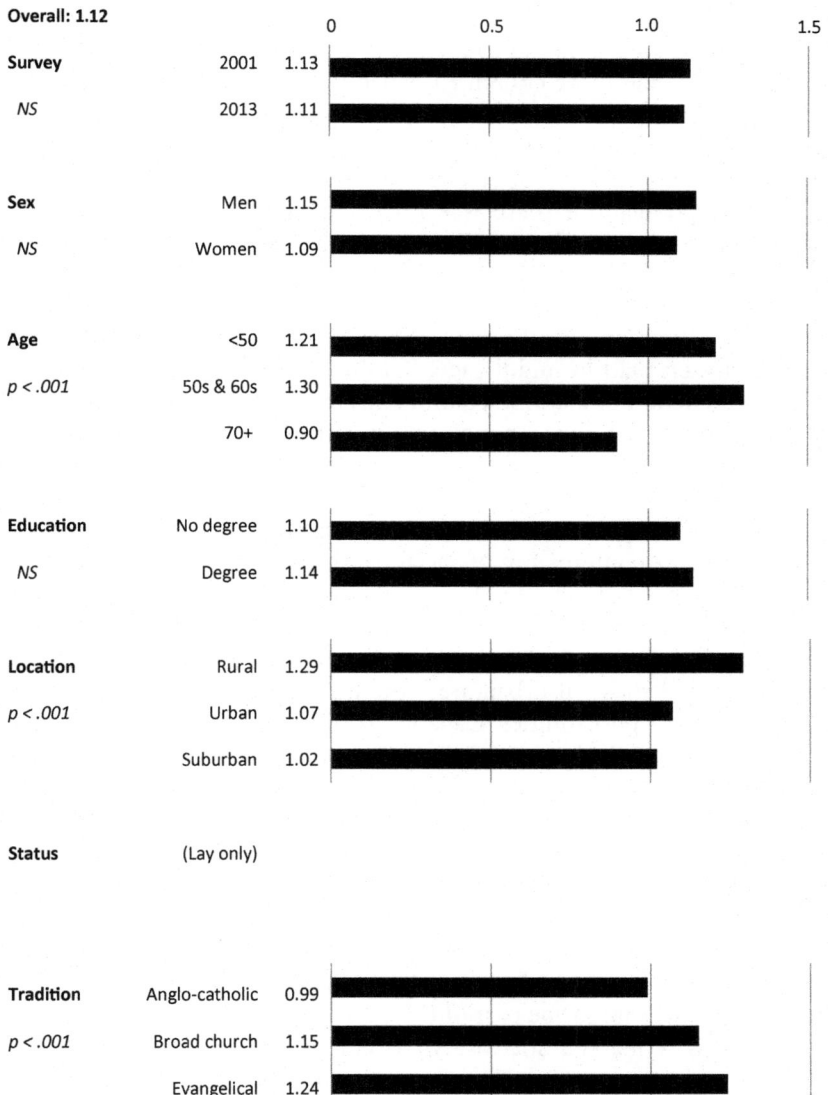

Fig. 9.9 Average number of leadership roles, laity: estimated means

than five. This kind of volunteering was less likely than having a church leadership role, or belonging to a church group. There was no evidence that those who had more church roles had lower activity beyond church, and indeed, the opposite was true. Busy people tend to be simultaneously busy in several different spheres of life. The differences between groups reflected the sorts of results expected from similar work among the general population: there was no overall difference between men and women, but differences in all the other categories were statistically significant (Fig. 9.10).

The age difference was in line with church groups, but less marked. Those over 70 or under 50 were less likely to have an unpaid role outside the church than in middle age. This age trend is in line with studies of the general population. Volunteering may be demanding and may therefore decline with age, though you might expect that the silver generation, who these days are fitter than their predecessors of that age and who have more time than those of working age, might be the most likely to volunteer. The greater voluntary activity of those with degrees is usually ascribed to a combination of social background, capacity, and opportunity. Graduates not only tend to be more able to volunteer, but also have social networks that may encourage them to do so.

Those in rural areas had the highest number of unpaid roles outside the church, and those in urban areas the least. This may reflect the sort of volunteering opportunities available in these different locations, and the age and social background of the sample. Lay people from Broad churches were the most likely to volunteer outside the church. There have been suggestions from the USA that certain church traditions (notably conservative Protestants) tend to foster church-based activity more than activity beyond the church. This is not supported more widely, though in this sample the tradition difference might suggest that those most closely bonded to a distinct tradition are least likely to volunteer outside the church. Evangelicals tended to socialize more in their churches, and this might be part of the explanation of the difference.

There was a marked increase in overall levels of voluntary activity between the surveys, which contrasts with the declines noted in this sort of activity in some UK studies (McCulloch, 2014). Cohort analysis (not shown) suggested the increase was across all age cohorts and all traditions.

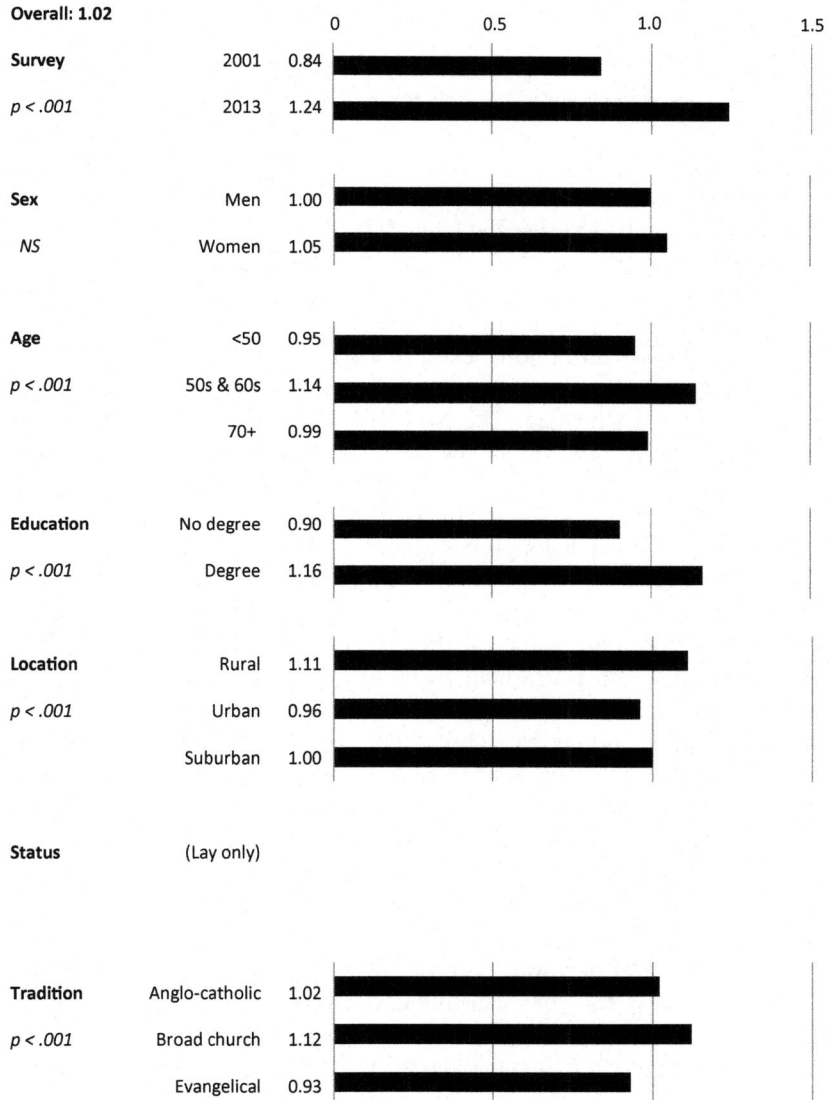

Fig. 9.10 Average number of unpaid roles, laity: estimated means

CONCLUSIONS

The Church of England is an established, national church and therefore tends to be the 'default' church for many people who attend only at Christmas or for the 'rites of passage' services such as baptisms, weddings and funerals. The *Church Times* surveys record the opinions of the core members who demonstrate the sort of commitment that the Church is aiming to achieve. On its website, the Church of England proclaims the importance of gathering with others and having fellowship (Church of England, 2017). The notion of the Body of Christ, expressed in the letters of St. Paul, is central to theological understandings that make belonging to a congregation more than an optional extra to discipleship. John Stott (2007, p. 19) famously wrote 'I trust that none of my readers is that grotesque anomaly, an unchurched Christian. The New Testament knows nothing of such a person. For the church lies at the very centre of the eternal purpose of God'. Promoting churchgoing, and more importantly church belonging, should, it seems, be a key task for the Church of England, even in a society where casual or 'virtual' belonging is becoming more important.

What do these results tell us about belonging to the Church of England at the start of the twenty-first century? The very high sense of belonging seems to be a common feature in these surveys, and levels of item agreement for the three measures here are in line with similar results from the Southwark Diocese *Signs of Growth* survey (Francis & Lankshear, 2015).[8] Given that these are people who attend church and/or care enough to complete a survey, a high sense of belonging is likely, so this may be nothing to boast about too loudly. What is perhaps more interesting is differences between groups. Given that congregations are predominantly female, it is surprising that there was no difference between the sexes in their sense of belonging or social life. Women belonged to slightly more groups on average, had a stronger sense of a caring congregation and felt less influence on decisions than did men. It seemed that laymen who do attend regularly feel they can influence decisions, even if they join in slightly fewer activities than do women. Women might be forgiven for thinking that in terms of gender disparity little has changed: women do

---

[8] The overall *Church Times* figures for belonging (91%), importance of social life (73%) and caring (77%) are all slightly higher than those reported for whole congregations in Southwark (88, 63 and 72%, respectively). Whole congregation surveys are more likely to include those who are less well bonded to congregations than self-selecting surveys of individuals.

the work and men are in charge, though given the size of the overall differences this may be pushing the point too far.

The most striking differences across most measures were related to age. Younger people, under 50, felt a lower sense of belonging, were less engaged socially and had a lower sense of a caring congregation than did older people, a result that was also true in Southwark (Francis & Lankshear, 2015, Table 2). On the other hand, they were involved in more church groups and felt they had more influence on decision-making (at least compared with those over 70). Some of the age disparity was most apparent in those from the Broad-church tradition, and there was little age difference in sense of belonging among either Anglo-catholics or Evangelicals. Young adults in these latter two traditions may have a sense of belonging that is derived from the distinctive beliefs or identity of these wings of the Church. Elsewhere, belonging may be more difficult to define in terms of distinctiveness within the denomination. Anglo-catholics and Evangelicals seemed to rely more on their church for their social life than did those in Broad churches, especially among younger cohorts. These are not teenagers, but mainly younger adults, who might be expected to rely mainly on non-church arenas for their social lives. The surveys could not tell if church as the main source of social life, or just an important source, but the relative difference between the traditions is interesting. The zeal for evangelism may be higher among committed Anglo-catholics or Evangelicals, but in terms of being networked beyond the church, it may be those from Broad-church congregations that are best positioned to invite non-churchgoing friends to attend a service or church-based course. If we are living in an age where face-to-face social contact is declining, then the Church of England may be well placed to buck the trend by offering a viable alternative lifestyle. This might be hampered if social activities are geared mainly to the very young or the elderly. Finding ways of capturing the interest and altruism of younger adults may be an important priority for congregations in the years ahead.

There were few differences between rural and urban churchgoers in terms of perceptions of belonging, caring and socializing. The idea that rural congregations are more close-knit may be a myth. What was evident was that lay people from rural churches tended to take on more leadership roles and felt a stronger sense of being able to influence decision-making. We often emphasize the downside of small rural churches in multi-parish benefices, but they do, albeit by necessity, allow lay people to have more control. In this sense, rural churches may be better at developing collaborative ministry than those elsewhere. The figures related to location bring out the difference between belonging to and running congregations. Older people generally seem to feel they belong, and the church is important for their social life. Younger people are busier in terms of belonging to groups, and they may have more say in what goes on, but they do not seem to always feel that they 'belong'. Perhaps this is because truly belonging takes time: there are lots of stories of people feeling they are 'incomers' even after years of attending. This may be a hard perception to overcome, because it is deeply rooted in human nature, but it is worth remembering that church surveys of this sort sample the 'remainers'; the leavers are often long gone and forgotten (Francis & Richter, 2007; Richter & Francis, 1998).

Issues around belonging are rarely, if ever, addressed to clergy. We assume they must have a strong sense of belonging, be socially involved and be able to influence decisions in their church. To be sure, this may be the case for active parochial clergy but not all, by any means, seem to want to socialize with their congregations. Not all clergy fit the mould of incumbents or curates, and it is worth reflecting on how other clergy groups answered these items.

The first group is retired clergy, who are forming an increasingly large proportion of the clergy.[9] This group had a similar sense of belonging and socializing to laity and parochial stipendiary clergy, but they felt much less able to influence decisions. Perhaps many who are retired but active in ministry simply turn up and do what they are told (or asked) to do by incumbents or churchwardens. They may be content to follow instructions and stay out of the decision-making process, leaving aside their expertise that could be the product of many years of parochial leadership. They might, on the other hand, be frustrated at being ignored. The traditional expectation is that retired clergy help out and keep quiet. As they now take an increasingly significant role in the lives of many congregations, this might be a *modus operandi* that needs to be reviewed.

The second group is extra-parochial clergy, who may be bishops, archdeacons or full-time diocesan officers. Their sense of belonging and socializing was much lower than any other group, and we might expect that if they are

---

[9] Figures from the Church of England 2016 Ministry Statistics show that the vast majority of those with permission to officiate are over 65 and therefore probably retired. The proportion of this group among the 'active' clergy rose from 32% in 2013 to 34% in 2016.

not tied to any one church as part of their ministry. Nonetheless, it raises the issue about how such people could and should be part of a congregation: How do they belong? Frequent attendance on Sundays may be difficult if duties call elsewhere in the diocese, but there may be other ways in which such clergy could be helped to feel part of the local church where they live.

The pattern of volunteering for unpaid roles outside church among the laity was much as we might expect for people in society at large. The effects of age and education seem to be a widespread phenomenon that must have particular causes in Western societies. The increase in levels of volunteering between surveys was small in terms of average numbers of roles, but represents a significant shift across all traditions and most cohorts. This seems to have been a genuine change in activity which has not, as far as these data suggest, been at the expense of levels of bonding and activity within congregations. It seems to be in line with some country-level surveys that have suggested that Putnam's pessimism about declining 'civic engagement' may have been unwarranted. Whether this trend represents a response of the Church of England laity to the Archbishop Rowan's call to work for the common good is unclear, but it is certainly what might be expected if such a call were being heeded.

REFERENCES

Archbishops' Council. (2004). *Mission-shaped church: Church planting and Fresh Expressions of Church in a changing context.* London: Church of England.

Church Army's Research Unit. (2013). *An analysis of Fresh Expressions of Church and church plants begun in the period 1992–2012.* Retrieved November 20, 2014, from http://www.churchgrowthresearch.org.uk/UserFiles/File/Reports/churchgrowthresearch_freshexpressions.pdf.

Church Growth Research Programme. (2013). *From anecdote to evidence.* London: The Church Commissioners for England.

Church of England. (2017). *Going to church and praying.* Retrieved December 21, 2017, from https://www.churchofengland.org/our-faith/going-church-and-praying.

Clark, A. K. (2015). Rethinking the decline in social capital. *American Politics Research, 43*(4), 569–601. https://doi.org/10.1177/1532673x14531071.

Davie, G. (1994). *Religion in Britain since 1945: Believing without belonging.* Oxford and Cambridge, MA: Blackwell.

Dekker, P., & Van Den Broek, A. (2005). Involvement in voluntary associations in North America and Western Europe: Trends and correlates 1981–2000. *Journal of Civil Society, 1*(1), 45–59. https://doi.org/10.1080/17448680500166338.

Egerton, M. (2002). Higher education and civic engagement. *The British Journal of Sociology, 53*(4), 603–620. https://doi.org/10.1080/000713102 2000021506.

Francis, L. J., & Lankshear, D. W. (2015). Introducing the congregational bonding social capital scale: A study among Anglican churchgoers in south London. *Journal of Beliefs & Values, 36*(2), 224–230. https://doi.org/10.10 80/13617672.2015.1041786.

Francis, L. J., & Richter, P. J. (2007). *Gone for good? Church-leaving and returning in the twenty-first century.* Peterborough: Epworth.

Gumbel, N. (1994). *Telling others: The Alpha initiative.* Eastbourne: Kingsway Publications.

Heard, J. (2012). *Inside Alpha: Explorations in evangelism.* Eugene, OR: Wipf and Stock.

House of Bishops and Archbishops' Council. (2011). *Challenges for the new quinquennium (GS1815).* London: Church of England.

Howes, G. (1998). Urban problems and policy: An Anglican case study. *Social Compass, 45*(1), 43–55. https://doi.org/10.1177/003776898045001004.

Hunt, S. (2005). The Alpha program: Charismatic evangelism for the contemporary age. *Pneuma, 27*(1), 65–82. https://doi.org/10.1163/157007405774270329.

Kent, J. (1992). *William Temple: Church, state and society in Britain, 1880–1950.* Cambridge: Cambridge University Press.

Kettell, S. (2012). Religion and the Big Society: A match made in heaven? *Policy & Politics, 40*(2), 281–296. https://doi.org/10.1332/030557312x640004.

Kuhrt, G. W. (Ed.). (2001). *Ministry issues for the Church of England: Mapping the trends.* London: Church House Publishing.

Lay Ministries Working Group. (2017). *Serving together: The report of the Lay Ministries Working Group 2015/16.* London: Church of England.

Li, Y., Savage, M., & Pickles, A. (2003). Social capital and social exclusion in England and Wales (1972–1999). *The British Journal of Sociology, 54*(4), 497–526. https://doi.org/10.1111/j.1468-4446.2003.00497.x.

McCulloch, A. (2014). Cohort variations in the membership of voluntary associations in Great Britain, 1991–2007. *Sociology, 48*(1), 167–185. https://doi.org/10.1177/0038038513481643.

Mohan, J., & Bulloch, S. (2012). *The idea of a 'civic core': What are the overlaps between charitable giving, volunteering, and civic participation in England and Wales* (Vol. 75). Birmingham: Third Sector Research Centre.

Paxton, P. (1999). Is social capital declining in the United States? A multiple indicator assessment. *American Journal of Sociology, 105*(1), 88–127. https://doi.org/10.1086/210268.

Powell, R. (2013). *Trends in Protestant church vitality over twenty years (1991–2011)* (Vol. NCLS Occasional Paper 23). Adelaide: Mirrabooka Press.

Putnam, R. D. (2000). *Bowling alone: The collapse and revival of American community*. New York: Simon & Schuster.

Richter, P., & Francis, L. J. (1998). *Gone but not forgotten*. London: Darton, Longman & Todd.

Schwarz, C. A. (1996). *Natural Church Development: A guide to the eight essential qualities of healthy churches*. St. Charles, IL: ChurchSmart Resources.

Smith, D. H. (1994). Determinants of voluntary association participation and volunteering. *Non-profit and Voluntary Sector Quarterly, 23*(3), 243–263. https://doi.org/10.1177/089976409402300305.

Spencer, S. (2015, August 14). Goals for growth expose a vision's limitations. *The Church Times*, p. 10.

Stolle, D., & Hooghe, M. (2004). Inaccurate, exceptional, one-sided or irrelevant? The debate about the alleged decline of social capital and civic engagement in western societies. *British Journal of Political Science, 35*(1), 149–167. https://doi.org/10.1017/s0007123405000074.

Stott, J. (2007). *The living church*. Downers Grove, IL: InterVarsity Press.

Warren, R. (2004). *The healthy churches' handbook*. London: Church House Publishing.

Warren, R. (2012). *Developing healthy churches: Returning to the heart of mission and ministry*. London: Church House Publishing.

Wilkinson, A. (1999). New Labour and Christian Socialism. In G. R. Taylor (Ed.), *The impact of New Labour* (pp. 37–49). London, UK: Palgrave Macmillan. https://doi.org/10.1057/9780333983812_4.

Woolever, C., & Bruce, D. (2004). *Beyond the ordinary: Ten strengths of U.S. congregations*. Louisville, KY and London: Westminster John Knox Press.

CHAPTER 10

Church Schools

INTRODUCTION

The Church of England is deeply rooted in the English school system. There are **4664** Church of England schools that educate about 1 million children at any one time. Dioceses support the work of church schools through their boards of education, and the overall cost of funding this work amounts to some £15 million (Church of England, 2018). It was sensible, therefore, to ask *Church Times* readers how much they supported this aspect of the Church's mission. The Christian faith has also been part of the wider school system since mass education began in England, with religious education (RE) and school assemblies being largely based upon Christianity and Christian moral teaching. In a society where fewer and fewer people admit to any religious faith, and where other religions have an increasingly high profile, it is also worth asking how far members of the established church are comfortable with this traditional practice continuing into the twenty-first century. Before looking at the results of some of the survey items related to church schools and education, it is worth setting the scene in terms of what was happening to school education generally around the time of the two *Church Times* surveys. This is partly about understanding the history and development of church schools, partly about noting what was happening with national education policy, and partly about being aware of the wider debate that developed over faith schools from the turn of the century.

© The Author(s) 2018
A. Village, *The Church of England
in the First Decade of the 21st Century*,
https://doi.org/10.1007/978-3-030-04528-9_10

Christianity and Church Schools in the English Education System

The impulse to develop mass education originated primarily with church groups, rather than from the state. The British and Foreign School Society, founded in 1807 by nonconformists, and the National Society, founded in 1811 by the Church of England, were instrumental in establishing schools that offered basic education to the poor. During the next 150 years or so the state increased its grant aid to church schools, as well as building so-called board schools where church school provision was inadequate (Chadwick, 1997; Murphy, 1971). As standards and expectations rose, the Church found it increasingly difficult to raise the money necessary to maintain schools and employ teachers. A 'dual system' emerged by the start of the twentieth century whereby both state and church were partners in expanding the national education service, with church schools being partly subsidized by local rates on condition that the newly formed Local Education Authorities (LEAs) would have some control in appointing school managers and inspecting standards (Chadwick, 1997). The 1944 Education Act was key moment that saw the rationalization of the system so that the LEAs took the bulk of the responsibilities for running and maintaining church schools. Church schools could opt to be 'voluntary controlled', that is, fully funded by their LEA but with reduced Church control over governance, or 'voluntary aided', that is, with the Church funding a percentage of building and maintenance costs in return for more Church control over governance. Controlled schools could, if parents requested, offer specific denominational instruction, or they could use the LEA agreed RE syllabus. Aided schools were free to decide their own RE syllabus. At this point, the Church of England decided to maintain the bulk of its provision in the primary rather than the secondary education (in contrast to the Roman Catholic Church), and this bias has continued down to the present time.[1]

The long-standing role of churches in education has meant that the Christian faith has a privileged position in English schools. The 1944 Act recognized this by specifying that all schools, state or voluntary, should include a daily act of collective worship and religious instruction.

---

[1] According to the Church of England website (accessed 16 July 2018), the Church has around 2000 voluntary controlled schools, of which 20 are secondary, and around 1700 voluntary aided schools, of which 53 are secondary.

Underlying the reforms was a sense that schools needed to be responsible for the spiritual and moral development of children within a context that has been described as 'Christian-civic humanism' (Sundermann, 2015). School assemblies are moments when pupils and teachers from the whole school (or parts of a large school) gather in one place. They are opportunities to exchange information, but also moments that express something of the ethos and atmosphere of a school. The requirement that all schools must have a daily collective act of worship that is largely Christian in character reflects the sort of assemblies that I experienced at a local authority secondary modern school in the 1960s. Every morning the whole school gathered, we sang a hymn, said prayers and listened to a teacher giving a short homily on something that might or might not be based on a Bible story. We then heard school notices and were, often as not, berated about something by the headmaster. We were virtually all white and for most of us Christianity was the only religion we knew.

In the cultural context of the 1940s, there was little opposition to the idea that RE meant Christian education, and worship was Christian worship. The post-war growth in multiculturalism and secularism would severely test those assumptions and make the Christian-centric nature of education appear anachronistic. Nonetheless, the widespread reforms introduced by the Thatcher Conservative governments in the 1980s held onto the traditional practice of school assemblies being essentially a focus of Christian worship. The Education Reform Act 1988, to the dismay of many teachers and delight of many traditionalists, specifically required that 'all pupils in attendance at a maintained school shall on each school day take part in an act of collective worship' and that worship would be 'wholly or mainly of a broadly Christian character' (ERA, 1988), a stipulation that remains in place today (Cumper & Mawhinney, 2015). For Church of England schools, an overtly Christian orientation might seem to be in line with what they would want to do anyway, but this is not always the case, particularly in voluntary-controlled schools. The tendency to reduce the ethos of Church schools to a general ideology to suit everyone, at the expense of specifically Christian ideas, has been noted by a number of reports and individual commentators (Church Schools Review Group, 2001; Cox, 2011; Jelfs, 2013).

In the years after the 1944 reforms, many church schools developed a reputation for high standards of teaching and behaviour, making them attractive to parents and often oversubscribed. At primary level, church schools would often take all pupils from their parish or catchment area if they could, and only apply faith-based selection criteria to additional places if they were oversubscribed. Church secondary schools were often oversubscribed and many applied some faith-based selection criteria. Parish priests became used to parents suddenly appearing in church at certain times of year, asking for a letter of support in order to get their children into a particularly popular school. The perceived high standard of church schools is perhaps one reason why successive governments encouraged the dual system to continue, but it is also one reason why they have attracted criticism. Some who would want churches to continue to have a role in running schools would nonetheless like to remove any selection of pupils that uses faith-based criteria.

The first *Church Times* survey coincided with a major review of Church of England schools commissioned by the Archbishop's Council in 2000 and chaired by Lord Dearing. At that time the system was much as it had been for the previous few decades: there was a mix of voluntary-aided and voluntary-controlled schools (with about 44% being aided rather than controlled), and over 95% of Church of England schools were in the primary rather than secondary sector. The review group report, which was widely welcomed, made a number of key recommendations (Church Schools Review Group, 2001). The main thrust was to emphasize the importance of schools as part of the mission of the Church and therefore to suggest an expansion of church schools. The dearth of secondary-level church schools was seen as a particular problem, and the report set an ambitious target of creating around 100 new church secondary schools over a ten-year period. The cost was estimated to some £25 million, which would need to be found by a national fund-raising campaign. This sort of expansion would have seemed impossible to an earlier generation that had handed over control of impoverished schools to the government in 1944. By the turn of the century, however, the educational landscape in England was changing, and successive governments had laid the groundwork that would allow a new system of funding and controlling schools. In the following decade, these changes began to make a real difference to the involvement of faith groups in education, and the Church of England has not been slow to take advantage of the new climate.

Changes in the Funding of Education from 1988

Most commentators trace the beginnings of the current education funding system to the Thatcher governments of the 1980s, which strove to push up standards and to introduce diversity and choice (Chitty & Dunford, 1999; West & Bailey, 2013). The term 'neoliberalism' is often used in the context of these changes to describe an ideology that favours the corporatization and commercialization of state institutions, something that has been evident in the field of education for some time (Jones, 2016). The key change introduced by the Conservative government's Education Reform Act 1988 was to encourage schools to opt out of LEA control and be funded directly by grants from central government. The creation of City Technology Colleges (CTCs) went a step further by envisaging schools that were created by private sponsors who would help to build specialist schools in poorly performing urban areas and then receive central government funding for the running costs (West & Bailey, 2013). Crucially, these schools were free to set their own curriculum and admissions policy, thereby creating a precedent that some saw as dangerously divisive. The CTC programme was not a great success, failing to attract many private sponsors from industry, though one notable sponsor was Peter Vardy, a Christian entrepreneur from Gateshead, who worked with a group of Evangelicals to set up the Emmanuel CTC (Walford, 2008). Here was a model for the way that religious groups might work in partnership with the state to promote schools with a particular ethos that could influence the lives of pupils (see, e.g., Burn, 2001, who was headteacher at Emmanuel CTC).

The crucial impetus for change along the lines created by Thatcherism came from New Labour under Tony Blair. His focus on education and the need to drive up standards meant that more direct government funding became available to enable schools to change, especially those who were deemed to be underperforming. The specialist school programme, whereby schools could become centres of excellence in particular curriculum areas (and receive extra government funding), was expanded so that by 2010 nearly 9 out of 10 secondary schools had achieved that status (West & Bailey, 2013). In 2000, Labour revived the CTC idea into what became City Academies, and then simply 'academies'. Levels of government support were increased, and the restriction on a technology focus was relaxed, paving the way for a range of interest groups to become involved in sponsoring school education. Geoffrey Walford (2008) has argued that Blair's own Christian faith and his view that religious faith should have a central role in society were important factors in encouraging faith-based organizations to sponsor academies. The rise of academies was further driven by the Conservative Liberal-Democrat coalition government's Academies Act 2010, which moved the focus away from converting just underperforming schools and which made it much easier for schools to convert to academies. Primary schools were then included in the scheme, which was by then an intention to bypass LEAs altogether and move all schools to the new funding model. The size of primary schools meant that few could operate as independent academies, so the notion of 'Multi Academy Trusts' became commonplace as a way of schools sharing overall governance and leadership. The result was that by 2012 some 41% of secondary schools were academies (West & Bailey, 2013). Academies are non-fee-paying schools that are state funded but independent of local authorities. Each academy operates according its particular funding agreement, which usually allows them to decide how to prioritize applications if they are oversubscribed. Academies do not have to follow the national curriculum and are responsible for hiring and employing staff.

Churches and other religious groups have generally been encouraged to act as sponsors for academies (Department for Education, 2016), though, as we shall see, the very existence of faith-based schools has been strongly opposed by some. The Church of England has used the funding system to its advantage in recent years to promote the aims of the Dearing report that were related to growing the number of church secondary schools and to increasing the Church's role in education. To date, the main changes have been to encourage church schools to convert to academy status: by 2018, there were 656 such 'converter academies', 88 of which were secondary schools. Specifically sponsoring academies gives the Church more control over the content of teaching than is the case in converter academies, and the Church of England was also involved in 250 sponsored academies, 42 of which were secondary schools (Church of England, 2018). The opportunities to shape the nature of education by being involved in the academy system were apparent from early on (Chadwick, 2001; Hand, 2012), and when the Church formulated a new vision for education, it was deeply informed by its values and theology, rather than simply by more secular visions that focus on intellectual attainment (Church of England, 2016). One development which emerged alongside the move to academies was the notion of 'free schools', which were academies that started as new state schools that were also outside local authority control. Some of these were designated 'faith schools' and allowed to give priority to children from particular faith backgrounds if they were oversubscribed. The Church of England had opened ten such schools by 2016 (Sherwood, 2016).

The move towards diversity in the schools sector, with more direct state funding of schools that are managed by independent trusts, has opened the way for the Church of England to regain some of the influence it lost over education in the latter part of the twentieth century. At the same time, the changed cultural context of the UK has meant that a door has opened for other religions to set up free schools. Changes that were primarily aimed at improving educational standards have also enabled particularity and specialization across more than just academic subjects. Over the period of the *Church Times* surveys the issue of faith and schools came under political and academic scrutiny as never before. Understanding some of the arguments in this debate will help to interpret the survey results.

Opposition to Church (Faith) Schools

The arguments for and against state-funded faith schools have been well rehearsed elsewhere (Berkeley, 2008; Cairns, 2009; Cairns, Lawton, & Gardner, 2005; Jackson, 2003; King, 2010), and there was a particular urgency to the question in the period between the two *Church Times* surveys. Some of the reasons for opposing such schools are long-standing ideological objections from secularists who see no place for the state sponsoring the mission and proselytizing of religions, or from liberals who are concerned about the threat to the autonomy of pupils who might be exposed to limited and particular opinions in schools that are tied to a particular faith (MacMullen, 2007). The notion that school segregation by faith might pose a particular problem for social cohesion became especially important in the first decade of this century. In the summer of 2001 there were riots in northern towns such as Bradford, Burnley and Oldham which arose out racial tensions between Asian and white communities (Cantle, 2001). Four years later the 7/7 bombings in London, which were perpetrated by extremist Muslims who were born and grew up in England, further heightened awareness of the difficulties of creating a society where people of all faiths and no faiths could live together in peace (Abbas, 2007; Modood, 2005). From 2005, the perception of a threat from homegrown Islamic extremism heightened tensions and negatively impacted on the perception of Islam (Hussain & Bagguley, 2012; Van de Vyver, Houston, Abrams, & Vasiljevic, 2016). There was a tendency to link issues of social cohesion with preventing violent extremism, which was focused particularly on Muslim communities (Dwyer & Parutis, 2013).

This context has shaped perceptions of faith schools in some quarters. The link between schools segregated by faith and a breakdown in social relationships was picked up in a report by the Runnymede Trust (Berkeley, 2008). The report was pessimistic about the ability of faith schools to encourage a sense of belonging in society generally, to develop a positive appreciation of diversity, to remove barriers to equality, or to build partnerships between people of different backgrounds. The history of segregated Catholic and Protestant schools in Northern Ireland seemed to be the paradigm for the way that faith-based schools can perpetuate religious and ethnic divisions in wider society. On that basis the report recommended that faith-based selection in schools should be abolished and that RE should follow a prescribed common curriculum. Around the same time, the fear that some schools might be inculcating values on children that were at odds with those assumed to be part of a liberal democracy led the Department of Education to insist that teachers should not undermine the 'fundamental British values' of democracy, the rule of law, individual liberty, mutual respect and tolerance of those with different faiths or beliefs (Elton-Chalcraft, Lander, Revell, Warner, & Whitworth, 2017). Schools became a focus in the battle to preserve these values, and schools with a religious character came under particular scrutiny.

The underlying assumption that faith schools are incapable of promoting social cohesion while holding onto a distinctive religious tradition has been questioned by some (Everett, 2013; Halstead & McLaughlin, 2005) and refuted by some empirical studies (Dwyer & Parutis, 2013; Francis & Village, 2014). Traditionally, most Church of England schools have tended to have open admission policies that reflect an ethos of serving their local communities by offering education within a particular moral framework. In general, this looks distinctly different from the sort narrow sectarianism that some seem to associate with faith-based schools. However, the ability of some academies and free schools to create greater religious distinctiveness does raise questions about where this might lead and whether is it good for the nation as a whole. It offers the Church more opportunities to control the ethos and distinctiveness of its schools, but could also lead Church of England schools to become more narrowly denominationally focused and less useful as instruments of mass education. So the question remains as to whether or not the Church should be investing more money and effort in creating church schools.

Church Schools in the Church Times Surveys

The two *Church Times* surveys contained several items related to the place of Christianity in schools generally and to the place of church schools in particular. Two items referred to who should pay for church schools ('The Church of England should fund more schools' and 'I am in favour of state-funded church schools'), the former being particularly relevant to the proposals of the Dearing report, which emerged around the time of the first survey. The other items were about the place and nature of religion in schools: 'Religious education should be taught in all schools', 'Religious education in schools should teach only about Christianity' and 'Schools should hold a religious assembly every day'. Given the growing debate about pluralism and multiculturalism in British society in the decade covered by the surveys, it would be interesting to see if there was a declining appetite for maintaining traditional links between Christianity and the educational system.

EXPLORING THE DATA

Virtually everyone (94%) in both surveys agreed that RE should be taught in schools, and there was also very strong support (85%) for state-funded church schools. In contrast, very few people (7% across both surveys) supported the idea that RE in schools should teach only Christianity. Opinions changed little from 2001 to 2013: there was a slight increase in support for teaching RE in all schools (93–95%), a slight decline in support for state-funded church schools (86–84%), and a decline in support for teaching only Christianity (9–6%). The other two items in the survey had less universal support or rejection, making the patterns of difference and change more useful to explore in detail.

The Church of England Should Fund More Schools

Overall, support for this idea was high (72% across both surveys), with relatively little difference between groups (Fig. 10.1). There was no significant difference by sex, location or between clergy and laity. Those aged 70 or older were slightly more likely to support funding schools than were the younger age groups (75% versus 71%), as were those without degrees (74%) compared to those with degrees (70%). Anglo-catholics (73%) and Evangelicals (75%) showed more support than those

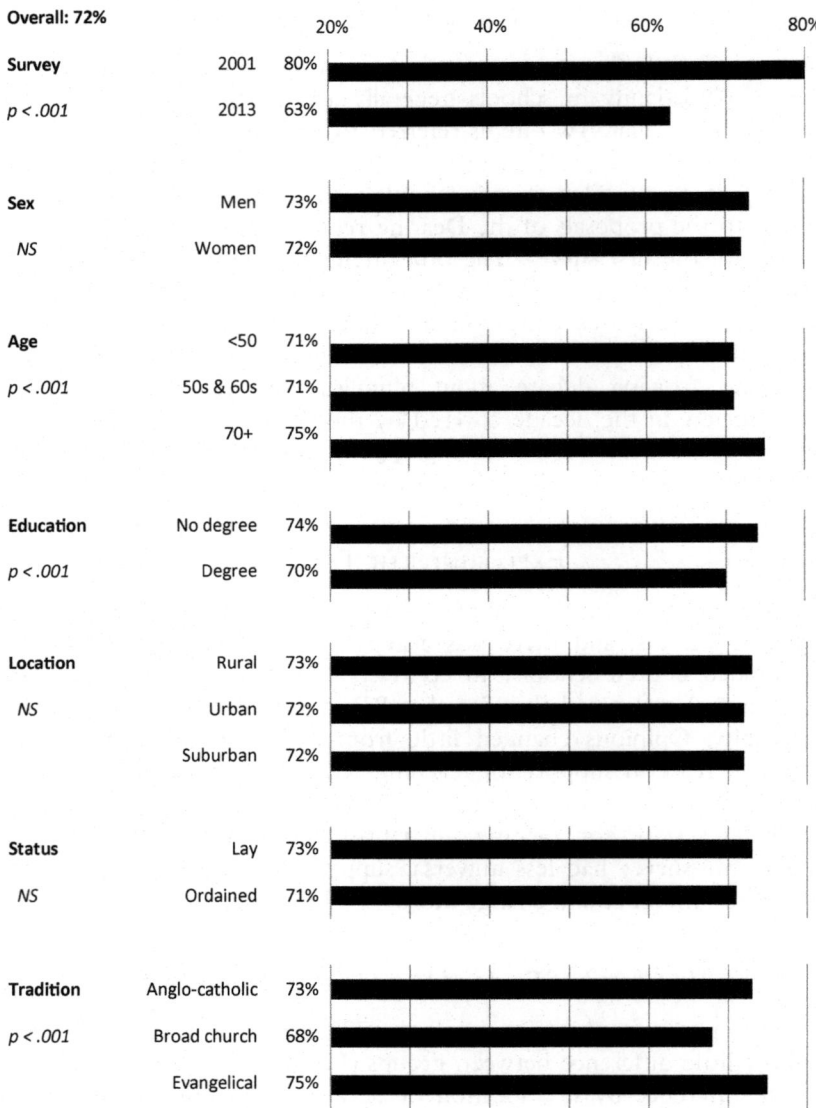

Fig. 10.1 The Church of England should fund more schools: estimated means

in the Broad church (68%), but this difference was dependent on some marked changes in cohorts between the two surveys (Fig. 10.2). The decline in support for funding schools was marked (80% in 2001 to 63% in 2013) and resulted in a different picture between traditions. In 2001, there was little difference between the three traditions, and little systematic difference with age: across the age cohorts, Anglo-catholic support was 79–87%, Broad church 69–83% and Evangelical 71–87%. By 2013, support had declined in most cohorts, but especially those born before the 1960s. It was in the younger cohorts that changes were most intriguing. Younger Anglo-catholics showed a smaller decline in support, so by 2013 they were more likely to be in favour of funding church schools than their older counterparts. Among the other two traditions the opposite was true, with a marked fall in support among more recent birth cohorts, so here the age trend was in the opposite direction compared to Anglo-catholics. As a result, by 2013 older Evangelicals were more supportive than equivalent cohorts in the other two traditions, whereas younger Anglo-catholics were more supportive than equivalent cohorts in the other two traditions.

Schools Should Hold Religious Assemblies Every Day

This item echoed some specific requirements of the 1944 and 1988 education acts, which were still in force when both surveys took place. It showed less overall support than the previous item (66%) and there were more differences between groups, apart from men and women, where there was no difference (Fig. 10.3). Those aged 70 or older were more supportive of the idea than those under 50 (72% versus 57%), as were those without degrees compared with graduates (71% versus 61%). Those who lived in rural areas were slightly more in favour than those who lived elsewhere (69% versus 64%) as were lay people compared with clergy (68% versus 64%). The difference with tradition again saw least support among the Broad church (61%) compared with the other two traditions (68%). There was a slight decline in support between surveys (67–64%), which cohort analysis suggested was most evident among older Anglo-catholics and younger Evangelicals, with little change among the Broad church (Fig. 10.4).

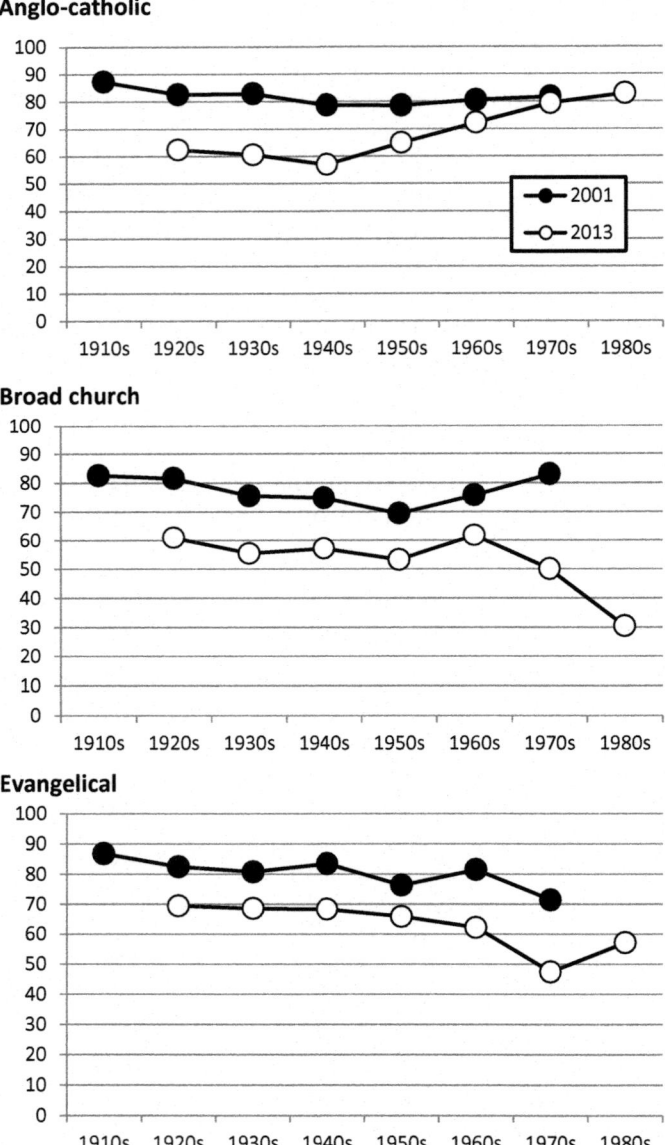

Fig. 10.2 The Church of England should fund more schools: cohort changes

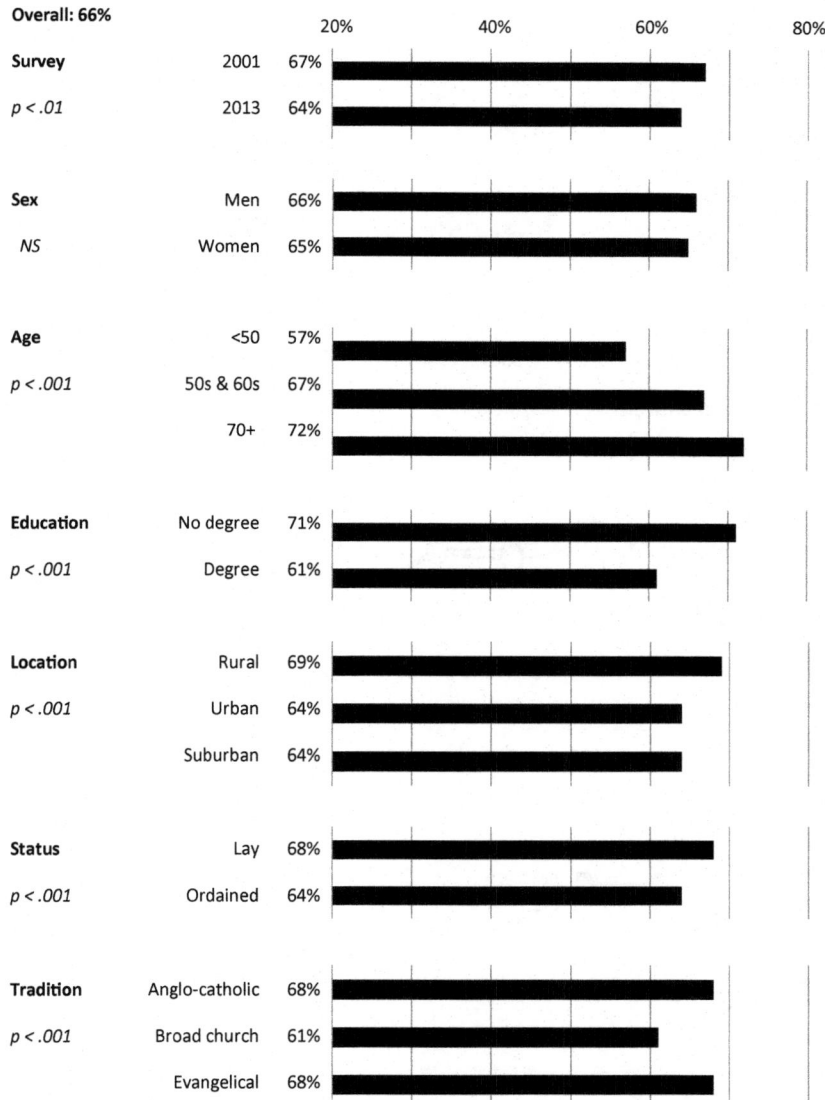

Fig. 10.3   Schools should hold religious assemblies every day: estimated means

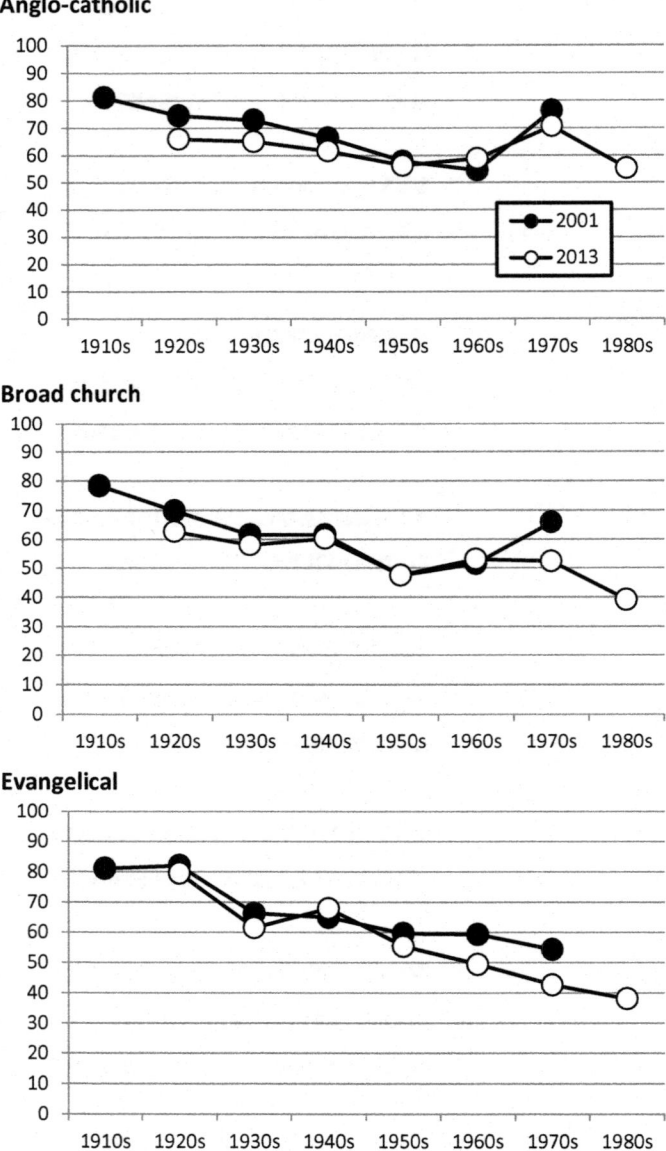

Fig. 10.4   Schools should hold religious assemblies every day: cohort changes

CONCLUSIONS

The first thing to note about the survey results is the very high level of support for the idea that RE should be taught in schools, and the very low level of support for the idea that this should be only about Christianity. Hardly surprising to those who know the Church of England, but useful to show that a sample of what must some of the more committed members of the Church hold the view that knowing about religion is important, and that learning about other faiths is also important. More detailed explorations of this issue have looked at the impact on children of teaching them about many different faiths, rather than just one. To teach just Christianity may inculcate children to the idea that it is the only religion, or at least the 'normative' religion against which others are to be judged. Introducing children to the idea that Christianity is one of many religions, and that religious faith is one of many different worldviews, may prepare them better for life in multicultural Britain in the twenty-first century. While some argue that this is important even from an early age, Ian MacMullen (2007) takes a slightly different view. Although he is strongly in favour of allowing pupils to make critically informed choices about religion (as part of the desire to develop their autonomy), he also accepts that younger children are not capable of dealing with the intellectual demands of weighing the different perceptions and beliefs of multiple religions. Instead, he argues for a limited selection of religions (no more than three) to be taught at primary level, leaving the broader picture until secondary school, where pupils should be more able to critically weigh the beliefs of multiple religions. This seems sensible from the standpoint of someone who wishes to engage with religion intellectually and critically, but it does not address the issue of positionality, which is so crucial for church schools. Part of what it means to be a church school is to teach about religion from a standpoint that is unashamed to privilege Christian belief and Christian moral values.

The advent of church-sponsored academies and free schools raises the possibility that the RE syllabus in church schools could become more exclusively Christian than it might have been under previous arrangements.[2] The move to academies was only just beginning to take hold in

[2] Schools under LEA control must deliver an 'agreed syllabus' on RE, which is monitored by the Standing Advisory Council of Religious Education (SACRE). Free Schools and academies are required in law to provide RE and collective worship. Academies with a faith designation must provide RE in accordance with their designated faith, but could use the agreed syllabus. Voluntary controlled schools that convert to academies must use the agreed syllabus, but could switch to RE based on their faith designation if parents agree to this.

2013, and the implications of this change of church-school RE syllabuses may take some years to emerge. On the current evidence, there is little appetite for restricting teaching to just Christianity, but any future surveys on this topic may need to take account of the changing context in which religion will be taught in schools over the next decade or so.

Support for schools holding religious assemblies every day was much lower than for teaching RE, but still gained two-thirds support overall. It is perhaps on this issue that the Christian tradition that lies behind the English schools system is most evident. When the question 'Do you think the requirement to provide a daily act of collective worship in schools should be enforced?' was asked of the general public in England in 2011, only 36% said yes, though this rose to 51% among those aged 65 or over (ComRes, 2011). The *Church Times* survey (using a slightly different question to the ComRes poll) showed higher levels of support, as might be expected, but similar trends with age, especially among the Broad church and Evangelicals. Younger people may have experienced school assemblies in a context where religion in general, and Christianity in particular, was becoming increasingly at odds with society at large. It was among the younger Evangelicals that support had most obviously eroded between the surveys. This group emerged across the 2013 surveys as being the most conservative, so it is perhaps surprising that they showed such relatively low support for collective acts of worship in schools. It might be that the content of such worship, which tends towards secular humanism, might be seen to be doing more harm than good if it fails to promote Christianity in a particular conservative Protestant mould. Herein is the conundrum for Evangelicals who feel that exposing young people to 'civic' Christianity can inoculate them against its radical call to personal and total commitment to Christ. Against this would be the view that in a country that is still emerging from its Christian roots it is still appropriate to expose young people to ideas and values that have been so influential on older generations.

There was strong but not universal support for the state funding of church schools. The 15% who did not support the idea were younger people and especially younger Evangelicals in 2013. An analysis of national polling data from 2007 related to faith schools generally found lower support for an item stating 'The government should fund single religion schools if parents want them' (Clements, 2009). Support was higher among those who were most religiously committed, but even among the most committed less than half the sample agreed with the statement. The high support for state funding of church schools in the *Church Times* sample may be because it specifically asked about church schools.

There was slightly less support for the idea that the Church of England should fund more schools, and this support eroded between 2001 and 2013. Without more detailed questions (not possible in a survey of this type) it is hard to know for sure what caused this general decline. The 2008 financial crisis hit parish and diocesan finances, which were in deficit from 2009 to 2011 (Research and Statistics, 2016), so there may have been an enduring sense that extra expenditure in financially strained times was not prudent. The Dearing report had set an ambitious target of raising £25 million in seven years to fund 100 new secondary schools. A report to General Synod in 2011, ten years after the Dearing report, suggested that some seventy schools had received financial support from the fund to develop their Christian ethos, but the amount used to create new schools was not clear because much of it was raised independently to fund new academies (Pritchard, 2011). The report suggested that 54,000 more children were in secondary education in Church of England establishments than in 2001, though how much of this was due to new schools was not specified.

The pattern of change by cohorts suggested that there was more to the change than a simple reluctance to support financial commitment to this work. Anglo-catholics have traditionally supported church schools, more so than Evangelicals who tended to stress the home and Sunday school as the places to foster faith in children (Worsley, 2013). Support declined among older Anglo-catholics between the surveys, but less so among younger cohorts. Support declined among older cohorts in the other two traditions, but the decline was most marked among the younger cohorts. In the emerging generations of the Church of England support among the Broad and Evangelical traditions, which together constitute the majority of clergy and laity, is lower than it ever seems to have been. So at a time when Church sponsorship of academies is growing, giving it greater responsibility and control for schools than it has had for many decades, support for this work may be declining among the rank and file. The very different pattern of involvement with schools that has come with the move to academies may not have fully permeated the Church yet, and it may take some years before the nature of this change is fully understood. If increased control leads to a move away from a typical ethos of 'Christian-civic humanism' and teaching pupils of all faith backgrounds towards an ethos that stresses the distinctive nature of Anglican faith and the need for personal commitment, then it may find more support among those who seemed in this survey to be less enthusiastic about investing in church schools.

REFERENCES

Abbas, T. (2007). Muslim minorities in Britain: Integration, multiculturalism and radicalism in the post-7/7 period. *Journal of Intercultural Studies, 28*(3), 287–300. https://doi.org/10.1080/07256860701429717.

Berkeley, R. (2008). *Right to divide? Faith schools and community cohesion.* London: Runnymede Trust.

Burn, J. (2001). Church schools: A critique of much current practice. In J. Burn & B. Griffiths (Eds.), *Faith in education: The role of the churches in education* (pp. 37–50). London: Civitas.

Cairns, J. (2009). *Faith schools and society: Civilizing the debate.* London: Continuum.

Cairns, J., Lawton, D., & Gardner, R. (2005). *Faith schools: Consensus or conflict?* Abingdon, Oxon: Routledge.

Cantle, T. (2001). *Community cohesion: A report of the independent review team.* London: Home Office.

Chadwick, P. (1997). *Shifting alliances: Church and state in English education.* London: Cassell.

Chadwick, P. (2001). The Anglican perspective on church schools. *Oxford Review of Education, 27*(4), 475–487. https://doi.org/10.1080/03054980120086185.

Chitty, C., & Dunford, J. E. (1999). *State schools: New labour and the conservative legacy.* London: Woburn Press.

Church of England. (2016). *Church of England vision for education: Deeply Christian, serving the common good.* London: Church of England Education Office.

Church of England. (2018). *Church schools and academies.* Retrieved July 17, 2018, from https://www.churchofengland.org/more/education-and-schools/church-schools-and-academies#na.

Church Schools Review Group. (2001). *The way ahead: Church of England schools in the new millennium.* London: Church House Publishing.

Clements, B. (2009). Understanding public attitudes in Britain towards faith schools. *British Educational Research Journal, 36*(6), 953–973. https://doi.org/10.1080/01411920903275873.

ComRes. (2011). *Worship in school study.* Retrieved July 19, 2018, from http://www.comresglobal.com/wp-content/themes/comres/poll/BBC_Religion_Worship_in_schools_results_(plus_regions)_July11.pdf.

Cox, J. (2011). *More than caring and sharing: Making a church school distinctive.* Stowmarket: Kevin Mayhew.

Cumper, P., & Mawhinney, A. (2015). *Collective worship and religious observance in schools: An evaluation of law and policy in the UK.* AHRC (Online).

Department for Education. (2016). *Memorandum of understanding between the National Society and the Department for Education.* London: Department for Education.

Dwyer, C., & Parutis, V. (2013). 'Faith in the system?' State-funded faith schools in England and the contested parameters of community cohesion. *Transactions of the Institute of British Geographers, 38*(2), 267–284. https://doi.org/10.1111/j.1475-5661.2012.00518.x.

Elton-Chalcraft, S., Lander, V., Revell, L., Warner, D., & Whitworth, L. (2017). To promote, or not to promote fundamental British values? Teachers' standards, diversity and teacher education. *British Educational Research Journal, 43*(1), 29–48. https://doi.org/10.1002/berj.3253.

ERA. (1988). *Education Reform Act 1988.* Retrieved July 19, 2018, from http://www.legislation.gov.uk/ukpga/1988/40/pdfs/ukpga_19880040_en.pdf.

Everett, H. (2013). Can church schools promote tolerance in the twenty-first century? In H. J. Worsley (Ed.), *Anglican church school education: Moving beyond the first two hundred years* (pp. 209–222). London: Bloomsbury.

Francis, L. J., & Village, A. (2014). Church schools preparing adolescents for living in a religiously diverse society: An empirical enquiry in England and Wales. *Religious Education, 109*(3), 264–283. https://doi.org/10.1080/00344087.2014.911623.

Halstead, J. M., & McLaughlin, T. (2005). Are faith schools divisive? In J. Cairns, D. Lawton, & R. Gardner (Eds.), *Faith schools: Consensus or conflict?* (pp. 61–73). Abingdon, Oxon: Routledge.

Hand, M. (2012). A new dawn for faith-based education? Opportunities for religious organisations in the UK's new school system. *Journal of Philosophy of Education, 46*(4), 546–559. https://doi.org/10.1111/j.1467-9752.2012.00878.x.

Hussain, Y., & Bagguley, P. (2012). Securitized citizens: Islamophobia, racism and the 7/7 London bombings. *The Sociological Review, 60*(4), 715–734. https://doi.org/10.1111/j.1467-954X.2012.02130.x.

Jackson, R. (2003). Should the state fund faith based schools? A review of the arguments. *British Journal of Religious Education, 25*(2), 89–102. https://doi.org/10.1080/0141620030250202.

Jelfs, H. (2013). Religious character in Church of England schools: The relationship between a religious tradition and its educational institutions. *Journal of Research on Christian Education, 22*(1), 52–74. https://doi.org/10.1080/10656219.2013.768170.

Jones, K. (2016). *Education in Britain: 1944 to the present* (2nd ed.). Cambridge, UK: Polity Press.

King, C. (2010). Faith schools in pluralistic Britain: Debate, discussion, and considerations. *Journal of Contemporary Religion, 25*(2), 281–299. https://doi.org/10.1080/13537901003750977.

MacMullen, I. (2007). *Faith in schools? Autonomy, citizenship, and religious education in the liberal state.* Princeton, NJ: Princeton University Press.

Modood, T. (2005). Remaking multiculturalism after 7/7. *Open Democracy.* Retrieved July 17, 2018, from https://www.opendemocracy.net/conflict-terrorism/multiculturalism_2879.jsp.

Murphy, J. (1971). *Church, state and schools in Britain, 1800–1970.* London: Routledge & Kegan Paul.

Pritchard, J. (2011). *Education and the church: Into the next 200 years.* London: Church of England.

Research and Statistics. (2016). *Parish finance statistics 2014.* London: Archbishops' Council.

Sherwood, H. (2016, July 10). Church of England is bidding to open scores of free schools. *The Guardian.* Retrieved from https://www.theguardian.com/education/2016/jul/10/church-of-england-bidding-open-free-schools.

Sundermann, E. L. (2015). *For God and country: Butler's 1944 Education Act.* Newcastle upon Tyne: Cambridge Scholars Publishing.

Van de Vyver, J., Houston, D. M., Abrams, D., & Vasiljevic, M. (2016). Boosting belligerence: How the July 7, 2005, London bombings affected liberals' moral foundations and prejudice. *Psychological Science, 27*(2), 169–177. https://doi.org/10.1177/0956797615615584.

Walford, G. (2008). Faith-based schools in England after ten years of Tony Blair. *Oxford Review of Education, 34*(6), 689–699. https://doi.org/10.1080/03054980802518896.

West, A., & Bailey, E. (2013). The development of the academies programme: 'Privatising' school-based education in England 1986–2013. *British Journal of Educational Studies, 61*(2), 137–159. https://doi.org/10.1080/00071005.2013.789480.

Worsley, H. J. (2013). High Church and Evangelical legacies to mission in church schools. In H. J. Worsley (Ed.), *Anglican church school education: Moving beyond the first two hundred years* (pp. 27–42). London: Bloomsbury.

CHAPTER 11

Conclusions

This book has reported on 28 items that were part of both the 2001 and 2013 *Church Times* surveys. The main chapters dealt with particular items related to the same topic and showed how the level of agreement with the item varied between different categories in groups defined by sex, age, education, location, ordination status and church tradition. This final chapter first looks at the results from a slightly different perspective by taking each of these groups in turn and asking what the results tell us about the nature of differences between categories in this group. For example, in general how much did men differ from women and was there a pattern in the direction of these differences? The chapter then looks at how far things changed between the two surveys and what the trajectory of change suggests for the Church of England over the next few decades.

DIFFERENCES BETWEEN CATEGORIES

The differences between categories within groups are shown in Table 11.1. As was found for the 2001 survey (Francis, Robbins, & Astley, 2005), in most groups there were significant differences between categories. The additional data for 2013 suggested that in most cases these differences persisted over the decade or so between the surveys. In many cases, the extent of the differences was not large in absolute terms, and the high level of statistical significance tends to reflect the large

© The Author(s) 2018
A. Village, *The Church of England
in the First Decade of the 21st Century,*
https://doi.org/10.1007/978-3-030-04528-9_11

Table 11.1 Summary of differences in percentage endorsement between categories for items in the *Church Times* surveys

Figures	Item	Survey		Sex		Age			Degree		Location			Status		Tradition		
	Group: Category:	2001	2013	M	F	<50	50-60	70+	No	Yes	R	U	S	L	O	AC	BC	EV
3.1	Jesus rose physically from the dead	-	+	-	+	+++	0	0	+++	---						0	0	+++
3.3	Hell really exists	+++	---	+++	---	+++	0	---	+++	---			+			0	0	+++
3.5	Christianity is the only true religion	+	-	+++	---	0	0	+++	+++	---	-	0				0	0	+++
3.7	All religions are of equal value	---	+++	-	+	+++	0	---	+++	---				+++	---	+++	0	---
3.8	All living things evolved	---	+++	-	+	-	+	0	---	+++						0	0	---
3.10	The Bible contains some human errors	---	+++	-	+	---	0	0	---	+++				---	+++	0	0	---
4.1	It is wrong for men and women to have sex before marriage	+++	---	+++	---	---	0	+++	++	--						0	0	+++
4.4	I am in favour of divorced people being married in church	---	+++		+++	+++	0	---	---	+++				---	+++	0	+++	0
4.6	I am in favour of divorced and remarried bishops	---	+++		+++	+++	0	---	---	+++				---	+++	0	+++	---

(continued)

Table 11.1 (continued)

Figures	Item	Group: Category:	Survey 2001	2013	Sex M	F	Age <50	50-60	70+	Degree No	Yes	Location R	U	S	Status L	O	Tradition AC	BC	EV
5.2	I am in favour of the ordination of women as priests		---	+++	---	+++	+++	0	---	---	+++				---	+++	----	+++	0
5.4	I am in favour of the ordination of women as bishops		---	+++	---	+++	+++	0	---	---	+++				---	+++	----	+++	0
6.2	It is wrong for people of the same gender to have sex		+++	---	+++	---	---	0	+++	+++	---				+++	---	----	0	+++
6.4	I am in favour of the ordination of practicing homosexuals as priests		---	+++	---	+++	+++	0	---	---	+++	---	0	+++	---	+++	+++	0	---
7.1	I have confidence in the leadership given by my diocesan bishop		+++	---	---	+++	---	0	+++			+	0	-	---	+++	----	0	0
7.3	I have confidence in the leadership given by the Archbishop of Canterbury		---	+++	---	+++	---	0	+++						---	++	----	0	+++
7.5	I have confidence in the leadership given by General Synod		+++	---	---	+++	---	0	+++	+++	---				-	+	----	0	+++

(continued)

Table 11.1 (continued)

Figures	Item	Survey		Sex		Age			Degree		Location			Status		Tradition		
Category:		2001	2013	M	F	<50	50-60	70+	No	Yes	R	U	S	L	O	AC	BC	EV
8.1	I would welcome more opportunities to learn about Christianity	---	+++	---	+++	+++	0	---	+	-				+	-	0	---	+++
8.3	I am growing in my Christian faith	+++	---	---	+++	0	0	---						---	+++	---	0	+++
8.5	I feel confident at explaining my faith to other people			+	-	+++	0	---	---	+++				---	+++	0	0	+++
9.1	I feel a strong sense of belonging to my church					---	0	+++								0	-	0
9.2	My church is important for my social life	---	+++			---	0	+++	+++	---				+++	---	0	0	+++
9.4	Members of my church care deeply for one another	---	++	---	+++	---	0	+++	+++	---				---	+++	0	0	+++
9.6	Average number of church roles			---	+++	0	+++	---			+++	0	0	Lay only		---	0	+++
9.7	I can influence my church's decisions			++	--	0	0	---	---	+++	+++	0	0	---	+++	---	0	+++
9.9	Average number of lay leadership roles					0	+++	---		+++	+++	0	0	Lay only		---	0	+++

(continued)

Table 11.1 (continued)

Figures	Item	Survey 2001	Survey 2013	Sex M	Sex F	Age <50	Age 50–60	Age 70+	Degree No	Degree Yes	Location R	Location U	Location S	Status L	Status O	Tradition AC	Tradition BC	Tradition EV
	Group: Category:																	
9.10	Average number of unpaid roles beyond church	---	+++			0	+++	0	---	+++	+++	---	0	Lay only		0	+++	---
10.1	The Church of England should fund more schools	+++	---			0	0	+++	+++	---						0	---	+++
10.3	Schools should hold religious assemblies every day	++	---			---	0	+++	+++	---	+++	0	0	+++	---	0	---	0

Note Table shows the direction of difference (+ or −) and the significance of the difference (+ = $p < .05$; ++ = $p < .01$; +++ = $p < .001$); blank group = no significant difference between categories. For groups with three categories, the table shows which categories scored significantly above (+) or below (−) the average (0) score. Sex: M = Male, F = Female; Location: R = Rural, U = Urban, S = Suburban; Tradition: AC = Anglo-catholic, BC = Broad church, EV = Evangelical

samples involved in the surveys. In other words, even if there was only a small difference between categories in the percentage of people endorsing the item, the large samples made it very unlikely that this difference was just a chance effect. These are small but real differences that suggest something is happening to cause this division of opinion. The nature of the statistical analyses underlying the tables ruled out the possibility that differences in a group were simply because of associations in distributions between groups. In other words, any difference between say clergy and laity could not be explained simply because the majority of clergy were men and the majority of laity were women.

Difference Between Women and Men

There were significant differences between the sexes in 19 of the 28 items tested. Sociologists and psychologists have long noted a widespread difference in religiosity between men and women in most Christian cultures (Francis, 1997; Loewenthal, MacLeod, & Cinnirella, 2002; Trzebiatowska & Bruce, 2014). Surveys suggest women are more likely than men to affiliate as Christian, to attend services, and to assent to core religious beliefs. In Church of England congregations, there are, on average, about twice as many women as men (Archbishops' Council, 2007). Explanations for the greater religiosity of women vary from those based on innate psychological preferences that predispose women to the ethos and activities associated with church, to those that attribute the difference to socialization and gender roles. Whatever the underlying cause of the difference, it seemed to emerge in the surveys. Among the laity, women had more church roles, on average, than did men, but there was no sex difference when it came to leadership roles or volunteering outside church. Women were less likely than men to feel that they had influence over church decisions, even though they seemed to be more active in the life of their congregations. There was an echo of this in Chapter 8, where women seemed more open to learning opportunities and more often felt they were growing in their faith, but were less confident in explaining their faith to others. Despite this, there was no difference in sense of belonging or in the importance of church to a person's social life. This may be a case of the persistence of gender roles, whereby men gain their sense of belonging through believing that they have some control over what goes on in their church, whereas women belong through active service that may not carry much influence in terms of leadership as traditionally understood. There was evidence that men may be resisting the gender change in leadership, insofar as they were less likely to be in favour of women priests or women bishops than were women.

When it came to beliefs and moral attitudes, women seemed generally to be more liberal than men, being more open to same-sex relationships and sex outside marriage, and less likely to believe that hell exists. This more 'tenderminded' attitude is generally associated with femininity (Francis & Wilcox, 1997), and a more detailed examination of the 2001 *Church Times* survey data showed how clergywomen tended to have more inclusive views on a wide range of issues than did clergymen (Robbins, 2007). If the growth in the proportion of women clergy continues, it may well be that the Church of England will become generally more inclusive and liberal in outlook, at least in terms of the direction given by local and diocesan leaders. If this marginalizes those who have a more tough-minded stance to faith, it is likely to push the gender ratio among laity further in favour of women in most congregations. This may be less likely to happen in those churches that resist the liberalization of values around sexuality and marriage. There is relatively little study of gender ratios in congregations of different traditions in the Church of England, and this would be a worthwhile issue to explore in more detailed future research.

Age Differences

Considering how important age profiles are for forward planning, there is remarkably little published data for adult lay people in the Church of England. The best there is comes from a large sample of parishes that took part in a 2007 study aimed primarily at examining ethnic diversity (Archbishops' Council, 2007). The survey questionnaire asked for age, but not by decade, making it difficult to compare profiles with other studies. In the sample of about 110,000 adults from across the Church of England, 47% were 65 or older, 21% were 55–64, 13% were 45–54, and 18% were 18–44. Given the likelihood of an ageing profile across the Church since 2007 (see Chapter 2), it is safe to conclude that well over half the laity of the Church of England are now 70 or older, making this the numerically dominant age group. Age was a consistent predictor of variations in attitudes, beliefs and practices, with every one of the 28 items showing some sort of significant difference between the three age groups (<50, 50–60 and 70+). In most cases, the trend was for the under 50s to be at one extreme, the 70+ group at the other and the 50–60 group between these two. In a few cases, it was one group that was different from the other two, who were about the same. The differences with age largely reflect those reported for the 2001 survey (Francis et al., 2005), though the cohort analysis (discussed later in this chapter) suggests that some of the age effects found across the surveys may be changing over time.

Older people felt more at home and were more deeply rooted socially in their church than were younger people. They were less active in terms of belonging to groups or leading activities and less active in volunteering beyond the church. In these aspects, it was the 50- to 60-year-olds who dominated, and this is in line with what is found in many societies when it comes to institutional membership or voluntary activity (Smith, 1994). Middle-aged people may have more time than younger people to be involved, as well as more experience and better networks; older people may have less capacity to help. In the *Church Times* surveys, the 70+ group felt less able to influence what is happening in their church. Older people were less likely to want to learn more about their faith, were less likely to feel they were growing in faith and felt less confident at explaining it to others. They were, however, more confident in the leadership of the Church, be that at local or national level.

The relationship between age and moral attitudes is much as you might expect: the 70+ group was consistently more conservative when it came to attitudes related to marriage, sexuality, the role of women in leadership and church schools. In terms of basic beliefs, the trends were less clear: older people tended to be less religiously plural than younger people, but it was the younger age group who stood out in being more conservative in several core beliefs.

The picture that emerged was of a large majority, the over 70s, for whom church life feels like 'home', but who are slightly less involved in group activities and who have less say in what happens. Looked at another way, younger people are not so strongly hefted to their church, probably do more than older people, though not as much as the middle-aged, but feel they have some influence. To some extent, older people are holding on to tradition, though this may be changing as we shall see when we look at changes between surveys. A key group in terms of running the church are those in their 50s and 60s, who tended to be the most likely to be involved in groups, leadership and voluntary work.

In nearly every case, their attitudes and beliefs fell somewhere between the youngest and oldest age groups. They may, therefore, be key people when it comes to bridging between the sometimes very different outlook of the old and young in the Church.

The Church needs to manage a situation in which there is a mismatch between attitudes, belonging, activity and influence. Keeping congregations comfortable for the social life of the majority (i.e. the elderly) may make it a place that the under 50s find harder to belong to, and which may make them less inclined to shoulder the responsibilities of leadership in middle life. On the other hand, alienating the elderly risks losing those who are most likely to be in church on Sundays. Fresh Expressions has been an attempt to re-engage a new generation, by offering alternative forms of church that may or may not be connected to long-standing congregations. It was noticeable in the survey that younger birth cohorts had shifted so they were more likely agree that church was important for their social life and to agree that their congregations cared deeply for each other, and this might reflect a new context in which the under 50s are building social and caring networks. There was some work on Fresh Expressions as part of the Church Growth Project in 2013 (Church Army's Research Unit, 2013), but more detailed works need to be done to understand whether and how newcomers or their congregations are linking to what is still the majority of the Church laity, the 70+ group.

Education

The measure of an individual's educational experience employed in the two surveys was slightly different because the 2013 survey asked about the highest level of education, whereas the 2001 survey simply asked participants if they held a degree or the equivalent, so this was the measure used here. Graduates were not randomly distributed across the sample: men were more likely than women to have degrees (74% versus 62%) as were the under 50s (83%) compared with those in their 50s or 60s (70%) or those aged 70 or older (58%). The relationship of degree status with age and sex was complicated because in the oldest group men were much more likely to have degrees than women, but this differences had all but disappeared among the under 50s. Clergy were also more likely to have degrees than were lay people (83% versus 63%), and there was a slight difference with location whereby 68% of those in rural areas had degrees compared with 70% in urban areas. The only group with no difference in the proportion of graduates was church tradition, where in all three traditions 68–69% had degrees. These figures are much higher than the population at large, where the proportion of graduates in England in the 2011 National Census was just 27% (ONS, 2012). The proportion of graduates in the workforce rose from 24% in 2002 to 35% in 2013 (ONS, 2017), but in the *Church Times* surveys, there were actually fewer graduates in 2013 (66%) compared with 2001 (70%). This may have reflected the age profile of the Church over this period, with cohorts with low levels of qualifications not being replaced by younger, better qualified people.

After controlling for the differences in graduates in various groups, education remained a significant predictor in 21 of the 28 variables tested. Graduates were generally no more or less likely than others to feel they belonged in their church, though their church was less important for their social life. They had the same average number of church roles or leadership roles as non-graduates, but were more likely to feel they could influence their church's decisions. This may be because graduates have a confidence and articulateness that gives them the ability to influence others, even if they are not as heavily involved in the life of their church. This confidence was apparent in other areas: graduates were less likely to want more opportunities to learn about their faith but more likely to feel confident in explaining their faith to others. Graduates were also more likely to be involved in unpaid roles beyond the church, and this trend for greater volunteerism among the better education seems to be widespread (Smith, 1994). Graduates had similar confidence to non-graduates in the leadership of diocesan bishops or the Archbishop of Canterbury, but less confidence than non-graduates in the leadership of General Synod.

Graduates in the surveys also displayed the sorts of more liberal beliefs and attitudes that are predicted for this group from studies among populations generally (Phelan, Link, Stueve, & Moore, 1995; Reimer, 2010). They expressed more liberal views on things such as the bodily resurrection, existence of hell and biblical inerrancy. They were more willing to accept the ordination of women priests and bishops, and more willing to accept divorce and remarriage, sex outside marriage and same-sex relationships. When it came to schools, they were less enthusiastic about the Church-funding schools or schools having religious assemblies.

In many ways, the graduates in the *Church Times* surveys seemed typical of graduates in the population generally. Their education experience (or perhaps the fact that they had the opportunity to go to university in the first place) may inculcate particular views associated with liberal values that prize reason, inclusivity and personal freedoms. This should not be taken to be true for every graduate in the Church of England, however, because there are an increasing number of studies (including detailed analysis of the data reported here) that show that the effects of education operated differently in different church traditions (Village, 2007a; Village & Baker, 2018). Evangelicals tend to retain their conservative theological, biblical and moral stance whatever their level of education, whereas those from Anglo-catholic or Broad-church traditions tend to be more liberal if they have higher levels of education. In these surveys, for example, when it came to support for ordaining practicing homosexuals as priests, the difference between graduates and non-graduates was greater among Anglo-catholics (47% support among graduates versus 30% among non-graduates) and Broad church (41% versus 28%) than among Evangelicals (10% versus 12%). This pattern was repeated across many of the issues that marked out Evangelicals as being different from the rest of the Church.

Part of what will shape the Church of England in the coming decades will be the rise in the proportion of the general population that has a university education. Those who preach and teach the faith will need to be aware of what this might mean in terms of enabling members of the Church to develop a faith that has meaning and salience in their everyday lives. This will be a task made more complex because of the very different effects of education in different traditions within the Church. In some traditions, education will alter faith perspectives, and those with experience of Higher Education may need to develop faith in a way that coheres with the kind of critical thinking and reasoning they have learnt. Among Evangelicals, however, graduates will need to develop a faith that can make sense of the disconnection between what they would perceive as a 'biblical worldview' and the increasingly liberal and secular world view of English society. For some, this will be about how to make belief meaningful if it seems to be indistinguishable in many ways from the secularism of society at large. For others, it will be about how to make faith reasonable and convincing to unbelievers.

Location

In the latter part of the twentieth century, the Church of England published two seminal reports, *Faith in the City* (Church of England, 1985) and *Faith in the Countryside* (Church of England, 1990), that influenced the Church for the next 25 years or more (Church of England, 2006; Smith & Hopkinson, 2012). Each demonstrated the particular social issues of urban or rural areas, and the specific tasks of ministering in each. The underlying assumptions that developed from these reports are that being a member of the Church in inner cities is very different from being a member in the countryside. It was therefore natural to ask those who took part in the *Church Times* surveys whether they came from urban, suburban or rural areas. As you might expect, the profiles of lay participants differed by location because there was a higher proportion of women, lower proportion aged under 50s, higher proportion aged over 70, lower proportion of Anglo-catholics and higher proportion of Broad church among those from rural areas compared to elsewhere. Most of these trends also held for clergy. These figures may represent something of the different nature of congregations in the countryside compared with inner cities or suburbia. Countryside ministry is certainly different, and this was reflected in the survey data, where rural lay people had more church roles, leadership roles, voluntary roles and influence on their church's decisions than those from other locations. The smaller congregations and fewer clergy per congregation in rural areas clearly have an impact in terms of requiring greater involvement and leadership from lay people.

Despite the different nature of urban and rural parishes, there were very few differences in attitudes and beliefs between locations. Only eight of 28 variables showed any differences, and four of those were ones just mentioned. The others were belief in the existence of hell and being in favour of homosexual priests (less likely in rural areas and more likely in suburban areas), confidence in diocesan bishops (more likely in rural areas and less likely in suburban areas) and religious school assemblies (more likely in rural areas than elsewhere). There was little evidence of greater conservatism among rural people after allowing for the different demographic profile of this group, so location per se did not seem to influence theological or moral beliefs. The exception might be same-sex relationships, which might reflect a generally greater conservatism about sexuality in rural areas, or a difference in the likelihood of encountering homosexual clergy in rural compared with urban environments. The lack of much difference between people living in very different sorts of communities may be testimony to the level of exchange between rural and urban communities, or the effects of improved communications that expose people to ideas and news irrespective of where they live. Those who read the *Church Times* are, by definition, likely to be engaging with the media and to be aware of what is happening beyond their immediate locality, so a different sort of sampling might reveal more attitudinal differences between city and country dwellers.

Ordination Status

As we saw in Chapter 2, clergy and laity in the Church of England have different profiles in terms of the gender balance, age ratios and education levels. Some of the more detailed work on the 2001 survey data has been based just on one group rather than including both clergy and laity (Robbins, 2007; Village & Francis, 2009). In the analyses presented here, I have mostly treated clergy and laity together (apart from when looking at roles within and beyond church), in order to see if their attitudes and opinions varied after allowing for the different profiles of the two groups. There were differences between clergy and laity in 18 of the 25 items tested. The different responses to social life, sense of a caring church and influencing decisions have been discussed in some detail in Chapter 9, which examines the figures for different types of clergy. The trends in other items suggest that clergy have more liberal views than laity when it comes to issues related to divorce and same-sex relationships. Despite lower proportion of women among clergy, clergy were slightly more in favour of women's ordination than were lay people. When it came to basic beliefs, there was relatively little difference between the two groups: clergy were less likely to see all religions as being of equal value and more likely to accept that the Bible includes some human error. Clergy were generally more positive about the hierarchy than were lay people, having greater confidence in the leadership of their diocesan bishop, the Archbishop of Canterbury and (to a lesser extent) the General Synod. They were less keen on schools holding a religious assembly every day, perhaps in the light of experience of seeing what that might entail or having to lead such assemblies themselves.

The picture that emerged is perhaps unsurprising given that clergy are drawn from the laity (and are therefore likely to share similar beliefs and values) but are selected and trained (so their attitudes and beliefs may be shaped by that process). Clergy selected for training have for some years had to accept that the majority of the Church welcomes the ministry of women priests, and it is unlikely that many opposed to women's ministry would offer themselves for ordination in a Church that was clearly moving towards the ordination of women bishops. The analysis of the 2001 survey data noted the disparity between clerical and lay attitudes to the ordination of remarried divorcees or practicing homosexuals: 'In some sense the committed laity may be looking for more conservative standards of sexual behaviour among the clergy than the clergy are looking for among themselves' (Francis et al., 2005, p. 56). The idea that clergy should show stricter moral codes is explicit in official Church documents related to areas such as remarriage and same-sex relationships (House of Bishops, 1991, 1999, 2003). While there may be some logic behind this, it is rather flimsy logic and tends inevitably to erode whatever moral standard it was intended to uphold. Clergy may be the first to see through the pretence of claiming to uphold a moral ideal of marriage while de facto accepting the remarriage of divorcees, or non-celibate same-sex relationships, among lay people.

Church Traditions

Of all the fault lines identified in the 2001 *Church Times* survey, that between Anglo-catholics and Evangelicals was perhaps the starkest (Francis et al., 2005, Chapter 7). The analysis was restricted to clergy and just the two wings of the Church. Here, I have included clergy and laity as well those who fell into the Broad church category. The combined survey data showed significant differences between traditions in all 28 of the items tested. In two cases, the remarriage of divorcees in church and holding religious school assemblies, it was the Broad church that stood out as being, respectively, more in favour and more opposed than were the other two traditions, which scored more or less the same. In all other cases, it was one or both of the two wings of the Church that differed from the Broad Church and/or from each other. Evangelicals showed their theological and moral conservatism in all items related to basic beliefs, marriage and same-sex relationships. Anglo-catholics were more liberal in these matters, being generally similar to those in the Broad church except when it came to same-sex relationships, where they were distinctly more liberal. When it came to the ordination of women, it was the Broad church that was most in favour, the Anglo-catholics who were most opposed, and Evangelicals that fell between these extremes. The surveys give empirical support to the positions that have emerged over the years from people who have spoken on behalf of the various wings of the Church. They give more voice to those who would see themselves as neither Anglo-catholic nor Evangelical. This group perhaps exemplifies the 'via media' that is said to be so characteristic of Anglicanism, but this should not be misunderstood. When it comes to some issues, it is the Broad church that leads the way and calls for radical change in the face of opposition from the two other traditions.

Evangelicals seemed to be more at home in their churches, more active and more comfortable with the leadership of the hierarchy. Anglo-catholics were less comfortable with the leadership, reflecting no doubt their sense of marginalization as issues dear to their heart, notably the ordination of women, moved forward despite their opposition. Some Evangelicals have opposed women's ordination and are even more opposed to ordaining practicing homosexuals, but this has not yet resulted in the same loss of confidence in leadership. This might reflect the fact in both surveys the Archbishop of Canterbury was someone from the Evangelical stable.

Evangelicalism seems to foster the desire to learn about faith and confidence in explaining it. Evangelical lay people were more active within their churches, but less active beyond them, something that has been noted in studies of Evangelicals from other denominations in the USA (Beyerlein & Hipp, 2005, 2006). This may not betoken a dangerous inward-looking attitude, but might reflect the fact that Evangelicals often do work in the community through their church rather than apart from it. It was Broad-church lay people who were most engaged in volunteering beyond their church, perhaps making this part of the Church the best place to foster the current aim of the Church to serve communities for the common good.

THE CHANGING FACE OF THE CHURCH OF ENGLAND

One of the key aims of the study was to see whether and how opinions changed between 2001 and 2013. The changes were examined both overall and by birth cohorts within each of the three traditions. After allowing for the different profiles of the two survey samples, there were significant changes in 23 of the 28 items tested. In some cases, the overall extent of change was relatively small, in others there were major shifts in opinion.

Changes between surveys were sometimes due to changes across the board and sometimes because of change in particular traditions or birth cohorts. This section summarizes the extent of overall change and change within particular birth cohorts for the items reported in Chapters 3–10.

Basic Beliefs

For basic beliefs such as the bodily resurrection and existence of hell, there was a tendency for these to be more likely to be held by younger than older people and, if anything, this difference may have increased between surveys because younger birth cohorts for Anglo-catholics and Broad church seemed to be more orthodox in 2013 than they were in 2001. There was also a marked increase among these two traditions in the proportion that believed Christianity is the only true religion, something that was always believed by younger Evangelicals. This might be the effect of the high and negative profile of Islam in the period between surveys, which may have disproportionately affected younger people. The move to greater acceptance of evolution was marked in all cohorts, even among Evangelicals, where acceptance was generally low. The period between the surveys included celebrations related to Charles Darwin that raised the issue of evolution in the public domain. Younger Evangelicals remained more resistant to accepting evolution than were Evangelicals born before 1960. Beliefs about evolution, creation and the environment are linked to beliefs about the Bible (Village, 2015b), but there was little corresponding reduction in belief about biblical inerrancy in the 2013 survey. The main change was a slightly greater acceptance of the possibility of human errors in the Bible among Evangelicals.

In general, there was relatively little movement in basic beliefs, and the pattern of greater traditional orthodoxy among Evangelicals than among the other traditions remained. This had always been most evident among younger Evangelicals, but the period between the surveys also saw some evidence of increasing orthodoxy among younger people in other traditions. The accommodation to widely held ideas such as evolution was evident, but young Evangelicals remained the least accepting of this idea.

Marriage and Divorce

In the first survey, there was a strong relationship with age in most of these items, with older people in all three traditions being generally more conservative about sex outside marriage, trial marriage or remarriage after divorce. By 2013, there has been some softening of attitudes generally, but most notably among the war and pre-war cohorts. In some cases, as with remarriage in the Anglo-catholic and Broad church traditions, these virtually removed the age effect, so that young and old were equally supportive. Evangelicals remained the most conservative tradition in these matters, but younger cohorts were especially resistant to change, so that the age effect was weakened or in some cases was almost reversed. Although the issues of cohabitation, trial marriage and remarriage after divorce are widely accepted in society and rarely mentioned in Church debates these days, they remain contentious for some. The ideals related to marriage that the Church proclaims are things that some feel should be asserted in practice. The proportions that do so are now relatively small in some traditions, but remain high in some sectors of the Church. Even in 2013, a third of all respondents felt sex before marriage was wrong, and even fewer agreed with trial marriage. Opinion may be liberalizing in these areas, but not as universally as some might imagine.

Women in Leadership

The surveys spanned the time when women priests were becoming commonplace, but the issue of women bishops was contentious and not yet resolved. Acceptance of women priests had been high in 2001 (82%), so it did not have much room to change, though it did increase to 91% by 2013. For women bishops, acceptance was much lower in 2001 (65%) and the shift that much greater (87%). This was due to movement in virtually all birth cohorts as people of all ages came to accept the leadership of women and parish, diocesan and national levels. The one exception was again younger Evangelicals, who if anything seemed to become more opposed as time went by. Anglo-catholics have generally been seen as the most opposed to women's leadership, but most birth cohorts in 2013 were about 80% in favour (on a par with pre-war Evangelical cohorts), and younger cohorts were only slightly less in favour. It may be that the figures reflect an exodus of the most conservative younger Anglo-catholics, whereas younger Evangelicals have remained in the Church.

Sexual Orientation

The patterns of change related to homosexuality were the most dramatic in the survey, as might be expected given the rapid changes in English society in the period between the surveys. Evangelicals have been the strongest objectors to any change in teaching about same-sex relationships, and in 2001, there was uniform opposition across all birth cohorts. By 2013, the pre-war cohorts had again softened a little, but younger cohorts were if anything more opposed. Among the other two traditions, there has been more acceptance, especially by younger people in 2001. Opinion moved dramatically among older birth cohorts by 2013, so that by 2013 only 10–25% of any given cohort would agree that same sex was wrong and 50–80% of any given cohort would be in favour of the ordination of practicing homosexuals as priests. The level of acceptance among some Anglo-catholic cohorts has been even greater than you would expect from their peers in society at large. In contrast, younger Evangelicals are widely at odds with the view of their peers outside the Church.

The Church will soon need to come to terms with the fact that same-sex marriages are now legal in England, Wales and Scotland, so the pressure to allow them to be solemnized in church can only continue to mount. The ability to resist this on theological grounds is weak, given that the Church moved to allow the remarriage of divorcees, something for which the biblical prohibition is if anything more explicit than for same-sex marriages. This issue highlights the impossibility of maintaining an ideal vision (in this case of life-long, monogamous union between a man and a woman) while at the same time accommodating pastorally and liturgically the needs of those who do not fit this ideal pattern. It is quite possible that in the next decade or so the third plank of the marriage ideal, monogamy, will also be challenged if what is now a tiny minority view becomes more mainstream (Jeffries, 2012). If this does happen, it will be interesting to see how far opinion-shifts among churchgoers mirror those that have happened for same-sex unions.

Confidence in Leadership

The picture here was mixed, possibly due to the particular circumstances that surrounded the changes in Archbishop between the surveys. Confidence in the leadership of the Archbishop of Canterbury improved in all three traditions between surveys, but this may have been because there was new and untested person in post in 2013 (Justin Welby) and a battle-weary person in post in 2001 (George Carey). In between times, Rowan Williams had come and gone, and although his legacy remained, it was not clear how far it would have affected this particular item. In contrast, confidence in leadership from other sources fell, especially General Synod. To some extent, this reflected the way that decisions over key issues had gone, with those who opposed change (as in allowing women bishops) having little confidence if Synod was allowing change, and those who wanted change (as in allowing practicing homosexual clergy) having little confidence if Synod blocked change. In some ways, Synod could not win and was bound to upset some whatever it did. More importantly, it points to a decline in collective responsibility, with the rank and file seemingly being less likely to abide by what the majority decides. Depending on your point of view, individual rejection of collective decisions may be a healthy resistance to an heretical consensus for change, or the ungodly triumph of individual self-assertion over the careful discernment of the Body of Christ. When it comes to controversial matters, the Church and the wider Anglican Communion have tried to resist change until there is virtual unanimity, which means upsetting those who long for change and see no good reason for delay. However, it is often necessary to wait until there is overwhelming pressure for change because this suggests grassroots opinion has already made the transition from old to new beliefs. For example, the survey results related to same-sex relationships suggest that those who oppose now are likely to change their opinions in the next decade or, so Synod may be wise to proceed firmly but slowly if it feels that change must come eventually. In the meantime, it must accept the fact that trying to run the Church of England is not likely to endear you to the rank and file whichever way the votes go.

Discipleship

Although the issue of how to create new disciples and support disciples in their journey of faith has been a key one since the turn of the century, it has not resulted in any great changes in items related to this topic. There have been more courses created at diocesan and national level, but the average number of different types of courses attended fell, as did the appetite for more opportunities to learn about Christianity. Alongside, this was a slight fall in the percentage that felt they were growing in their faith. On the positive side, confidence in being able to explain faith to others remained high between the surveys. More detailed study has shown that confidence in faith is shaped by a complex mixture of the 'givens' of personality and the experiences of life, including experience of education for discipleship (Village, 2015a). Understanding how faith is created and nurtured is crucial because it is likely to be something that is changing all the time. The way that the Church promotes Christianity to the public at large must adapt to the way society is now (Graham, 2018), and this may require different sorts of learning opportunities and different ways of speaking about faith.

Belonging, Leading, Serving

The few items that remained constant between surveys were mainly those in Chapter 9, such as sense of belonging, influencing church decisions and the number of roles lay people had in their church. The size of congregations reported by lay people declined slightly between surveys: in 2001, 34% reported their Sunday congregation was less than 50, whereas in 2013 this figure had risen to 40%. With no significant increase in the roles per person, there was no evidence from these data that declining attendance was leading to more work for fewer people. Given that the sample was of committed members of the Church, it was hardly surprising that sense of belonging remained high. Those who feel they do not belong because they disagree with what they hear, or because they have a different personality profile to the majority, may be likely to leave (Francis & Robbins, 2012; Village, 2007b). One interesting change that may be important was a slight trend for church to be a more important part of the social life of younger birth cohorts, especially in Anglo-catholic and Broad churches. It would be useful to know what is causing this shift, and whether or not it reflects changes that have come about through the Fresh Expressions movement. *Church Times* surveys may not be the best way to capture this sort of information, and more detailed study of the social lives of these birth cohorts is needed. There are two sides to having people embed their social life in their church: one side might foster this because it is a context in which to express the reality of being part of the Body of Christ, and all that means in terms of giving and receiving love. The other side might resist this because it can disconnect people from the secular world, thereby making them less able to share their faith with unbelievers. Part of the success of the Alpha programme was based on using converts from one course as leaders on the next because their social networks were still heavily rooted in non-church people (Hunt, 2005a, 2005b).

Church Schools

The period between the surveys saw big changes in the funding of schools in England, to which the Church of England responded by trying to increase the number of church secondary schools (see Chapter 10). This was also the period of the global financial crash in 2008, and the austerity that ensued had a noticeable effect on church finances at parish and national level. Added to this was a growing debate about whether religious schools in general were bad for social cohesion, especially in relation to the growth of schools funded by Muslims. For these reasons, the generally high support for funding more church schools in 2001 had eroded somewhat by 2013 (80–63%). This at a time when the Church was trying to increase the number of church secondary schools, and to take more direct control of existing church schools through the new rules for academies. This might be a case of the Church needing to be more aware of its support base and keep people better informed of the opportunities that arise through changes in the funding rules for schools. The decline in support for funding more church schools was more or less across the board, though less so in younger Anglo-catholic cohorts and more so in younger cohorts of Broad church and Evangelicals. What had been an issue with broad support across the Church is now less supported and may be one where a gap will open up along party lines in the future.

There was a slight decline in support for the rules that insist that schools hold religious assemblies every day, again among more recent cohorts in the Broad church and Evangelical traditions. Younger people were generally unenthusiastic about this idea, and this negative attitude may increase as time goes on. The time may come when the support for this idea is gone even in the Church of England, which would make it seem unviable for society at large. Perhaps the Church should be working proactively to suggest what might be useful legislation to help schools without a religious character to deal with the issues that this rule intended to address. How far is it still appropriate to express corporately in such schools an implicit assumption of religious faith and the values and beliefs of Christianity?

FUTURE SURVEYS IN THE CHURCH OF ENGLAND

The two *Church Times* surveys have proved valuable sources of information about the state of the Church of England at two particular moments in time. The size and complexity of the questionnaires has not prevented a relatively high response rate, and this has allowed not only a detailed snapshot of belief (Francis et al., 2005), but also some more detailed analysis on specific issues (Robbins, 2007; Village, 2011, 2012, 2013, 2015a, 2015c, 2016; Village & Francis, 2008, 2009, 2010). The Church of England has for many years collected a wide range of statistics related to attendance and ministry, but these do not indicate the attitudes and beliefs that are assessed by the *Church Times* surveys. This book has shown how such surveys can give empirical evidence of shifting opinions and changing attitudes in a way that is not possible simply by listening to commentators and those in the hierarchy of the Church. Although some might say the results are in many cases predictable, they do quite often indicate trends that might otherwise have been missed. For example, the repeated pattern of increasing conservatism among younger Evangelicals, in contrast to increasing liberalism in older Evangelicals, is something that may point to important changes that cry out for more detailed investigation.

Future surveys will need to create new items that reflect the changing face of the Church of England in the twenty-first century. More information on Fresh Expressions and updated items related to church schools are just two examples among several others. New moral issues are likely to come to the fore, such as choices for the end of life and the option of having multiple simultaneous marriage partners. At the same time, there is virtue in retaining the same items to see how opinions change over time. If more surveys emerge over several decades, it should be possible to show more clearly how opinions evolve within particular birth cohorts. Another consideration might be to spread the survey more widely beyond the *Church Times* to bolster the sample of those (such as Evangelicals) who are probably under-represented among readers of the newspaper. Having a better idea of what is going on at the grass roots of the Church does not make it easier to decide what to do about the controversial issues that have to be confronted, nor will it of itself reverse the decline in numbers. What it might do is to help the Church reflect better on what it is and what it believes.

References

Archbishops' Council. (2007). *Celebrating diversity in the Church of England*. London: Church of England.

Beyerlein, K., & Hipp, J. R. (2005). Social capital, too much of a good thing? American religious traditions and community crime. *Social Forces, 84*(2), 995–1013. https://doi.org/10.1353/sof.2006.0004.

Beyerlein, K., & Hipp, J. R. (2006). From pews to participation: The effect of congregation activity and context on bridging civic engagement. *Social Problems, 53*(1), 97–117. https://doi.org/10.1525/sp.2006.53.1.97.

Church Army's Research Unit. (2013). *An analysis of Fresh Expressions of Church and church plants begun in the period 1992–2012.* Retrieved November 20, 2014, from http://www.churchgrowthresearch.org.uk/UserFiles/File/Reports/churchgrowthresearch_freshexpressions.pdf.

Church of England. (1985). *Faith in the city: A call for action by church and nation.* London: Church House Publishing.

Church of England. (1990). *Faith in the Countryside.* Worthing: Churchman Publishing.

Church of England. (2006). *Faithful cities: A call for celebration, vision and justice.* Peterborough: Methodist Publishing House.

Francis, L. J. (1997). The psychology of gender differences in religion: A review of empirical research. *Religion, 27*(1), 81–96. https://doi.org/10.1006/reli.1996.0066.

Francis, L. J., & Robbins, M. (2012). Not fitting in and getting out: Psychological type and congregational satisfaction among Anglican churchgoers in England. *Mental Health, Religion & Culture, 15*(10), 1023–1035. https://doi.org/10.1080/13674676.2012.676260.

Francis, L. J., Robbins, M., & Astley, J. (2005). *Fragmented faith? Exposing the fault-lines in the Church of England.* Milton Keynes: Paternoster Press.

Francis, L. J., & Wilcox, C. (1997). The relationship between Eysenck's personality dimensions and Bem's masculinity and femininity scales revisited. *Personality and Individual Differences, 25*(4), 683–687. https://doi.org/10.1016/s0191-8869(98)00085-3.

Graham, E. (2018). How to speak of God? Toward a postsecular apologetics. *Practical Theology, 11*(3), 206–217. https://doi.org/10.1080/1756073x.2018.1460522.

House of Bishops. (1991). *Issues in human sexuality: A statement by the House of Bishops of the General Synod of the Church of England.* London: Church of England.

House of Bishops. (1999). *Marriage: A teaching document.* London: Church of England.

House of Bishops. (2003). *Some issues in human sexuality: A guide to the debate.* London: Church of England.

Hunt, S. (2005a). The alpha course and its critics: An overview of the debates. *PentecoStudies, 4*(1), 1–22.

Hunt, S. (2005b). The Alpha program: Charismatic evangelism for the contemporary age. *Pneuma, 27*(1), 65–82. https://doi.org/10.1163/157007405774270329.

Jeffries, S. (2012, November 10). The sex issue: Is monogamy dead? *The Guardian.* Retrieved from https://www.theguardian.com/lifeandstyle/2012/nov/10/sex-is-monogamy-dead.

Loewenthal, K. M., MacLeod, A. K., & Cinnirella, M. (2002). Are women more religious than men? Gender differences in religious activity among different religious groups in the UK. *Personality and Individual Differences, 32*(1), 133–139. https://doi.org/10.1016/s0191-8869(01)00011-3.

ONS. (2012). *2011 census: Key statistics for local authorities in England and Wales.* Retrieved July 31, 2018, from Office for National Statistics. https://www.ons.gov.uk/peoplepopulationandcommunity/populationandmigration/populationestimates/datasets/2011censuskeystatisticsforlocalauthoritiesinenglandandwales.

ONS. (2017). *Graduates in the UK labour market: 2017.* London: Office for National Statistics.

Phelan, J., Link, B. G., Stueve, A., & Moore, R. E. (1995). Education, social liberalism, and economic conservatism: Attitudes toward homeless people. *American Sociological Review, 60*(1), 126–140. https://doi.org/10.2307/2096349.

Reimer, S. (2010). Higher education and theological liberalism: Revisiting the old issue. *Sociology of Religion, 71*(4), 393–408. https://doi.org/10.1093/socrel/srq049.

Robbins, M. (2007). Clergymen and clergywomen: The same inclusive gospel? *Journal of Beliefs & Values, 28*(1), 55–64. https://doi.org/10.1080/13617670701251561.

Smith, D. H. (1994). Determinants of voluntary association participation and volunteering. *Non-profit and Voluntary Sector Quarterly, 23*(3), 243–263. https://doi.org/10.1177/089976409402300305.

Smith, A., & Hopkinson, J. (Eds.). (2012). *Faith and the future of the countryside.* Norwich: Canterbury Press.

Trzebiatowska, M., & Bruce, S. (2014). *Why are women more religious than men?* Oxford: Oxford University Press.

Village, A. (2007a). *The Bible and lay people: An empirical approach to ordinary hermeneutics.* Aldershot and Burlington, VT: Ashgate.

Village, A. (2007b). Feeling in and falling out: Sense of belonging and frequency of disagreeing among Anglican congregations. *Archive for the Psychology of Religion, 29,* 268–288. https://doi.org/10.1163/008467207x188865.

Village, A. (2011). Factors predicting relationship with society among Anglicans in England. In L. J. Francis & H.-G. Ziebertz (Eds.), *Public significance of religion* (pp. 215–240). Leiden: Brill. https://doi.org/10.1163/ej.9789004207066.i-495.82.

Village, A. (2012). English Anglicanism: Construct validity of a scale of Anglo-catholic versus evangelical self-identification. In F.-V. Anthony & H.-G. Ziebertz (Eds.), *Religious identity and national heritage: Empirical-theological perspectives* (pp. 93–122). Leiden: Brill. https://doi.org/10.1163/9789004228788_007.

Village, A. (2013). Traditions within the Church of England and psychological type: A study among the clergy. *Journal of Empirical Theology, 26*(1), 22–44. https://doi.org/10.1163/15709256-12341252.

Village, A. (2015a). Nature or nurture? What makes people feel confident in faith? *Rural Theology, 13*(1), 82–93. https://doi.org/10.1179/1470499415z.00000000043.

Village, A. (2015b). Was White right? Biblical interpretation, theological stance and environmental attitudes among a sample of UK churchgoers. *Journal of Empirical Theology, 28*(1), 1–26. https://doi.org/10.1163/15709256-12341321.

Village, A. (2015c). Who goes there? Attendance at Fresh Expressions of Church in relation to psychological type preferences among readers of the Church Times. *Practical Theology, 8*(2), 112–129. https://doi.org/10.1179/1756074815y.0000000007.

Village, A. (2016). Biblical conservatism and psychological type. *Journal of Empirical Theology, 29*(2), 137–159. https://doi.org/10.1163/15709256-12341340.

Village, A., & Baker, S. (2018). Rejecting Darwinian evolution: The effects of education, church tradition, and individual theological stance among UK churchgoers. *Review of Religious Research.* https://doi.org/10.1007/s13644-018-0335-8.

Village, A., & Francis, L. J. (2008). Attitude toward homosexuality among Anglicans in England: The effects of theological orientation and personality. *Journal of Empirical Theology, 21,* 68–87. https://doi.org/10.1163/092229308x310740.

Village, A., & Francis, L. J. (2009). *The mind of the Anglican clergy: Assessing attitudes and beliefs in the Church of England.* Lampeter: Edwin Mellen Press.

Village, A., & Francis, L. J. (2010). An anatomy of change: Profiling cohort-difference in beliefs and attitudes among Anglicans in England. *Journal of Anglican Studies, 8*(1), 59–81. https://doi.org/10.1017/s1740355309990027.

INDEX

/

Printed by Printforce, the Netherlands